Praise for the book

'I consistently cite the "Incredible India" campaign as a masterstroke of international branding. And who better to tell the story than the man who created it. Amitabh Kant's book is insightful, thought-provoking, superbly researched, and deftly crafted. While it's an engaging story of how he made India a tourism juggernaut – and a textbook battleplan for anyone who wants to know how to brand a country – it's much more. Kant is an engaging writer who combines the nuts and bolts of tourism strategy with a deeply felt sense of India and its singular personality. Yes, he did a brilliant job of selling India, but he did it because he loves it. And his passion shows on every page.'
Keith Bellows, Editor in Chief, *National Geographic Traveler*

'Incredible inspiration. Amitabh Kant's account of branding India is a must-read not just for those in the tourism and advertising industries but also to all of us who want to experience the authentic richness of a continent that could well be the key to all our futures.'
Sarah Miller, Editor, *Condé Nast Traveller*, UK

'Nothing builds brands better than passion. Amitabh Kant's passion for both Brand India and Kerala is bubbling in every line and between the lines. The book proves that brands don't just need a face, they also need a body, arms, legs and a very big heart.'
Piyush Pandey, Executive Chairman & National Creative Director, Ogilvy & Mather

'Countries are becoming increasingly aware of travel and tourism and its untapped economic and social potential. This is a remarkable saga of how to attract the attention of overseas and domestic customers.'
Jean Claude Baumgarten, President, World Travel & Tourism Council

'Few campaigns have impressed me as much as "Incredible India" in its uniqueness, creativity, impact and effectiveness. Visualized and implemented by Amitabh Kant, the campaign took Indian tourism to new heights. The book provides deep insights into the formulation of the campaign and how a crisis can be converted into an opportunity. The lucid, open-hearted, first-person account makes interesting and informative reading for academics and practitioners alike.'
Francesco Frangialli, Secretary-General, UN World Tourism Organization (UNWTO)

Branding India

Branding India

An Incredible Story

Amitabh Kant

Design:
V. Sunil

COLLINS BUSINESS
An Imprint of HarperCollins Publishers

First published in India in 2009 by Collins Business
An imprint of HarperCollins *Publishers* India
a joint venture with
The India Today Group

Copyright © Amitabh Kant 2009

ISBN: 978-81-7223-809-4

2 4 6 8 10 9 7 5 3

Amitabh Kant asserts the moral right to be identified
as the author of this book.

HarperCollins *Publishers*
A-53, Sector 57, NOIDA, Uttar Pradesh – 201301, India
77-85 Fulham Palace Road, London W6 8JB, United Kingdom
Hazelton Lanes, 55 Avenue Road, Suite 2900, Toronto, Ontario M5R 3L2
and 1995 Markham Road, Scarborough, Ontario M1B 5M8, Canada
25 Ryde Road, Pymble, Sydney, NSW 2073, Australia
31 View Road, Glenfield, Auckland 10, New Zealand
10 East 53rd Street, New York NY 10022, USA

Printed and bound at
Thomson Press (India) Ltd.

Photo courtsey: Xavier Zimbardo (www.xavierzimbardo.com)

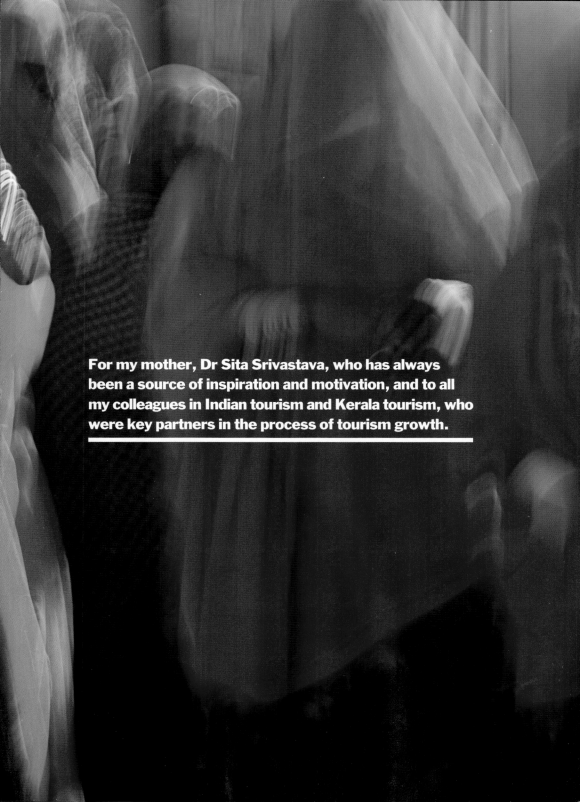

For my mother, Dr Sita Srivastava, who has always been a source of inspiration and motivation, and to all my colleagues in Indian tourism and Kerala tourism, who were key partners in the process of tourism growth.

Contents

Acknowledgements

I am deeply grateful to V. Sunil for having captured the essence of the text through his innovative, creative and contemporary design of this book. Sunil is a creative whiz kid and has been the key driver behind the unique 'Incredible India' campaigns. I am also thankful to his colleagues Rajesh Bhargava and Kishore Kumar of Wieden+Kennedy, Delhi, for putting their heart and soul in designing the book. Sincere thanks are due to Swarup B.R. from Stark Communications for assisting me in the research and for providing inputs on complex issues. I am also thankful to Vishwa Sharma and K. Narayanan for typing, correcting and going through the manuscript meticulously.

I acknowledge with thanks the permission accorded by the ministry of tourism, government of India, and Kerala tourism to use the creatives of the 'Incredible India' and 'God's Own Country' campaigns in this book.

The book would not have been possible without the encouragement and support of my family – my wife, Ranjeeta, and my daughters, Vedica and Vanshica.

Preface

This is the story of how the largest democracy in the world, with twenty-eight states, seven union territories, eighteen official languages and 1.12 billion people spread across 3.29 million square kilometres of breathtaking geography and history, was brought together under the realm of tourism by a simple branding exercise that unified this magnificent diversity.

Put in a line, this sounds simple and nice. But in fact it was an unbelievably complex and intricate exercise. As tourism is a multi-sectoral activity, it required intervention from every possible government sphere – infrastructure, urban development, health, culture, railways, shipping, rural development, environment and forests, civil aviation, roads and highways, home affairs… the list is endless. To achieve a synergy, however minimal, among these departments and move ahead without making too many compromises was a huge task. That it was accomplished was, of course, thanks to many colleagues in the government and the private sector, who battled all odds for the cause of Indian tourism.

This was the period (2002 to 2008) when a paradigm shift was made towards strengthening tourism infrastructure at key destinations, civil aviation was radically liberalized, e-business made travel and tourism click, leading hotel chains entered India, young entrepreneurs blossomed and innovations such as medical and rural tourism and cruises added to the diversity of the Indian experience on offer. This was also the period when tourism was increasingly viewed as an instrument of employment creation and sustainable development.

All this was backed by a perfect environment. The country was on a roll. India Inc. was at its best – stock markets were soaring, infrastructure projects were thriving, foreign direct investment was pouring in, entrepreneurship was flourishing, and disposable incomes had hit never-before highs. And most importantly, perhaps, people started investing big-time in travel – in experiences that added value to their lives.

The best part was that 'God' taught me the basics in his own country. My experience in Kerala (as its tourism secretary from 1997 to 2001) was a blessing in more ways than one. After having partnered Kerala's incredible journey from an unknown destination to India's No. 1 tourism hotspot, moving to the tourism ministry in Delhi in late 2001 was the perfect challenge for me. However, the dynamics and scale of this challenge, as I discovered in no time, were frightening.

The biggest challenge was the task of holding the entire canvas together with one powerful idea that would help achieve the vision of unifying India as an aspirational destination. After almost a year of research, debates, discussions, public contests, focus groups and what not, that idea was christened

'Incredible India!'. Thus began a journey that spanned over six years – during the course of which India metamorphosed into one of the top destinations of the world (*CondeNast Traveler* Readers' Award ranked India as the World's No. 1 preferred holiday destination in 2007).

That journey today faces unprecedented trials and challenges.

The economic downturn and the cowardly terror attacks in Mumbai have adversely impacted tourism. Inbound tourist inflow during the first three months of 2009 has seen a decline of around eighteen percent as compared to the same period last year. The Taj and Oberoi hotels became targets because they were in the heart of the city, were easily accessible, and were prestigious targets as they were full of foreigners and local elite. Most importantly, the targeting of international tourists generates a great deal of media attention, leading to tourists avoiding the destination. It is to achieve this result that not merely the Taj and the Oberoi in Mumbai but the Grand Hyatt and the Radisson in Aaman, the Hilton in Taba, the Marriot in Jakarta and Islamabad and the Serena in Kabul have been attacked by terrorists. The attack in Mumbai will force the travel and tourism industry in India to fully prepare for security threats and, in many ways, alter the way the tourism industry works.

A remarkable feature of the attack on the Taj and the Oberoi in Mumbai was the exemplary courage and selfless service displayed by the hotel staff. They went beyond the call of duty – caring, guiding, advising and even supervising operations during the long drawn out attacks. Several leading chefs and staff members lost their lives while saving the lives of the guests. Karambir Kang, general manager of the Taj in Mumbai, lost his wife and children and yet worked through the crisis to help guests. These are the men and women who have made Indian tourism proud.

In many ways, tourism is an antidote to terrorism; it is a catalyst for employment creation, income redistribution and poverty alleviation. In fact, one of the best ways to fight the terrorists is to support travel and tourism.

After the 2001 attack in New York, the then Indian prime minister, Atal Behari Vajpayee, speaking at a chief ministers' conference on tourism, had stated:

'Now we know why terrorism has hit tourism the most. Tourism is a foe of terrorism. Whereas terrorism feeds on intolerance, tourism breeds tolerance and empathy. Terrorism has no respect for human life. In contrast, tourism teaches us to savour and celebrate all that is beautiful in nature and human life. Terrorism seeks to erect walls of hatred between faiths and communities. Tourism breaks such barriers. Terrorism detests pluralism, whereas tourism celebrates it. Terrorism has no respect for human life. Tourism pays a tribute to all that is beautiful in nature and human life. Terrorism may have temporarily hit tourism in this metaphorical battle between the two. But tourism will make a major contribution to the eventual defeat of terrorism and all other manifestations of fanaticism.'

I have no doubt that the tourism industry will be resilient and bounce back as it did post-September 2001. Tourism has a unique capacity to adapt and survive. It has constantly demonstrated its extraordinary resistance and ability to overcome crises. External events impact tourism only temporarily – they redistribute it geographically and alter the product use but are not able to bring it to a halt. The need for travel, for business as well as leisure, is an intrinsic part of our lives. The latest VISA / PATA Asia Pacific Travel intentions survey, 'Determining Travel Preferences in 2009 and Beyond', found that while the global economic scenario will impact tourism, it is unlikely to bring travel to a standstill. It establishes that travellers will be more creative in their selection of destinations. The survey found that thirty-six percent of the people surveyed did not expect to make any changes in their travel plans in the near future while sixty-four percent of respondents were reviewing their plans in the light of economic uncertainty. Among those respondents reviewing their plan, fifty-seven percent stated that they would still travel but would look for cheaper alternatives while thirty-eight percent said that they would travel within their own country instead. Only thirty-six percent said that they would postpone their travel as a result of economic uncertainty.

The present crisis also presents an opportunity. The 'Incredible India' campaign emerged from the crisis that confronted Indian tourism in 2001-02. The 2008 terror attack requires another cohesive, concerted response. Till the mid-nineties, Kerala was nowhere close to being a tourism destination. Its emergence in great measure was due to traffic diversion from the terror-prone Jammu and Kashmir. Kerala was ready for this – it had developed new products like the backwaters and ayurveda; its entrepreneurs had created experiential boutique resorts; and proper infrastructure had been created. There is a need for more states to emerge as tourism destinations by enhancing the quality of experience on the ground, by improving their infrastructure and creating new sub-brands.

The massive potential of travel and tourism as an employment creator still remains untapped. The dynamism of an emerging economy, the impact of demographic changes, the rise of the urban middle classes, the shift towards experiential tourism, the role of climate changes and the evolution of technology, open up vast opportunities.

In the context of India, the vast potential of tourism as an employment creator and wealth distributor still remains untapped. The size of the tourism industry worldwide is US$4.6 trillion whereas the software industry globally is a mere US$500 billion. The tourism industry globally generates over 250 million jobs whereas the software industry generates only 20 million jobs. As India grows and expands its base in travel and tourism, it will generate many more jobs and the sector will become a major catalyst for India's growth.

Welcome to this incredible journey.

Amitabh Kant

March 2009

'There will be times in life when impossibility is felt, but then there are dreams – and dreams allow us possibility.' Jeffrey David Lang

Crisis as catalyst: the making of a brand called 'Incredible India'

I had no idea what was in store for me when I was posted as joint secretary, ministry of tourism, in the summer of 2002. The pride of having contributed to Kerala's emergence as a premier tourism destination had made me very optimistic and I wanted to contribute my bit to India. But in no time I realized that things were not so simple. What welcomed me was a severe crisis. Looking back, I am certain it was this dire situation that catalyzed Brand India.

A crisis of massive magnitude had gripped Indian tourism in 2001-02. The year 2002 had seen a decline of six percent in tourist arrivals and three percent in foreign exchange earnings in US$ terms as compared to 2001, which itself had witnessed a fall of 4.2 percent in arrivals and 7.6 percent in foreign exchange earnings over 2000. Hotels in India had gone down to 25-30 percent occupancy, international tour operators had removed India from their sales brochures and inbound Indian tour operators had, on account of lack of business, switched to outbound operations. The common refrain was that there was no consumer demand in the key source markets of India. This was a consequence of several disastrous events, one after another – the attack on the World Trade Center in New York, the war in Afghanistan, the attack on Parliament House in Delhi, the troop mobilization at the Indian border and travel advisories leading to withdrawal of schedules by airlines from India.

This was also a period when global tourism, for the first time in history, saw a sharp decline and leading National Tourist Organizations (NTOs), such as Thailand, Singapore and Malaysia, sharply cut their advertising, promotion and marketing budgets. For India, this was a time for reflection. It was a moment for action. The need of the hour was a strong national policy for tourism. The need was to acknowledge tourism's potential for revenue and employment generation. The 'Incredible India' campaign was launched at the peak of this crisis to bring back consumer demand, generate momentum and enhance growth in the tourism industry.

From the difficult days of 2002, let me transport you to the International Tourismus Bourse (ITB) Berlin in March 2007 – the world's largest travel and tourism show – where India participated as a partner country. The campaign used the entire city as a canvas, decorating it with large billboards, vibrant graphic art and 3D installations, with even taxis and buses being covered with advertisements. Signalling a new level of sophistication in India's branding strategy, the ITB campaign overwhelmed the international media and trade. The Indian pavilion did unprecedented business and the Indian hotels were virtually sold out. In October 2007, Indian tourism, in partnership with the Confederation of Indian Industry (CII), organized Incredible India @60 in New York. The event coincided with the United Nations General Assembly meeting and Brand India was unleashed in New York with all its 'Incredible' colours, while the world sat up to welcome India in what was a dazzling display of its culture, tourism wealth and intellectual power. As *Fortune* magazine put it, 'the bullishness of India's business Brahmans was in display in New York city.... It presented the picture of a confident nation ready to engage with the world.'[1]

What had changed so radically between 2002 and 2007? The lack of consumer demand in 2002 had revealed that Indian tourism lacked a meaningful identity in the global market place, which meant that there was an imperative need to position and brand India as an attractive destination. A strong and clear image could increase consumer confidence and enhance the desirability of its tourist products.

A comprehensive body of literature discusses brands and branding: for example, Aaker (1991),[2] Aaker (1996),[3] Aaker and Joachimsthaler (2000),[4] Duncan and Moriarty (1997),[5] Gardner and Levy (1955),[6] Keller (1998),[7] Kotler (1997)[8] and Levitt (1980)[9]. Kotler has suggested that the positioning task consists of three broad steps: identifying a set of possible competitive advantages upon which to build a position, selecting the right competitive advantages, and effectively communicating the positioning to the target audience. Aaker expands this model and suggests that a brand encompasses many variables, all of which influence the brand's value – credibility, brand customer relationships and the brand's positioning.

To apply a generic brand definition to a tourist destination context, the following conceptualization offered by Keller (1998) is suggested: 'A brand is a product but one that adds other dimensions, differentiating it in some way from other products designed to satisfy the same need. These differences may be rational and tangible – related to product performance of the brand – or more symbolic, emotional or intangible – related to what the brand represents. Brands themselves are valuable intangible assets that need to be handled carefully.'

With reference to 'related to what the brand represents' in the above definition, a tourist destination brand concept should convey the promise of a memorable travel experience that is uniquely associated with the destination (Ritchie and Ritchie, 1998).[10]

Sleeping Giant

In the global tourism industry, India had often been referred to as a 'sleeping giant' or a sleeping elephant. The country's many assets had been eulogized at every international trade platform, and its prospects and potential were deliberated at every global tourism meet, yet India's performance was far from laudable. For more than a decade, till 2002, India's share of the world tourist traffic had remained static at about 0.38 percent. The chasm between potential and performance was widened as a result of various factors, the worst being the perception that tourism was an elitist activity set in the background of five-star hotels, recreation and pleasure. Somehow the actual benefits of tourism – its multiplier effect on employment, infrastructure, community growth – all seemed to have been miserably lost.

Until 2002, India had eighteen tourism offices abroad. There was no positioning, common branding or a clear, precise message. One foreign office called it 'Spiritual India', another termed it 'Cultural India' and the third 'Unbelievable India'. The clichéd visuals, such as saffron-clad sadhus in the Himalayas and rope-tricks performed amidst crowds, reinforced the traditional image of India rather than giving the contemporary feel of a young nation and focusing on a defined segment of the market. By then, several destinations in the Southeast Asian region had indeed become brands with an emotional appeal. It was obvious that the branding process was working as their tourist arrival figures were going up phenomenally.

In 1999, Malaysia had launched its 'Malaysia – Truly Asia' brand as a long-term image-building process to position it in the international travel arena. It reflected a distinctive cultural diversity and projected

Malaysia as a microcosm of Asia. Since then, the campaign has continued to evolve and enrich the original brand personality. This has enabled Malaysia tourism to strengthen its appeal and penetrate new markets.

The 'Live it up Singapore' campaign of Singapore, launched in 2000, created the essence of a dream holiday categorized under five main experiences: The City of Diverse Culture, The Garden City, The Fun City, City of the Arts and the Gateway City. This has now been replaced by the 'Uniquely Singapore' campaign, which cuts across all sectors and positions Singapore as a destination unique in itself. It asserts itself as distinctive both in terms of the economic power that enables it to attract high-value investments as well as its multicultural synthesis of east and west, old and new.

The 'Amazing Thailand' brand campaign launched in 1998 was remarkable for its creativity, focusing on the cultural elements of Thailand. The visual language of the campaign promoted it as a fresh, natural and diverse destination. Unfortunately, it was replaced by a disastrous campaign entitled 'Heaven on Earth', but good sense has prevailed, with the Thailand tourism think tank bringing back 'Amazing Thailand' with its inimitable style.

To my mind, the finest destination branding campaign in recent times has been the '100% Pure New Zealand' campaign, which presented a series of authentic experiences. The theme in all the visuals connects the traveller with New Zealand's diverse landscapes, people, cultures and scope for adventure. While '100% Pure New Zealand' is the principal campaign line, a number of derivatives and extensions such as '100% Pure Romance' and '100% Pure Spirit', have evolved. The campaign has been backed by a superb interactive web presence, a brilliant consumer-orientated public relations (PR) strategy that proclaims itself as the 'Best Supporting Country in a Motion Picture' through the *Lord of the Rings* film trilogy. Advertising, effective PR and an appealing web presence have enabled New Zealand to create a strong brand relationship, interactively engaging visitors. '100% Pure New Zealand' is today a powerful, interactive and emotionally appealing brand.

Vision for Indian Tourism

In 2002, the government of India defined its vision for the development of the tourism sector (see Box A). It aimed to 'achieve a superior quality of life for India's people through tourism, which would provide a unique opportunity for physical invigoration, mental rejuvenation, cultural enrichment and spiritual elevation.'[11]

Box A

Key Strategic Objectives

- Position tourism as a major engine of economic growth;
- Harness the direct and multiplier effects of tourism for employment generation, economic development and for providing an impetus to rural tourism;
- Focus on domestic tourism as a major driver of tourism growth;
- Position India as a global brand to take advantage of the burgeoning global travel trade and the vast untapped potential of India as a destination;
- Acknowledge the critical role of the private sector with the government working as a pro-active facilitator and catalyst;
- Create and develop integrated tourism circuits based on India's unique civilization, heritage and culture in partnership with the states, private sector and other agencies.

There was clearly a need for Indian tourism to develop a strong identity that encapsulated India's special attributes and created a definable profile. There was an imperative need to differentiate India from other destinations in the world. The vision was to produce a clear identity, a unique brand, which would drive all marketing strategies. It would pervade all forms of communication and stimulate the travel consumer's behaviour and decision-making processes to competitively position India in the global market place. As a result, in October 2002, Indian tourism launched the 'Incredible India' campaign.

The Vision Statement of the campaign envisaged the following objectives:
- Put India on the world tourism map and develop it as a premier holiday destination for high-yielding tourists;
- India should be a global brand, with worldwide brand recognition and strong brand equity, especially in the trade and among the target audience.

The rationale and justification for this approach was that the mass market would follow the high-yielding tourists. Markets are deferential and responsive to the views and requirements of upscale tourists, which in turn will have a positive impact on the destination itself. A visible inflow of upscale tourists will induce accelerated investments in tourism and attract tourism management talent into the sector.

While it is easy to position and brand single-product destinations like the Maldives and Mauritius or a wildlife destination like South Africa, it is extremely difficult and complex to establish a clear, precise identity for a multiproduct destination like India. India is a land of contrasts, a combination of tradition and modernity – a land that is at once mystical and mysterious. India is bigger than the twenty-three countries of Europe put together and every single state of India has its own unique attractions. 'Incredible India', therefore, necessarily had to be the mother brand with the states establishing their own brand entity and emerging as sub-brands.

The rich tapestry that is India cannot be captured in a single word or expression but 'Incredible' comes close enough. At times overwhelming, but always 'Incredible'. The initial phase of the exercise was to create a distinct image for India and an effective style of communication. This style was created with the logo 'Incredible !ndia', where the exclamation mark forming the 'I' of India was used innovatively. The credit for thinking big, focusing on professional promotion and marketing, and creating an environment of working with the best creative minds goes to two senior officials with whom I was closely working – the then secretary of tourism – Rathi Vinay Jha, and the then director-general, tourism – V.K. Duggal.

The first task was to create a content-rich website which would constantly upgrade the visitor with information and provide value-add-ons and tie-ups with competent travel sites capable of handling online bookings and offering packages. The attractive and functional website {www.incredibleindia.org} became the base for a series of online campaigns. The assessment of these campaigns was based on click through rates (CTRs), page views of the site and tracking of every single consumer who came on the site. These consumers were sent regular e-newsletters and focused information on the destination. The print media campaign was integrated with the website through a series of contests. For instance, the yoga ad, using yoga as part of the USP of India, got an overwhelming response of 42,867 participants worldwide on the website. Subsequently, a series of micro-sites were created as well. (For a glimpse of the campaigns visit www.incredibleindiacampaign.com).

8

Incredible !ndia   Incredible !ndia

Incredible !ndia   Incredible !ndia

Incredible !ndia   Incredible !ndia

9

Incredible !ndia   Incredible !ndia

Incredible !ndia   Incredible !ndia

Incredible !ndia   Incredible !ndia

Incredible India

An ode to eternal love, crafted in the finest marble known to man. Also, the most photographed monument

Incredible India

t. Do come for an experience that's truly incredible! www.incredibleindia.org contactus@incredibleindia.org

Incredible !ndia

Incredible !ndia

Global Campaign 2002-03

Incredible India

The Indian Himalayas. Highly recommended for mountaineering. Rock climbing. Rafting. Skiing. Honeymooning. Do come for an experience that's truly incredible! www.incredibleindia.org contactus@incredibleindia.org

14

Incredible India

A few thousand-year-old recipe for eternal youth. You'll find unanimous approval from your mind, body and soul. Do come for an experience that's truly incredible! www.incredibleindia.org contactus@incredibleindia.org

Research formed an integral component of the campaign. On the basis of analysis, Indian tourism had clustered a list of fifteen countries into three groups – markets that needed to be defended, those that needed aggressive investment and yet others that needed to be seeded before they could be invested in (see Box B).

Box B

Key Marketing Challenges

- Markets
- Move from a low-volume, low-value marketing strategy to a high-value marketing strategy;
- Defend and enhance India's share in traditional long-haul markets;
- Develop strong short-haul markets;
- Penetrate the key source markets in Asia.
- Consumers
- Target the age group of forty to sixty-five years belonging to affluent, well-educated, married, white-collar segments for a value-based strategy;
- Convert business travel to business-cum-leisure travel;
- Target Persons of Indian Origin (PIOs) in the US and Canadian markets;
- Position and differentiate strongly vis-à-vis key competitors in the region – China, Thailand, Singapore and Malaysia.
- Ensure active management of goodwill and the country's image.
- Build strong sub-brands as key components of a risk minimization strategy.
- Develop spending avenues to capture higher value from each tourist.

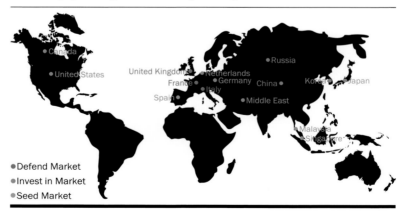

More Than Mere Advertising

The campaign started with a meagre outlay of Rs 15.71 crore in 2002-03. Its impact and delivery led to increased outlays for the tourism ministry, and by the year 2008-09, the total outlay for overseas marketing had increased to Rs 220 crore, with Rs 110 crore being spent on the 'Incredible India' campaign. The campaign itself had taken a 360-degree perspective, encompassing not merely print and electronic communication and the internet, but also public relations, outdoor hoardings, in-flight television advertising and a special Buddhist campaign in the short-haul markets of Southeast Asia.

It must be emphasized that the 'Incredible India' campaign was more than just mere advertising, which, in fact, played only a marginal role. The brand-building process comprised personal relationships with international tour operators and journalists, partnerships, promotions, contests, use of interactive media and an aggressive communication strategy. All these have helped build the 'Incredible India' experience. In the tourism ministry, our roles were not merely those of government officials but of brand managers orchestrating the future progress of the brand, motivating the private players, outmanoeuvering competition and constantly trying to ensure that the tourist to India got the best possible experience. We also blended strong elements of Indian culture while promoting and marketing India. At ITB Berlin, an awestruck audience gave a standing ovation to the musical genius of the percussionist Shivamani after his performance. At the World Travel Market (WTM) in London, it was Vikku Vinayak Ram and his group of eight traditional instrumentalists who left the entire hall spellbound, while the magic of Indian classical dancers was unveiled at the Lincoln Auditorium in New York during Incredible India @ 60. The bold and powerful colours of India were on full display on taxis in London, trains in Amsterdam and tourist buses in Berlin and New York, giving potential tourists a glimpse of the vast cultural and scenic treasures of India.

16

In reality, the 'Incredible India' campaign encompassed a new corporate culture, increased accountability, performance measurement and partnership with the industry through the Experience India Society and a clear customer focus. The society is a private sector initiative of leading hoteliers like the Taj, Oberoi, ITC, Hyatt and tour operators like Kuoni and Thomas Cook. The thrust for private-public partnership

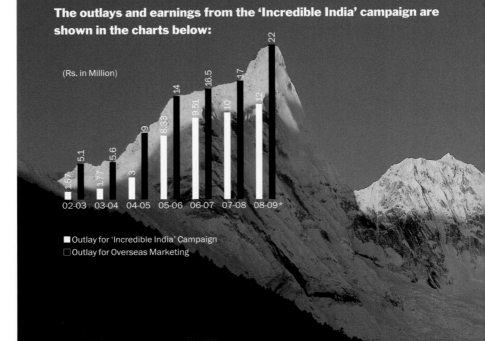

The outlays and earnings from the 'Incredible India' campaign are shown in the charts below:

(Rs. in Million)

Year	Outlay for 'Incredible India' Campaign	Outlay for Overseas Marketing
02-03	5.1	1.57
03-04	5.6	1.77
04-05	9	3
05-06	14	8.33
06-07	16.5	9.51
07-08	17	10
08-09*	22	12

■ Outlay for 'Incredible India' Campaign
□ Outlay for Overseas Marketing

The 'Incredible India' campaign led to increased outlays for both overseas marketing and 'Incredible India' campaign from 2002-03 onwards

(Foreign exchange earnings increased from 2003 – the year the campaign took off)

Source:- Tourism statistics, Ministry of Tourism. Image is digitally manipulated.

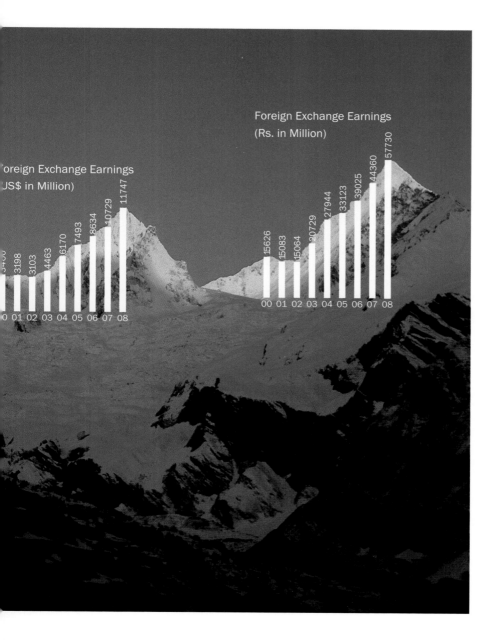

Foreign Exchange Earnings
(US$ in Million)

3198
3103
4463
6170
7493
8634
10729
11747

00 01 02 03 04 05 06 07 08

Foreign Exchange Earnings
(Rs. in Million)

15626
15083
15064
20729
27944
33123
39025
44360
57730

00 01 02 03 04 05 06 07 08

18

in tourism was provided by Krishna Kumar, the progressive head of Taj Group of Hotels, P.R.S. Oberoi, the visionary chairman of the Oberoi group and the meticulous Sushil Gupta of Hyatt. They had the vision to raise private sector resources to complement government outlays for destination marketing of India. Of course, developing a strong and distinctive image called for creativity, brilliant execution and constant innovation, which became

World's top outbound countries: 2020		
Country	Arrival generated worldwide	Market share
1. Germany	163.5	10.2
2. Japan	141.5	8.8
3. USA	123.3	7.7
4. China	100.0	6.2
5. UK	96.1	6.0
6. France	37.6	2.3
7. Netherlands	35.4	2.2
8. Canada	31.3	2.0
9. Russia	30.5	1.9
10. Italy	29.7	1.9
Total (1–10) above	788.9	49.2
Total all countries	1602.0	100.0

Source: UNWTO, Tourism Vision 2020

the hallmark of the campaign. As Indian tourism worked with some of the finest creative minds in the advertising world to create a strong destination image, the brand had to be constantly kept alive and fresh. Every year a new creative campaign was unleashed in the global markets. The objective was always to create an impact on the consumers in a focused, targeted manner, using print backed by electronic media advertising, reinforced by online publicity and further enhanced by outdoor media. There are two advertising stalwarts who played a stellar role in the evolution of the campaign – V. Sunil, who brought freshness, innovation and sophistication to the 'Incredible India' branding, and Bharat Bala, whose commercials captured the vibrancy, flavour and essence of India (for V. Sunil's perspective, see Box C). Bharat Bala's commercials pulsate with India's energy and have gone on to win several international awards (his vision is expressed in Box D).

The campaign focused on markets in three distinct phases:

Phase 1: India-aware, Western and short-haul markets – the US, UK, France, Spain, Italy, Germany, Singapore, Malaysia and UAE.

Phase 2: India-aware, culturally linked markets – China, Japan and South Korea.

Phase 3: India-unaware, high international traveller market – Russia.

Box C

'To be truly powerful, a brand must express itself not just in terms of a product benefit, but in terms of a greater socio-economic truth. Apple told a brave new world to reject big blue IBM and "Think Different". Nike told flabby, procrastinating city-dwellers everywhere to stop making excuses and "Just Do It", following it up with the brilliant "swoosh" icon, a graphic device that expressed energy and inspired sport without a word.

The "Incredible India" campaign belongs to this generation of branding. Visually, it uses the "!" Symbol to convey the mind-boggling depth and intensity of the Indian experience. Every aspect of India – be it its ever-accelerating GDP, extreme geography, kaleidoscopic culture, deep-rooted spirituality or even photogenic chaos, even – is summed up by the simple yet profound exclamation mark.

The campaign is also noteworthy in terms of tone. Headlines such as "Not all Indians are polite, hospitable and vegetarian" are more than just witty advertising copy. They are symptomatic of a much bigger social phenomenon – an optimistic and extroverted new India, eager to make its presence felt in the global community. This India is a far cry from the meek, tentative, "offshore" destination of the last decade. It is this sub-text that transforms "Incredible India" from a mere branding exercise into a pop culture milestone, denoting a turning point in the evolution of one of mankind's greatest civilizations.'

V. Sunil, Executive Creative Director, Wieden+Kennedy

20

'Today, India cannot be thought of without acknowledging the irony of it being an ancient country with a modern outlook. The film was shot bearing this in mind; we were careful to preserve the eternal quality of its people and landscape, yet remained modern in its execution. There was a clear intent of veering away from the traditional advertising approach. As opposed to staging unrealistic scenarios, the core motivation of the film was to reflect the people, landscape and emotion of India with a sincere honesty and simplicity. This simplicity extended across the visuals and onto the soundtrack that would accompany them.

One of the primary goals was to achieve a film that would

onestly depict the landscape and people of India as visiting
ravellers would find them when they arrived. We endeavoured
o portray the very same, completely real emotions they
would feel when they experienced India for themselves.
ll the moments shown in the film, in that sense, are real
nd readily accessible to those who seek them.

 We chose yoga to punctuate and enhance the visuals for
s ancient stature and enduring association with the spiritual
hilosophy that is at the core of the land. The serene grace
nd strength of the postures reflect the integrity of mind,
ody and soul that we believe visitors would discover when
hey experienced India.' Bharat Bala, Film Director

The UN World Tourism Organization's analytical research of the world's top outbound countries by 2020 had clearly demonstrated that Japan and China would be the key focus points of world tourism apart from the European nations, the US and Canada, while Russia would emerge as an important new source market with an expected 30 million outbound tourists by 2020.

India also had to focus on the growing intra-ASEAN travel market and capitalize on the short-haul travel segment in markets like Singapore, Malaysia and the Middle East.

An Integrated PR Exercise

A highly integrated public relations exercise also played a significant role in harnessing the power of the international media. The 'Incredible India' campaign started with small outlays in the attempt to create a global brand by competing not merely with other destinations, but with other global brands for consumer mindshare. A new brand like 'Incredible India' had to out-think rather than out-spend competition. It was necessary to be intensely creative, focus on the right clientele and ensure that the campaign was featured in select media. Public relations offered a highly cost-effective and credible method to raise awareness of India as a tourist destination. The Indian tourism ministry invited leading writers, editors, tour operators and opinion-makers as its guests and pampered them from their arrival to the point of their departure. This led to India being extensively featured in almost all leading journals in key source markets, but the PR exercise that had an immense impact in the British market was the Jade Goody letter campaign in the UK.

During the airing of the popular Celebrity Big Brother TV show in the UK, there were a number of negative and outdated views expressed about India by a leading participant, Jade Goody, in the show. As her strident comments led to controversy, the viewership rose phenomenally. India's tourism office in London considered it an opportune time to attract the attention of the media and the readers of the broadsheets through a message to Jade Goody. It published an open letter to Jade Goody and her friends, inviting them to India. The open letter (see Box E) was published in leading papers like the *Times, Guardian, Independent, Daily Telegraph* and others.

The advertisements had an immense impact on the print and

electronic media. The campaign was discussed on almost all the TV channels (ITV, Sky, BBC, Channel 4, CNN), radio stations and digital media. As many as 200,000 websites discussed the open letter. Never before in history had any Indian tourism advertisement been discussed on so many websites, radio and television shows and in newspapers and magazines. The approximate publicity returns were to the tune of £5 million as against the £50,000 spent on the campaign.

Growth of Infrastructure

There were two other major factors that had an impact on the growth and expansion of Indian tourism. First, the radical opening of the Indian skies and second, the sustained growth of India as an economic power. The new policy initiatives led to acquisition of new aircraft, the emergence of new low-cost carriers for the benefit of consumers, permitting of private scheduled carriers to operate on international routes and gradual discontinuance of the practice of mandating commercial agreements on new services.

The quality of airport infrastructure is critical in the process of maintaining India's international competitiveness. The development plans for the Delhi and Mumbai airports envisage an investment of Rs 5270 crore and Rs 6130 crore respectively. Greenfield projects at Bangalore and Hyderabad have already become operational and the Airport Authority of India is developing thirty-five non-metro airports. This new airport infrastructure will be the key driver of tourism growth in future.

The quality of the national highways will also play a major role in sustaining the growth momentum in the tourism sector. The government has approved a programme of upgrading 40,000 kilometres of national highways and constructing 1000 kilometres of new expressways. This programme includes six-lane roads connecting the Golden Quadrilateral. Domestic tourism, already at a high level of 430 million tourists, will receive a further impetus with the radical improvement in the transport network.

The Indian Railways is the largest mover of people by rail worldwide, transporting more than five billion people every year, or around 157 million passengers a day. It has witnessed an immense turnaround and will benefit from an investment of Rs 200,000 crore for the modernization, capacity increase and completion of new projects

Tourist arrivals in millions

Tourist arrivals started showing growth from 2003 onwards –
the year the 'Incredible India' campaign took-off.

2.54
2001

2.73
2003

2.65
2000

2.38
2002

3.46
2004

25

3.92
2005

4.45
2006

5.02
2007

5.38
2008

26

An Open Letter to Jade Goody and Friends from the India Tourism Office

Dear Jade Goody,

Once your current commitments are over may we invite you to experience the healing nature of India. Being one of the world's oldest civilizations, our land is one where the ancient and the modern co-exist and a multitude of religions live in harmony. We have a modern thriving culture and offer an amazing wealth of sights and sounds, tastes and textures making our country a place like no other.

With everything from bustling cosmopolitan cities to the quiet countryside, we have destinations that offer a backdrop of unmatched beauty. Our country is blessed with everything from snow-clad mountains and crystal glaciers to thick forests rich in wildlife and long sandy coastlines, offering something for everyone.

As a beauty therapist, you may be especially interested in visiting one of the many spas where you can cleanse your stresses away, enjoy yoga in the land that invented it and experience Ayurvedic healing which promotes positive health and natural beauty.

The best way to understand Incredible India is to visit and we look forward to welcoming you soon.

Yours sincerely,
India Tourism Office

during the eleventh Five Year Plan. The Indian Railways is presently upgrading twenty-six major railway stations as world-class stations throughout the country, including four metropolitan cities. There will be separate departure and arrival facilities for passengers, world-class waiting rooms, multilevel parking, malls and other facilities.

Parallel to 'Incredible India', a complementary campaign, entitled 'Atithi Devo Bhavah' or 'Guest is God', was launched domestically to create a sense of pride in India as a tourism destination and qualitatively improve the services provided by taxi drivers, guides, immigration and custom officials (see Box L). The campaign, using India's leading film actors – the popular Shah Rukh Khan and now, the versatile Aamir Khan – has been broadened, focusing on aspects such as garbage collection and stopping defacement of monuments. Emphasis has been laid on enhancing the visitor's experience at major tourist sites such as Ajanta-Ellora, Mahabalipuram, and the Buddhist Circuit.

In December 2006, CNN commissioned an Advertisement Effectiveness Campaign Survey, investigating the viewers' recall of the 'Incredible India' campaign as well as their message comprehension and overall perception of India as a travel destination (see Box F). In November 2006, BBC World conducted a tracker survey on 'Incredible India' advertising on BBC across various regions. The campaign's viewership and its impact are shown in Box G.

A marketing-led strategy has created the necessary demand and it is imperative that the infrastructure at tourist sites as well as hotel accommodation keep pace so that Indian tourism constantly evolves to higher levels of growth. The challenge is to create 100,000 star category hotel rooms in the next three years. This requires the states

Box F
Awareness of 'Incredible India'

The proportion of those who knew the campaign very well/a fair amount in March 2006 was 270% bigger than those who had 'never heard' of it – in Feb 2005.

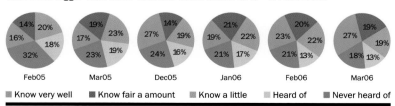

Tracker: Advertiser: Incredible India: Awareness (Target Regions, Heavy Viewers)

to create land banks and make them available on a long-term basis. An innovative initiative – the 'Incredible India Bed and Breakfast' scheme – with the objective of creating additional capacity before the Commonwealth Games in 2010 – has already been launched. India has gradually transformed itself into a 365-days-a-year destination with increased emphasis on medical tourism, Meetings-Incentives-Conventions-Exhibitions (MICE) and adventure tourism. There are no off-seasons and tourists are visiting India in large numbers during the lean months. Major emphasis has to be given on improving the quality of the experience of tourists, so that there is word-of-mouth publicity. Political and administrative will is necessary to convert at least three major tourism sites in each state into centres of excellence. The success of these projects will have a demonstrative impact and spread the gains of the 'Incredible India' campaign to the hinterland. Tourism has an immense multiplier effect and if India's growth study has to be accompanied by employment creation, tourism provides the answer – as amply demonstrated by the economic research carried out by the World Tourism and Travel Council (WTTC) (see Box H).

The 'Incredible India' campaign has enabled India to emerge as a destination of choice for the discerning traveller and enhance its market share. I have never been a great believer in the numbers game. India, given its vast wealth of heritage and culture, should focus not

Box G

'Incredible India' campaign – remember seeing advertising

Levels of high familiarity jumped up by 36% globally – 83% of heavy viewers in target regions had seen it

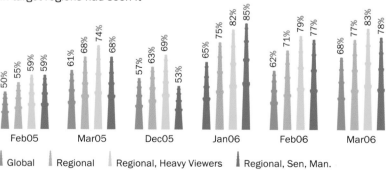

| | Global | | Regional | | Regional, Heavy Viewers | | Regional, Sen, Man. |

Source: BBC World

On an Employment Scale

Countries expected to generate the largest amount (in absolute terms) of Travel & Tourism Economy Employment:

T&T Economy Employment, 2008 (000 jobs)

1	China	74,498
2	India	30,491
3	USA	14,933
4	Japan	6,833
5	Mexico	6,633
6	Indonesia	5,936
7	Brazil	5,500
8	Vietnam	4,891
9	Russia	4,126
10	Thailand	3,911

Source: World Travel & Tourism Council (WTTC) –Progress & Priorities 2008/09

Box H

on mass but foreign tourists spending more time and money here. The branding campaign did precisely this. By targeting the upmarket clientele India's unit value realization went up radically. In 2007, the 5 million tourists who arrived in India spent nearly US$ 11 billion. In contrast, while Malaysia and Singapore attracted higher numbers of tourists – 20.02 million and 10.2 million respectively – their foreign exchange earnings were substantially lower – US$ 10.1 billion and US$ 9.16 billion respectively. The World Tourism Organization (WTO) Tourism 2020 Vision had projected that India's total arrivals by 2010 would be 5.08 million and by 2020 reach 8.9 million. However, India has achieved the 2010 target in 2007 itself. Despite the economic downturn India will in all likelihood achieve the 2020 target by 2010. India's share of the world tourism market and the Asia-Pacific market will rise at a much faster pace. The WTO therefore needs to re-analyse and revise its projections.

The campaign has won several accolades (see Box I), such as the coveted Pacific Asia Travel Association (PATA) Grand Award for Best Destination Marketing Worldwide in 2007. The jury observed that it was 'a memorable, evocative and emotive campaign. The campaign leveraged India's colour and cultural diversity and intelligent use of traditional and interactive media including micro-sites and online contests and targeted the international visitor to drive a double-digit growth in foreign visitor arrivals'. India also won the No. 1 position at the prestigious *Condé Nast Traveller* UK Readers' Award 2007. India led the band with (94.55) followed by Italy (93.95), Thailand (93.55), Australia (93.00), New Zealand (91.85) and South Africa (91.66).

Kate Slesinger, publisher of *CondeNast*, stated, 'The success of India among the UK's most influential travellers is due to the fact that the product now matches the dream crafted so artfully by advertising and public relations. The reality of India in 2007 is that it represents a kaleidoscope of experiences to be enjoyed in utmost comfort and luxury.' The Future Brands Country Brand Index 2006 ranked India among the top ten country brands. 'Incredible India' figured seven times across nine parameters and forty-five countries considered in the index. It was the numero uno brand in terms of authenticity (see Box J).

The campaign promoted and enhanced India's 'soft power' by influencing the behaviour of people through cultural and ideological means. The term 'soft power' was first coined by the Harvard professor, Joseph Nye, who remains its most prominent proponent in his book, *Bound To Lead: The Changing Nature of American Power.* He further developed the concept in *Soft Power: The Means To Success in World Politics* (2004), defining soft power as a term that distinguishes the subtle effects of culture, values and ideas on behaviour from other coercive means such as military action.

Building Blocks

Looking back, there were a few building blocks on which the 'Incredible India' brand strategy was evolved. These were:

1. Clear definition of value proposition

The campaign differentiated India as a tourism destination based on its inherent strengths. It established what India stood for and differentiated its value proposition. Experience had become the most significant force in tourism. The campaign focused on the authentic cultural heritage and spiritual experiences that India provided.

2. Consistency in communication strategy

A consistent transmission of messages across all channels of communication (electronic/print/net) was sent to key markets across the world. The ministry and all its foreign and domestic offices adopted the same positioning and the same creatives. The temptation of changing the brand message every six months merely to establish that the ministry was dynamic, and changing the tagline after any change of officers and ministers, was avoided. This helped in sending a simple, consistent message, thereby creating a long-standing impact on the target audience.

3. Constant research and innovation

Substantial resources were spent on an annual basis to undertake research on how the travel world was evolving and the changes occurring

Box I

Accolades

PATA Grand Award – 2007
Best Destination Marketing Campaign Worldwide

CondeNast Traveller – UK Readers' Award 2007
World's No.1 Preferred Holiday Destination

World Travel Awards – 2006
1 'Incredible India' – Best Destination
   Market Campaign
2 Rural Tourism – Most Responsible Tourism
   Project
3 'Incredible India' TV Commercial – Best Tourism
   TV Commercial
'Incredible India' Best Mice Destination

Lonely Planet
India Amongst the Top 5 Destinations in
Survey of 167 Countries

Travel + Leisure
Highest Recall Advertisement Worldwide

ABTA (Association of British Travel Agents)
India is No.1 Amongst Top 50 Places for 2006

PATA Gold Awards – 2005
1 Best Print Advertisement Campaign
2 Best Destination Marketing Campaign

32

in major short- and long-haul markets. This led to constant modification in both the media plans and the finalization of creatives. Based on inputs from travellers, foreign offices and the trade, a new campaign was launched on an annual basis. New and innovative strategies were adopted in web marketing, outdoor publicity and by placing India vigorously on You Tube and other new sites in the arena of social marketing.

4. Commitment to continuous support for brand building

The biggest challenge was to convince senior officials of the Planning Commission and finance ministry to constantly provide adequate outlays. Several destination brands have died a natural death or experienced a sharp and natural decline on account of lack of continuous financial support. Our attempt was to constantly measure the impact of brand communication and assess the return on every individual investment. Quite often it was difficult to do so. However, the overall impact in terms of increased traffic flows and enhanced earnings was so impressive that outlays were willingly enhanced, both for infrastructure improvement and for promotion and publicity of India as a tourism destination.

5. Constant interaction with travellers / travel writers and editors

Most travellers perceive a destination in their own unique, emotional terms. It was therefore essential as a brand manager to constantly and relentlessly monitor how India as a destination was being perceived. It was necessary to regularly respond to mails, spend time with tour operators and writers and interact with editors of leading international journals at WTM and ITB. This enabled us to monitor the evolution of the brand and close the gaps that existed between the conceived and perceived positioning of the brand.

6. Turning tourism officials into brand ambassadors

There was an imperative need to push the brand values all the way through the organization. This necessitated tourism officials working not as file pushers but as brand managers, constantly responding to complaints and queries and interacting with tour operators. There was a radical shift towards understanding the requirements of the traveller and providing him services.

Changes in Travel Trends

During this period, throughout the world, a change in travel trends was clearly perceptible. With growing levels of affluence in China,

India, Eastern Europe and America, people had higher disposable incomes as well as leisure to travel. However, behind these economic variables were a series of underlying social, cultural, political and technological factors that brought about changes in consumer attitudes and behaviour. Various tourism bodies across the world were exploring and analysing the major attitudinal and economic aspects that would affect consumers in key travel markets and shape the future of the global industry by 2020.[12] Besides affluence, individual attitudes and aspirations, the change from a 'purchase economy' to an 'experience economy', sociopolitical evolutions, cultural and environmental concerns, and technology, were all becoming key influences on global tourism.

The changing demography of travellers has led to a growth in demand for various niche products. More and more people are opting for shorter and more frequent holidays. Emerging economies are creating new tourism destinations and increasing competition. Climate change and increasing awareness are leading to eco-tourism and nature-based holidays. With the growth of cheaper worldwide communication, the internet will influence the next generation of travel and tourism product distribution. Although terrorist attacks and natural disasters are becoming a major concern for safety and security, opening up of the skies with new air routes and budget airlines is making more destinations accessible and travel cheaper. Slow, independent travel is becoming the 'in thing' rather than the hectic package tour.

 34

Does this mean the end of mass tourism? While there will be a trend towards diversification and fragmentation driven by affluent tourists seeking specialist offerings, there will still be a demand for less specialized holidays by families and individuals with less disposable incomes. However, even the traditional 'rest and relaxation' beach holiday will need to incorporate educational or cultural elements to meet the new aspirations of twenty-first-century tourists.

Is India ready for this newly evolved international traveller? The country definitely can offer the diversity to meet the 'demand for customized holidays and knowledge-rich experience' (see a tourism expert's viewpoint in Box K).

The challenge to Indian tourism, however, lies in maintaining the momentum of growth. This is dependent on five critical Cs: civil aviation (continued opening of Indian skies), civic governance (improving the quality of infrastructure), capacity building of service providers (taxi drivers, guides, immigration), communication strategy (constant innovation of the 'Incredible India' campaign) and convergence of tourism with other sectors of the Indian economy.

Anyone who knows India understands how unwieldy she is – not just for her sheer size, but for the multilayers of opinions, attitudes, resistance, dynamism, temperaments, governing bodies, individual egos and cultural nuances. No branding strategy, no national policy would be successful unless all these numerous elements are orchestrated to perform together. Only a mammoth multisectoral activity would ensure that we achieve 360 degrees of convergence – without going around in circles ineffectually.

Fortunately, people in the government are becoming increasingly aware of the social and economic benefits of tourism. It is increasingly becoming a mission for political leaders – big and small – to lead their constituencies into the lucrative world of domestic and global tourism. At close quarters, I have seen them vigorously pursuing the sanction and implementation of rural tourism and destination and circuit development projects of their constituencies. There is a realization that tourism is a big employment creator and has immense multiplier impact. Politicians, along with the private sector and even the common man, are coming together for the first time to create a new tourism story for

Box J

Authenticity		History		Art & Culture	
Presentation of distinctive, genuine & unique culture		Past accomplishments celebrated through museums & monuments		Archietecture, fine arts & performing arts abound	
1 India	1	1 Egypt	2	1 Egypt	3
2 New Zealand	2	2 Italy	1	2 Italy	1
3 Egypt	3	3 Turkey	4	3 India	9
4 South Africa	4	4 Greece	3	4 Greece	5
5 Thailand	5	5 India	6	5 Japan	
6 Costa Rica	6	6 Israel	10	6 France	2
7 Lebanon	7	7 United Kingdom	7	7 United Kingdom	4
8 Italy	8	8 China	5	8 China	6
9 Peru	9	9 Japan	9	9 Czech Republic	
10 Morocco	10	10 France	8	10 Turkey	

India. Some of these issues are discussed at length in the chapter 'Poverty Alleviation: Tourism as the Key Catalyst'.

While exploring the developing trends surrounding the branding of countries, Creenagh Lodge, chairperson of Corporate Edge, points out, 'For countries as for commercial organizations, the final element in a successful brand is its ability to inspire. That inspiration is the first step for growing self-esteem. And the confidence thereby produced is the power which drives the brand's success.'[13]

For the inspiration to succeed and to sustain productivity over a long period, countries require brand managers with the vision and ability to execute it efficiently. The Indian tourism sector needs to identify future brand champions and give them the tools to generate fresh ideas, innovate, develop courage to implement their ideas and partner the most competent and creative people.

In the long-term, India's branding exercise will succeed dramatically if the economy achieves constant levels of growth, its infrastructure radically improves, the gains of health and education systems are made widespread and poverty levels decrease. There can be no substitute for growth. Only growth will bridge the gap between the image and reality.

Incredible India

The meru danda, or the spine.

Ancient wisdom compares it with a shining golden
mountain called Meru, the axis of the universe.
The danda-asana straightens and strengthens the spine,
the axis of our mind, body and soul. Indeed,
like Yoga and Ayurveda, India offers many stopovers for
the traveller on a journey of self-discovery.
It's an experience that's truly incredible.

www.incredibleindia.org   contactus@incredibleindia.org

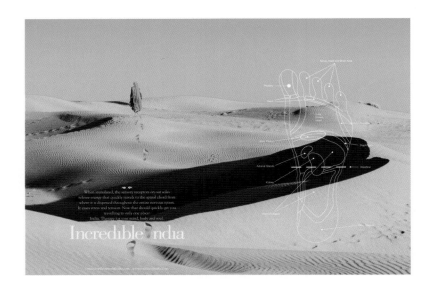

Global Campaign 2003-04

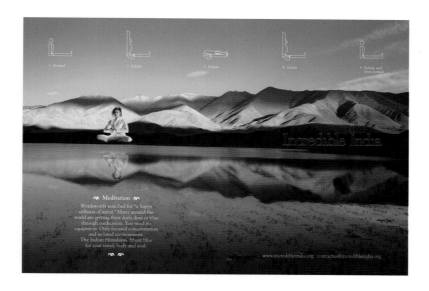

1. Normal   2. Inhale   3. Exhale   4. Inhale   5. Exhale and then normal

❧ Meditation ❧

Wordsworth searched for "a happy
stillness of mind." Many around the
world are getting their daily dose of bliss
through meditation. You need no
equipment. Only focused concentration
and isolated environment.
The Indian Himalayas. Sheer bliss
for your mind, body and soul.

❧ ❧

www.incredibleindia.org contactus@incredibleindia.org

40

This ancient science is the result of a flourishing
partnership between ayu (life) and veda (knowledge).
It is a simple way of outsmarting illness, by maintaining the
delicate balance between one's doshas (humours).
Where else will you find mystic wisdom that refuses to
grow old with time. Wisdom that is an incredible balm
for the mind, body and soul.

Sahasrara   Ajna   Vishuddhi   Anahata   Manipura   Swadisthan   Muladhara

Each one of us is a unique
composition of the five elements:
Vishuddha (Ether), Anahata (Air),
Manipura (Fire), Swadisthan
(Water) and Muladhara (Earth).

Incredible India

www.incredibleindia.org contactus@incredibleindia.org

'Long regarded as the sleeping giant of world tourism, India is now showing signs – not only of an awakening, but of a concerted and comprehensive approach to providing a firm foundation for future growth.

India is rich in what I think, especially in the case of India, to be rather trivially termed, "tourism assets" – unique and rich history and culture, grand edifices, spectacular scenery, artefacts and craftwork of unequalled beauty and painstaking skill, and a spiritual dimension that has seen the birth of half of the world's great religions and an enhancement of others. For many centuries India has been a major centre of world trade and its influence has spread to all corners of the world. But for all of this, India attracts less international visitors. What has been the anaesthetic that has led to this slumber, and has for too long robbed the country from assuming the benefits that a strong tourism industry can bring?

I would like to suggest, rather curiously, that India has not achieved its true potential, not in spite of, but because of the richness, the authenticity and the complexity of its core tourism assets, as well as the sheer size of the country. Less and less it seems the question is, "Where will I go or what will I do on my vacation?" More and more it is, "What will my holidays do for me?"

41

And in this evolution in the motivation to travel, lies the makings and the opportunity for a revolution in Indian tourism. The changes now being made by the government of India and its ministry of tourism and culture in the positioning and marketing of India are, in my view, very positive and promising.

Firstly, the move to establish a clearly defined brand for India will, for the first time, allow the unique essence, values and personality of India to be succinctly defined and communicated. It will allow the essence of India to really resonate within the perceptions of key targeted segments of the market.

Secondly, we are seeing a change from an emphasis on "what India has to offer" to one where there is a more direct understanding of and engagement with the customer by identifying their key holiday motivations, and fulfilling their needs and aspirations.

The change from promoting India's places and things, to one that promotes "spiritual and mental refreshment" is a significant one and one which, I am sure, will connect with the changing motivation for travel. But in making the necessary changes, this is just the first part of the task. We are seeing a defining of the promise to our customers – "Come to India and you will be spiritually and mentally refreshed". Even more importantly, we now have to define, facilitate and deliver a range of experiences that will fulfill that promise...

I look forward to India fulfilling its destiny as it emerges as one of the giants of world tourism.'

John King, Chairman, Tasmania State Tourism Board, Australia

Not all Indians are polite, hospitable and vegetarian.

The Royal Bengal Tiger is the undisputed king of wild India. The tiger apart, you can observe over 1,200 types of birds and more than 272 animal species at India's 84 national parks and 447 wildlife sanctuaries. Scared?

Incredible !ndia
www.incredibleindia.org

Global Campaign 2006-07

A Tale of Two Ministers – Contrasting Styles

The 'Incredible India' campaign was launched during Jagmohan's tenure as minister for tourism and culture from 2002-04. Jagmohan had a passion for infrastructure. Before he became tourism minister he had changed the face of pilgrimage destination at 'Mata Vaishno Devi'. He went about with missionary zeal to improve the quality of the tourism infrastructure in India. He travelled extensively, took his team of officers from all departments to destination sites, undertook comprehensive inspections and decided the road map and action plan for site development. Based on the field visits, the development projects were formulated and sanctioned. He then closely and rigorously monitored the projects and cracked the whip when time and cost overruns and implementation delays took place. He effectively converged the functioning of the ministry of tourism and culture, the Archeological Survey of India (ASI) and the Central Public Works Department (CPWD) and, in his short tenure, demonstrated that radical changes could be speedily brought about in the quality of experience at the destination level. Infrastructure improvements at Ajanta-Ellora, Mahabalipuram, Kurukshetra, Chittorgarh, Kumbalgarh, Humayun's Tomb and Haridwar are a consequence of his drive and determination.

Jagmohan, however, genuinely believed that marketing should be undertaken only after the heritage sites in India were radically transformed. He also felt that tourism officials preferred the softer option of promotion and marketing rather than undertaking the tougher task of infrastructure improvement at key destinations. Prior to the 'Incredible India' campaign, the marketing outlay of the ministry of tourism was distributed amongst its eighteen offices abroad. Each office had its own advertising agency and its own tagline – some termed it 'Unbelievable India', some called it 'Colours of India' and others termed it 'Spiritual and Cultural India'. There was no synergy, no uniformity, no brilliance in creativity, no convergence of media, and above all, a lack of positioning and branding of India as a tourism destination.

It required all the persuasive skills of Rathi Vinay Jha, V.K. Duggal and myself to convince Jagmohan of the need to launch a centralized marketing campaign with specific dedicated outlays. After several rounds of interaction, he agreed verbally but never really approved it on file. The file always came back with a query. So it was based only on his verbal consent that the 'Incredible India' campaign was launched. Soon thereafter, Jagmohan directed that the brand line should be changed to 'The Wonder that is India' based on A.L. Basham's magnum opus, *The Wonder that was India* and I had to finally tell him that consumer research by marketing experts had revealed that the phrase 'Incredible India' in its creative form would be catchy, appealing, contemporary and would make an impact.

To his great credit, it must be said that Jagmohan later attributed the entire success of the campaign to his officials. He became an active convert and vigorously promoted and marketed the new destinations he had created as an integral component of the 'Incredible India' campaign.

Ambika Soni, the minister of tourism and culture (at the time of writing), understood the need for effective marketing strategies. She had a sense of colour, design and visual appeal and gave the final approval to the creatives – almost to the extent of directing them herself – not because she wanted to interfere in the arena of creativity but because she had clarity of vision and a sense of direction on how India as a destination should be promoted and marketed. In many ways, notwithstanding her allergy to the dancing elephant in the 'Incredible India' commercial, she brought freshness and innovation to the campaign.

 44

The 'Incredible India @ 60' campaigns in New York and India as a 'Partner Country' in Berlin were conceptualized and driven with energy and clockwork precision by Ambika Soni. Both these events have had a tremendous and overwhelming impact on the consumer. In fact, no country in the world has attempted branding through events of such scale, size and dimension. She has taken this further and launched an integrated 'Incredible India' campaign and opened an Indian tourism office in China, which has emerged as the largest outbound market in the world, and focused strongly on the short-haul markets of Southeast Asia. An example of this is the 'Incredible India' event in Singapore. Ambika Soni has also effectively synergized and converged tourism's strength and resources with private bodies like the CII and Experience India Society. This has enabled a focused, concentrated attack on the key source and emerging market. In the long run, these initiatives will have a tremendous impact on the growth of inbound tourism to India.

The two ministers had, however, one thing in common – the highest levels of integrity I have come across in my twenty-eight years as a civil servant.

Incredible India

45

Incredible India

Global Campaign 2004-05

46

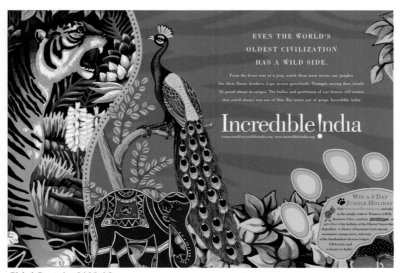

Global Campaign 2005-06

And to think these days
men get away with giving flowers and
chocolates to their wives.

A monument of love built by an inconsolable emperor, Shah Jehan, in memory of his wife Mumt
Arguably the world's most photographed monument, the Taj is one of India's twenty-six World H

Mahal is perhaps best experienced in moonlight.
...s. Do visit with a loved one.

Incredible !ndia
www.incredibleindia.org

Just how do you paint a canvas
that's ten feet high, weighs over four tons
and does not stand still.

Incredible India

49

One day, man will travel at
the speed of thought. Pity.

Incredible India

Global Campaign 2006-07

A step-by-step guide to salvation.

50

Don't panic.
There's always rebirth.

With some of the world's highest mountains, fastest rapids and a long coastline, India sets adrenaline rushing. Game? Incredible !ndia

reathe out.
reathe out.

e!ndia

London cab, part of 'Incredible India' campaign

Tram in Berlin at ITB 2007

Bus in New York, part of Incredible India@60

London cab, part of 'India Now' campaign

London bus, part of 'India Now' campaign

London bus, part of 'India Now' campaign

Box L

'Atithi Devo Bhavah'

In the latest Indian tourism commercial, Bollywood film icon Aamir Khan stops a young romantic couple from inscribing their feelings on the walls of a World Heritage site. Earlier, leading film actor Sharukh Khan had spread a powerful message against littering at heritage and tourism sites. These films, along with commercials for educating taxi drivers and guides, form an integral component of the social awareness 'Athihi Devo Bhavah' (Guest is God) campaign.

This was a customized integrated campaign to bring about attitudinal and behavioural changes amongst key stakeholders towards foreign tourists and to create social awareness of the benefits of tourism among the general public. The stakeholders had to be made to realize that if foreign tourists went back happy, then more tourists would make the effort to visit India, resulting in greater financial benefits for the stakeholders. The aim was also to bring about a positive change in the attitude towards foreign tourists.

The objective of the 'Atithi Devo Bhavah' campaign was to remind people about India's ancient belief that Guest was God, and to implement it in the context of tourists. The programme consisted of three components: (a) Training and certification, (b) PR, contact programmes and road shows and (c) Mass media communication.

Training and certification

This involved sensitizing the key stakeholders and training them in terms of changing their attitude and behaviour towards tourists.

The first segment consisted of taxi drivers, porters, baggage handlers and tour guides.

The second consisted of restaurant owners, staff of small hotels, shop owners and shop staff.

The third consisted of custom and immigration officials, airlines staff and tour operators.

The phase one training programme covered four areas:

(i) Hygiene: This included personal hygiene of the person and also that of the product/service.

(ii) Conduct and behaviour: Politeness and basic courtesies in interacting with foreign tourists.

(iii) Integrity: This aimed at ensuring that the service-provider did not cheat the tourist and charged a fair price for the specific service.

(iv) Safety and security: Personal safety and security of the foreign tourist.

In the first phase of the programme, the training was carried out in seven cities – Delhi, Mumbai, Agra, Jaipur, Goa, Hyderabad and Aurangabad. A total of 26,300 stakeholders were trained in this phase.

The people undergoing training were given certificates, a pledge (which they also verbalized), badges, stickers and a training manual. The certification was valid for six months, after which they had to get themselves retrained. 'Atithi Devo Bhavah' was to be used as a benchmark for quality and as a process of certification.

PR, contact programmes and road shows

A PR exercise was conducted to create awareness about the programme and the strong need for attitudinal changes towards foreign tourists. Contact programmes and road shows were undertaken to explain the concept to the tourist trade. These contact programmes were conducted in the seven cities mentioned earlier.

Mass media communication

Mass media tools were targeted at the general public, while focusing on the stakeholders of the tourism industry. The key communication objectives of the mass media campaign were as follows:
(a) Create awareness and bring about an attitudinal change in the behaviour of the target audience towards foreign tourists.
(b) Explain to the stakeholder how it is in their own interest that more foreign tourists should come to India, which would only be possible if they get good service and have a happy experience in India.
(c) Explain the concept of 'Atithi Devo Bhavah'.

Creative units

The creative initiatives consisted of the following:

1. A film and visual explaining the background and the need to carry out the programme in order to bring about an attitudinal and behavioural change among stakeholders in the Indian tourism industry towards foreign tourists. It was produced both in Hindi and English.
2. Two ad films for television: one focusing on taxi drivers and the other on tourist guides.
3. A four-ad campaign in Hindi and regional languages targeting taxi drivers, tourist guides and tour operators. These ads were released in the first phase.
4. In the second phase, a three-ad campaign was released in Hindi and regional languages to carry the communication forward and to explain in more direct terms the financial benefits accruing to the stakeholders from the foreign tourists.
5. Radio spots were also prepared and used on FM radio channels.

Results

The first phase of the 'Atithi Devo Bhavah' campaign ran during the period January 2005 to March 2005, when 26,000 stakeholders were trained in seven cities.

The mass media campaign created awareness and interest among stakeholders and the general public about the need to improve the behaviour towards foreign tourists.

The second phase ran from November 2005 to March 2006. In this phase, a total of 52,000 stakeholders were trained.

'The Malayali ethos is the same as the best of the Indian ethos: inclusive, flexible, eclectic, absorptive. Kerala has shown the way: may the rest of India follow.' Shashi Tharoor

'God's Own Country' shows the way: Kerala, where it all began

In more ways than one, Kerala takes credit for being the first state in India to comprehend the significance and importance of positioning and branding in the sphere of tourism. From being a non-entity in the mid-1980s, Kerala today has evolved into Indian tourism's superbrand and the country's most premium holiday destination – where the likes of Paul McCartney and Richard Branson holiday. The most written and talked about destination in India, Kerala's worldwide success represents the triumph of vision, professionalism and public-private partnerships in the volatile and turbulent world of tourism. I can talk with confidence about Kerala tourism's astounding growth because I was part of the quiet revolution that swept across the unbelievably green state.

Though I have seen most of India, there are three regions that have touched my life irreversibly. Uttar Pradesh, where I was born and brought up, surrounded by the mystique of the Himalayas, the Ganga and the Taj Mahal; New Delhi, where most bureaucrats end up at some point in their careers to walk the corridors of power and more importantly, perhaps, to experience a city that is a blend of several historical eras with its monuments, tombs and elegant tree-lined avenues; and Kerala, where I have lived and worked for long periods, spending almost two decades in the state, amidst breathtaking scenery and in the backwaters of 'God's Own Country'.

This long association has given me a deep insight into the Kerala psyche.

I can't put a finger on what exactly drew me to the state at first sight. It could be the simplicity and tranquillity of life there. It could be the soothing green that envelops you – especially for one used to the earthy brown of the plains. Kerala's luxuriant landscape is undiluted nature, and its magic lies in the fact that almost the entire state is a tourist destination, with the life of the people very much a part of its allure. The people of Kerala have always fascinated me. Almost always clad in shades of white, to me they represent a pristine land.

My fascination for Kerala also has a very personal reason – as the secretary for tourism, government of Kerala, I had the opportunity to build the brand called 'God's Own Country' in select national and international markets. I was lucky enough to witness the state scale new heights of glory, winning global recognition as 'one of the ten exotic paradises of the world', as *National Geographic Traveler* identified it in its millennium collectors' issue. As secretary of tourism, I enjoyed a close relationship with the state, and was fortunate to catch glimpses of the place that would otherwise have eluded me.

For me, Kerala is at her best during the monsoons. There is an endearing rawness about the state that comes alive during the monsoons, when the entire land is wrapped in rich green, and the people surrender to the rejuvenating powers of ayurveda. Onam is another time I treasure. The cool breeze, the fields golden with ripened crops, the occasional drizzle that plays havoc with the pookalams (flower decorations).... One can't overlook Kerala during the Onam festival and the best way to celebrate it is with the boat races the state is synonymous with. Call it a ballet or symphony, the sheer energy of the races never fails to surprise me.

Some of my most cherished memories have to do with Kerala. One of them relates to the first anniversary of the Babri Masjid incident. I was then the district collector of Calicut (now Kozhikode), a predominantly Muslim region. The town was tense; so was the administration. The highly volatile situation called for a delicate handling of events. That was when we decided to invite all the leading artists in Kerala to give form and colour to their perception of communal harmony on a hundred-metre-long canvas. The best part of it was the participation of India's celebrated artist, M.F. Husain, who had readily agreed to my spontaneous invitation.

Much to our surprise and relief, there was no untoward incident the next day. Instead, we saw thousands watching in awe as artists, led by the inimitable Husain, filled the massive canvas with images of peace and harmony. The transformation was electric and I can, to this day, feel the goodwill and harmony that infused the atmosphere. For me, the day was also a revelation of the power that pure art had on a people who had inherited one of the world's finest cultural riches. Only

'God's Own Country' is perhaps the most powerful positioning statement for an Indian destination. But it was not easy to pull it off. The opposition was stiff. 'How can India's first communist state be called "God's Own Country"?' 'Why are you targeting only pilgrims?' 'How can you own God?' 'What is the rest of the world then – the devil's?' There was no end to the criticism. But thankfully, the officials at the time had it in them to stick to the positioning that in reality was a brilliant springboard to showcase the myriad facets of Kerala's most powerful tourism product, nature. Written by the late Walter Mendez, it was T.K. Harshan, now the chairman of the Stark group of companies, who was instrumental in selecting, presenting and establishing this positioning. Since then, it has been used brilliantly as a creative platform by the Stark team lead by Swarup B.R. In fact, Stark has been instrumental in partnering with Kerala Tourism and building the brand over a decade by providing 360-degree support in terms of strategy, and creative and marketing services.

Keralites can immerse themselves this deep in art, for the plentiful natural surroundings have beautifully honed their senses, bestowing them with the sensibility to pause and appreciate the simple joys of life.

Convergence of Events

The story of tourism in Kerala is one of a serendipitous convergence of events. When Kerala launched its first aggressive print campaign in the late 1980s, everyone mocked us. 'What on earth do you have, other than an ITDC hotel in Kovalam?' they asked. Little did anyone know that the deliberate decision not to wait for the perfect situation to begin the campaign would be the first step towards creating a tourism model that the rest of India would emulate in the years to come. And never did anyone in Kerala think that in just over another decade, tourism would emerge as the most powerful industry in the state.

This campaign sparked off a chain reaction. To begin with, enquiries started pouring in (see Box A). With an alarming dearth of good hotels and resorts, the department of tourism had no option but to ask the Kerala Tourism Development Corporation to respond. Sensing the opportunity, a large number of travel agents across Kerala – who owed their existence to the exodus of Malayalees to the Middle East, starting in the early 1980s – decided to don the garb of tour operators as well. Soon, home-bred tourism entrepreneurs got into the act of creating a tourism infrastructure, especially focusing on resorts and hotels (see Box B).

Homespun entrepreneurship was of tremendous relevance twenty years ago. For a state that firmly believed – and still does – in shifting political allegiances between two warring parties every five years and that was notorious for its militant labour and dharnas and bandhs (strikes), it required the innate skill of a Keralite to navigate his project through the various labyrinthine channels that would put the backwaters to shame.

The department of tourism, in the meantime, stepped up its promotional activities and started participating in domestic as well as international travel and trade fairs. Very soon, the number of visitors started climbing. In 1995, charters started flying in, bringing in around 10,000 tourists – all of them heading to the beaches of Kovalam. Kerala looked ready to take off – albeit in the wrong direction. The charters accentuated mass tourism. The cluttered, unplanned development in Kovalam, triggered by the backpackers and the 'hippies' of the 1970s, became worse in the wake of mass tourism, which contributed little or nothing to the local economy. We had charters full of garbage-collectors from Manchester and cobblers from London taking more from the destination (gorgeous sun, sand and sea) than what they contributed to it (£15 a night). In short, high-volume, low-value tourism started to thrive.

When I stepped in as secretary to the government of Kerala in charge of tourism in 1999, there were two clear choices in front of me – to take the easy way out by pushing mass tourism, encouraging more charters, focusing on numbers to ensure success – or to take a tough stance in the long-term interest of the state and change the model of growth with a specific focus on quality tourism that was also sustainable, to ensure that the state would stay in the business of tourism. Though I knew that I might incur the wrath of many, I chose the second option.

I was working with a tourism minister, E. Chandrasekhar, who was an old-world communist – deeply committed to the ideology, yet practical, realistic and far-sighted. Fortunately, he endorsed my approach and provided all the support required to effect the critical shift in Kerala Tourism. My colleague, Dr Venu V, who was then the director of Kerala Tourism, and who later joined me in the tourism ministry in Delhi, shared the same vision and played a vital role in realizing it. My predecessor, K. Jayakumar (a creative whiz), and successor, T. Balakrishnan (who earlier made a tremendous impact as director of tourism), also played critical roles in the development of tourism in Kerala.

A detailed study of the situation revealed that the shifts we needed to make were many – and I was determined that we did everything from the perspective of building the brand called Kerala Tourism.

Targeting the Affluent

To begin with, we decided that we would do away with the whole concept of mass tourism. Charters were consciously discouraged – this was also to rejuvenate a rather tired Kovalam. In terms of overall marketing and promotion, the focus was shifted to the affluent, sensitive traveller, to whom Kerala was pitched as an upmarket destination. This was done with the specific intention of ensuring that the benefits of tourism percolated down to the common man.

Studies show clearly that backpackers and budget travellers pay for their entire holiday in the country of origin – they tend to spend

Homespun Successes

Though most of the leading hospitality brands, including the Taj, the Oberoi, the Leela, Le Meridian, the Radisson, the Ramada and the Banyan Tree, are in Kerala today, it is homebred innovators like the CGH Earth group (formerly the Casino Group) with sensationally good properties like the Coconut Lagoon, Spice Village and so on that set the ball rolling. The Dominic family, now headed by Jose Dominic (see also the chapter, 'Sustainability: the itinerary for the future') is the perfect example of a native creating hospitality environments that address the aspirations of new age travellers. Dynamic young tour operaters like E.M. Najeeb of Air Travel Enterprises, the Abad group of hotels, the Muthoot Group, Kumarakom Lake Resort, Travancore Heritage and a host of other entrepreneurs have done Kerala proud. What sets Kerala apart is the fact that home stays, which just offer anywhere between one and five rooms, are also doing extremely well.

The first and foremost is Klaus Schleusner, a professor of German language at IIT, Chennai, who created the Surya Samudra Beach Garden. He was the first one to painfully dismantle, assemble and restore a number of traditional, 200-300 year old wooden 'Tharwad' bungalows, to create a resort in beautiful natural surroundings. Klaus understood luxury, focused on the discerning traveller and resisted the greed to be big. Slowly and steadily, he created Surya Samudra amidst unfettered serenity and a gorgeous setting that totally cut you off from civilization. Klaus built a swimming pool carved out of a rock quarry with carvings underwater and water flowing out of the mouth of Lord Brahma. It was always a learning process to spend an evening with Klaus, and my own worldview and perspective of tourism evolved out of these interactions. Klaus has moved on in life and is in the process of launching another unique hideaway.

Then there are Victor and Jini Dey, who operate one of the finest home stays in India – Tranquil Plantations. Tranquil is nestled in a 400-acre private coffee and vanilla plantation within the remote and lush rainforest of Wayand, in the northern region of Kerala. The facility has eight rooms, a luxury treehouse and the experience here, amidst lush gardens, ablaze with scarlet hibiscus, birds of paradise, potted geraniums and three dogs, is truly invigorating. For the discerning traveller interested in eco-tourism with a unique flavour, Tranquil and its surroundings are unparalleled.

Joerg Dreschsel and his wife Txukxsu (pronounced Chukku) operate Malabar Escapes, the finest chain of small boutique and villa hotels in Kerala. The Malabar House in the heart of Fort Cochin is chock-a-block with antiques and art that you can only marvel at. It seamlessly combines tradition and contemporary design in each of its seventeen rooms and suites having their own eclectic mix of distinctive colour, designs, antiques and art. The hotel is a member of Relais Chateaux and is certified by Green Globe 21. A special feature of Malabar House is its gourmet restaurant, which blends South Indian cooking with Mediterranean cuisine against a background of live performances of South Indian dance and classical music. No wonder *Time* magazine termed it as the Best Boutique Hotel of Asia in 2007.

I would like to mention Moosa and his wife, Faiza, who operate Ayesha Manzil, a beautiful old colonial-style mansion overlooking the blue Arabian Sea in the charming little town of Tellicherry. I started my career in Tellicherry as a sub-collector, staying in a house made by Lord Wellesley, who later became the Duke of Wellington. Moosa became one of my earliest friends in Kerala. My wife Ranjeeta and I were frequent visitors to Ayesha Manzil and Ranjeeta learnt her first lessons in Kerala cooking from Faiza. Ayesha Manzil was built in 1862 by Murdoch Brown, an Englishman who came to Tellicherry as a trader of the East India Company. It was once the largest and most famous trading centre for spices, especially pepper, widely known as black gold, the most sought after spice in Europe. Tellicherry pepper can still be bought out of the supermarket shelves in Europe and is renowned for its pungency and flavour.

At Ayesha Manzil, time stands still as you witness the Arabian Sea in all its grandeur. The silence is only broken by some of the greatest Moplah dishes – mussels, clams, oysters, fish parathas and Motta Mala (a garland made out of egg yoke) – based on the local recipes of a renowned culinary expert – Faiza.

freezone
life in a new light

Infrastructure. **Golden beaches. Green shores. Yellow coconuts.**
Dream projects. **Catamaran rides. Hammock naps. Surfboard thrills.**
Prize catches. **Brown tans. White surf. Red shrimps.**
Cool incentives. **Dance dramas. Forays into historic forts. Fishing hamlet tours.**
Four-in-one-offers. **Beaches. Backwaters. Hill stations. Wildlife sanctuaries.**
Kerala. Your high-return hideaway.

One of the ten paradises of the world
- National Geographic Traveler

kerala
God's Own Country

info@keralatourism.org | Call: 1-800-425-4747 | www.keralatourism.org

highway
life in a new light

Life flows by at 10 kmph. No pollution. No horns. No gas stations.
Delightful rush hours. Fleets of ducks. Flocks of birds. Schools of fish.
Fast food fresh from the net. Pearlspot. Prawns. Mussels.
Houseboats for waterbeds. Park where you please. Float. Doze. Dream.
Faithful wake-up birds. Pelicans. Cormorants. Egrets.
Forty-four rivers stretch endlessly. No speed breakers. No traffic lights. No one-ways.
Kerala. Your road to peace.

One of the ten paradises of the world
- National Geographic Traveler

kerala
God's Own Country

info@keralatourism.org | Call: 1-800-425-4747 | www.keralatourism.org

less money once they are here, quite unlike affluent travellers. Backpackers also triggered a particular kind of development – the one-hundred-rupee-a-night rooms that mushroomed all over Kovalam when it became the haunt of backpackers. Affluent tourists, on the other hand, inspire world-class resorts that in Kerala are traditional in flavour but modern in amenities. In fact, this conscious shift in focus, which enhanced unit value, has been the foundation of brand Kerala. In December 2007, after hunting high and low across Kerala, the only room a friend of mine could manage to find to bring in the new year was a suite in Kumarakom, at Rs 30,000 a night. Kerala is one of the most expensive destinations in India today – especially between September and March.

The next step was to identify the products that were exclusive to Kerala – products that were the key to the success of tourism. Needless to say, the backwaters and the traditional system of ayurveda were chosen and these became the rallying points.

The extensive palm-fringed backwaters of Kerala, stretching to almost 1,000 kilometres, continue to charm the world. With houseboats entering the picture in the early 1990s, exploring the backwaters became one of the most enchanting attractions of Kerala. The 'kettuvallams' (traditional rice boats made without using a single nail) were converted into magnificent houseboats replete with open-air decks, bedrooms with attached bathrooms, kitchens and all the conveniences of a good hotel. The only difference was that you could check in and drift into a mesmerizing water-world of peace and quiet.

Ayurveda was God's prescription for Kerala. Not only did it rejuvenate the traveller, it also cured him of many ailments. Today, Kerala is the destination of choice for the authentic ayurvedic experience – be it cosmetic or therapeutic. In addition to increasing the duration of the traveller's stay in Kerala (up to three weeks or more), ayurveda has rapidly converted the traditionally lean June-July monsoon months to the main season for visitors. This trend is thanks to the fact that ancient texts clearly state that ayurvedic regimens are most effective during the monsoon when the body pores open out, making the application of medicinal oils and other treatments more efficacious.

The other key feature that made Kerala stand out was its wealth of culture. Where else could a visitor watch legendary maestros like Krishnan Nair and Gopi perform the majestic dance drama of Kerala,

Kathakali, till 4 a.m.? Kathakali is a metaphysical art form, a vigorous blend of dance, music, action, literature, and even painting. Then there is the perfect solo dance drama Thullal, which is characterized by wit and humour. Mohiniattam is another gentle and graceful classical dance form, its elegant costume being a cream sari with a wide gold border and traditional gold ornaments.

The classical dance forms of Kerala are a delicate fusion of ancient classical texts and folk traditions. Koodiyattam is the oldest surviving form of Sanskrit theatre, recognized by UNESCO as an 'intangible heritage of humanity'. There are also the Chakyarkoothu, Nangiarkoothu and Krishanattam forms. The most popular of Kerala's array of performing arts is the Theyyam, a ritualistic dance form of north Kerala. It is a devotional performance with a surrealistic representation of the divine. Kerala also has a unique literary flavour and has produced some remarkable writers, including Thakazhi Sivasankara Pillai, Vaikom Muhammod Basheer, G. Sankara Kurup, Pottekad and M.T. Vasudevan Nair.

Once the key products – the backwaters and ayurveda (along with a vast repertoire of art forms and exotic cuisine,the two other aspects that set Kerala clearly apart) were identified, a series of familiarization (FAM) tours were launched for leading tour operators and travel writers from key emerging markets relevant to Kerala. These tours yielded rich dividends. In addition to eminent tour operators featuring Kerala, the editorial coverage that Kerala enjoyed was truly valuable.

Turning Point

The turning point, however, happened when the *National Geographic Traveler*, after extensive research spanning two years, brought out a special issue at the turn of the century on the fifty destinations of a lifetime – the only destination that featured from India was Kerala (see Box C). The international trade suddenly woke up to 'God's Own Country' – and Kerala got a new lease of life. Of course, the social development indices of Kerala played a very important role – travellers as well as travel writers were more than impressed by the fact that Kerala has the highest literacy in India (close to hundred percent), the highest health standards in India (proven by the lowest infant mortality and highest life expectancy), the highest Physical Quality of Life Index (PQLI), the lowest crime rate and so on. As Noble Laureate Amartya Sen comments: 'There is also one state, where life expectancy is higher

BY BILL McKIBBEN

PARADISE FOUND

K ERALA IS A VERY EASY PLACE to simply sit back and
enjoy. The name means "land of coconuts," and the palms
shade nearly the entire state from the tropical sun; many
call the beach at Kovalam the best in India; visitors can spend
a day riding small ferries through the backwater lagoons or
watching elephants cavort in the wildlife sanctuaries; the spicy food may
be the best vegetarian cuisine on the planet.

But for me, the real reason to visit Kerala, which lies at the southwest-
ern tip of the subcontinent, is for the *intellectual* adventure: Kerala
is a bizarre anomaly among developing nations, a place that offers real hope

Elephants *(left)* at
a Hindu temple in
Vadakkumnathan
wear elaborate
dress during spring
festival season.

for the future of the Third World. Consider: This small state in India
much larger than Maryland, has a population as big as California's and
annual income of less than $300. But its infant mortality rate is low, its
among the highest on Earth, and its birthrate below America's and
Kerala's citizens live nearly as long as Americans or Europeans. Th
a land of paddy-covered plains, statistically Kerala stands out as the Mount Ever
development; there's truly no place like it.

In the mornings, from nearly anywhere in Kerala, you can hear loud music from the
ples, wailing muezzins at the mosques, and church bells ringing at the cathedrals. Rel
ance is just one reason for Kerala's success. The state government has effected sw

KERALA, INDI

Tra
large
backwa
like
Cochin
used
ar

"There is in the kingdom a great quantity of pepper and ginger   and cinnamon and nuts of India."—*Marco Polo*

Box C

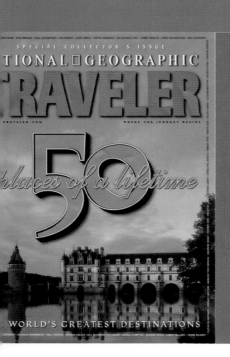

In its October 1999 special collector's issue, National Geographic Traveler selected Kerala as one of the 50 destinations of a lifetime. The feature by Bill Mckibben celebrated Kerala as a 'Paradise Found'.

than China (75 years at birth as opposed to China's 72) and infant mortality lower (12, as opposed to China's 28). Kerala has good state policies of supporting school education for all and making sure that it works; and has provided free health care for all for many decades now. Even though now many well-to-do families choose private medical care, everyone still has the option of having health care from the state.'[1]

The strategic shift in the profile of the traveller that Kerala started wooing and the new-found international recognition, were the two things that sparked off the award-winning 'Watercolours By God' campaign in 1998. The first-ever television commercial done by a tourism board in India, this breathtaking commercial captured the magic of Kerala and differentiated it dramatically from other states. It was shot by the internationally renowned cinematographer, Santosh Sivan. During those days, outlays for tourism were minuscule. With limited budgets, there was no way we could produce truly international commercials. I recall flying to Mumbai, meeting Santosh in the Taj Coffee Shop and convincing him to create something truly exceptional for his home state at virtually no cost. Santosh, a passionate film-maker, worked like an artist possessed and made a series of commercials which captured Kerala in all its moods and colours and which have been acclaimed as the finest destination commercials till date. Soon after the launch of the film, Kerala Tourism also became the first tourism board in India to venture into advertising on the internet.

The next major initiative to be launched was Synergy, the public-private partnership enterprise in tourism. Synergy sparked off a whole new world of opportunity, where the department and the trade ceased to function as independent duchies and joined hands to take Kerala Tourism forward. In fact it was Synergy that gave Kerala the strength to move out of the Indian tourism pavilion and set up an independent stall of its own at international trade fairs. Synergy also resulted in more trade members participating in domestic as well as international roadshows – on an average, fifty to one hundred trade participants attend the roadshows organized by Kerala Tourism. The partnership has been a critical force in implementing innovative initiatives in the industry. The tourism department has extended marketing, publicity and policy support to the trade, which in turn has ensured that tourism development is sustainable, friendly to the destination and preserves the culture and traditions of the land.

nightlife
life in a new light

Blazing torches. Searing music. Dancing flames. Swaying people.
Pulsating rhythms. Throbbing drums. Clashing cymbals. Glistening bodies.
Intoxicating vapours. White mist. All permeating. Sensuous.
Slowly everyone slips into a trance. Mind. Body. Soul.
And then as pilgrims they awake. Purged. Forgiven. Blessed.
Hindus. Christians. Muslims. All.
Kerala. Your path to nirvana.

One of the ten paradises of the world
- National Geographic Traveler

God's Own Country

info@keralatourism.org ¦ Call: 1-800-425-4747 ¦ www.keralatourism.org

workshop
life in a new light

First a test-drive to discover how your body has coped. With deadlines. Targets. Life in the fast lane.
Then the overhaul using Ayurveda. The 5000 year old system of medicine. 100% natural. 100% safe.
Rejuvenation regimens. Rasayana chikitsa. Shodhana chikitsa. Kayakalpa chikitsa.
Water wash. Medicated baths. Monsoon showers. Total cleansing.
Touch and polish. To wipe away the wrinkles of worry. The scars of pollution. The ailments of age.
And then you are road ready. Glowing body. Singing mind. Soaring spirit.
Kerala. Your trip to eternal youth.

One of the ten paradises of the world
- National Geographic Traveler

kerala
God's Own Country

info@keralatourism.org : Call: 1-800-425-4747 : www.keralatourism.org

The high point in the life of the brand was also sparked off by Synergy in the year 2000 – by an event called the Kerala Travel Mart (KTM).[2] For the first time in India, a single destination hosted a buyer-seller meet that turned out to be a resounding success. So much so that KTM has become a bi-annual event that today attracts over one thousand buyers – 400 from across fifty countries, and over 600 from the rest of India. The number of sellers has gone up steadily and embraces almost every entrepreneur who has a tourism product to sell internationally. In addition to giving the buyers a first-hand experience of the products and enabling the sellers to plan business for the next season by pre-selling room nights, KTM ensures equal opportunity for all the players in the tourism industry in Kerala. Young entrepreneurs like E.M. Najeeb and Jose Dominic have displayed visionary leadership in rapidly evolving it into one of the most powerful marts in the world. It is a brilliant example of what private-public partnership can achieve – with the government acting as a facilitator-cum-catalyst and the trade fostering entrepreneurship in the larger interest of sustaining and building the tourism sector for the good of all.

Over the years, product innovation by the trade has contributed substantially to Kerala's success. The list is quite long – the houseboat, the tree house, butterfly holidays, tiger trail holidays that won international acclaim because they converted poachers into guides, and many others. Meetings, Incentives, Conventions and Exhibitions (MICE) also started thriving, especially small and medium-sized groups. Monsoon tourism has also turned out to be a remarkable winner. A dedicated campaign was launched to promote the monsoon, the key impetus for the campaign being that the monsoon is traditionally the best time to practise ayurvedic regimens – both cosmetic and therapeutic. This slowly started yielding results – occupancy levels that normally hit rock bottom during the monsoon started picking up, raising the hope that Kerala would become a land where the season never ends.

With arrival figures climbing steadily, it became imperative to carry out a campaign within Kerala in order to sensitize Keralites about how tourism enriches the state. This multimedia campaign, in addition to highlighting the fact that tourism sustains art as well as the environment, also inspired the Malayalee to make an effort to understand his own culture – especially taking into consideration the fact that the international traveller often knew more about Kerala art forms and architecture

A few years ago, this lady from
    France fell in love with Kerala.
Today, she's married to Mohiniyattom.

Corinne Mathou, France

Corinne Mathou's devotion to Mohiniyattom is complete. And someday, she aspires to teach this dance form to others. Strange as it may seem, it was a German who compiled the first Malayalam dictionary three hundred years ago. It was a Dutch who first recorded our biodiversity two hundred years ago. Across time, many foreign nationals, fascinated by this land have settled down here and become more Keralan in their ways than Keralites. Today, over 66 lakh travellers who love our land, our customs and our traditions visit Kerala every year. The world certainly is proud of Kerala. Are you?

kerala
God's Own Country

Kerala Tourism Park View Trivandrum 695 033 Kerala Ph: 0471-2321132 Fax: 2322279
Email: info@keralatourism.org www.keralatourism.org

than he did. The campaign highlighted the presence of travellers like Louba Schild and Corinne Mathou, who were so fascinated with the art forms that they settled here to master Kathakali and Mohiniattam (see Box D).

New Destinations

The biggest thing that happened to tourism in Kerala was the opening up of three new destinations – Kumarakom, Munnar and Wayanad. In no time, these locations became hot favourites, with celebrities ranging from ex-Beatle Paul McCartney to the then prime minister of India, A.B. Vajpayee, holidaying here. Tourism was on a roll and investments poured into this sector. Destination management companies emerged and perception-wise, Kerala became the No.1 tourism destination in India.

One of the initiatives that fetched us tremendous mileage was that we invited M.F. Husain to spend a fortnight in Kerala to do a series of paintings, which he later titled 'Kalyanikuttiyude Keralam'. Husain's paintings were an exquisite evocation of Kerala – its lagoons, forests, cultural art forms and the many-hued greenery of the countryside with its emerald fields, banana groves and coconut trees. Replacing his trademark horses with elephants, Husain embodied the magic of Kerala through the dazzling fluency of his brush. These paintings were brilliantly interpreted by Shashi Tharoor in a special book on 'God's Own Country'.[3] Tharoor's essay was a nostalgic rendition by a writer who, despite being city born and bred, has an inordinate pride in the Malayali cultural heritage. The foreword that I wrote for that book summed it all up (see Box E).

Since then, the distinguished Indian artists, Yusuf Arakkal and Paresh Maitey, have painted canvasses of Kerala in all its vivid colours. Their works on Kerala have been viewed extensively and written about widely, capturing the imagination of the art world.

Maitey, in his book, *An Enchanting Journey*, describes his experience thus: 'Kerala has always fascinated me. It is beautiful, lyrical, romantic and mesmerizing like my native land. Kerala presents a multitude of magical and captivating images. Its majestic caparisoned elephants, the endless carpet of green paddy fields, the curving contours of the boats, the fishing nets filtering the sunrays into prisms of translucent lightness, the filigreed pattern of the coconut trees against the charcoal skies pregnant with the monsoon and ethereality of its backwaters.

'In the summer of 2000, when I was the tourism secretary in Kerala, we decided to invite select celebrities to Kerala as part of a brand-building exercise. Needless to say, the first name that came to my mind was none other than Husain. He was the best brand God's Own Country could be associated with. I invited him right away to do a series of paintings of Kerala. As always, he was delighted to accept the invitation. What touched me most was his simple statement, "No, I do not want any money. I'll do it because I love Kerala."

We travelled the length and breadth of Kerala. Beaches, backwaters, hill stations, waterfalls, wildlife sanctuaries, cultural centres. We dropped in on creative giants like Adoor Gopalakrishnan, Abu Abraham, M.T. Vasudevan Nair and O.N.V. Kurup. All along, Husain painted. "If Kashmir is all about men and mountains, Kerala is about women and nature," he said. Which is more than evident in his series of fascinating paintings, which he chose to call "Kalyanikuttiyude Keralam" – the Kerala of Kalyanikutti, the epitome of the ordinary, yet extraordinary Kerala woman.

It is this set of paintings that inspired this book. As you turn these pages, you'll discover the magic that Kerala, God's Own Country, inspires. You'll discover the ever-evolving Husain – white and grey, yet full of colour; feet on the ground (literally too), yet an imagination that's always soaring; a graceful eighty, yet a raring-to-go twenty. That's my Husainda. Your Maqbool Fida Husain.'

From my Foreword to *Kerala: God's Own Country*

M. F. Husain's Kerala

This is a visual memoir of my numerous visits to "God's Own Country".'

In more ways than one, brand Kerala had arrived. And it was nothing but the strength of the brand that helped it survive a series of onslaughts – 9/11, SARS (Severe Acute Respiratory Syndrome), the Gulf War and so on. While prices crashed in far-eastern destinations, Kerala was perhaps the only destination which held on visibly to the price line.

The brand's response to a crisis also speaks volumes. When the tsunami struck in December 2005, the entire world thought that Kerala was also badly hit – which was far from the truth. In less than forty-eight hours of the disaster, officials of Kerala Tourism went on CNN, BBC and on Indian channels to reassure travellers that there was no need to panic or make any cancellations. The massive PR effort paid off and the season went by without too many cancellations of bookings.

The Backwater World

The Kerala backwaters are the rarest and most delicate natural ecosystems on earth. Comprising five large lakes linked by canals, both manmade and natural, they are fed by thirty-eight rivers, and extend to virtually half the length of Kerala state. Fresh water from the rivers meets the sea water from the Arabian Sea, creating a unique ecosystem. In certain areas, such as the Vembanad Kayal, where a barrage has been built near Kumarakom, salt water from the sea is prevented from entering deep inside, keeping the fresh water intact. Vembanad Kayal is the largest of the lakes, covering an area of 200 kilometres, bordering Alappuzha, Kottayam, and Ernakulam districts. Kerala has over 900 kilometres of interconnected waterways, rivers, lakes and inlets that make up its backwaters. In the midst of this beautiful landscape, there are a number of towns and cities, from where backwater cruises begin and end.

The kettuvallams (literally 'a boat held together by ropes') in the backwaters are a prominent tourist attraction in Kerala. A marvel of traditional design, the boat

is made with pieces of wood from jackfruit trees, which are knotted together with thousands of coir ropes and coated with a waterproof resin made of boiled cashewnut shells. Not a single nail is used in its construction. The kettuvallams were traditionally used as grain barges, to transport the rice harvested in the fertile fields alongside the backwaters. Several innovative entrepreneurs offer the backwater experience to tourists and have adapted their traditional crafts into aesthetically furnished houseboats – without compromising on the timeless rules of design and structure. For instance, Rainbow Cruises, which provides the finest houseboats with Gold Star certification, uses solar power, its toilets have biodegradable systems, and garbage generated on the boats is brought onto the shore, segregated and disposed in a sewage treatment plant. Its houseboats are also equipped with global positioning systems and mobiles.

The challenge for Kerala Tourism is to ensure that the number of houseboats does not cross the accommodation capacity of this sensitive ecosystem and that all the houseboats conform to the requirements of responsible and eco-friendly practices.

The fact that Kerala has consistently projected itself as a stand-alone destination (like Bali in Indonesia) helped a great deal to insulate it from the issues affecting India.

A Growth Story

In fact, the growth figures for Kerala tell the story on their own.

Today, in addition to giving employment to over 12,00,000 people across skilled, unskilled and semi-skilled sectors, tourism in Kerala generates Rs 9126 crore for the exchequer and Rs 1988 crore as foreign exchange earnings. The only sector that is thriving in the state, tourism brings in investments to the tune of Rs 1000 crore annually. A Tata Consultancy Services (TCS) study brought out the economic impact of tourism in Kerala's economy – tourism had a multiplier effect of 2.4 on income and 4.2 on employment.[4] Thus, the impact of tourism was substantial.

More importantly perhaps, tourism today is rapidly reviving dying art forms, inspiring the new generation to study ethnic arts, sustain architecture and so on. Tourism is also opening the eyes of the average Keralite to the treasures in his backyard and to a certain extent, inspiring him to know more about his own land and his own traditions. And it has certainly given Keralites across the world something to be proud of back home.

Today, Kerala is the most lauded destination in India, a destination that has picked up the maximum number of awards in the tourism sector in India. And it is India's only tourism superbrand (see Box F).

In 2008 the house of Hermes unveiled a fragrance – Un Jardin Apres La Mousson (A Garden after the Monsoon) – which captures the scents of Kerala. The perfume is a blend of vetiver, ginger, tuberose and gardenia. Its note on the bottle romanticizes Kerala thus:

'In coastal Kerala, spices have been trafficked since the Romans rode on the winds of the monsoon seeking cardamom and pepper – black gold. Women wear their saris differently here than they do up north, draping them like Togas. And when the first monsoon blows in from the Arabian Sea – and it always seems to arrive in the first week of June, extinguishing the scorching rays of the summer sun and ushering in a joyful verdant renewal – the modest women of Kerala rush out in the rain and the saris cling close to the body.' The essence of 'God's Own Country' that inspired the Hermes' perfume, made and bottled in France, makes Kerala sound like the sexiest destination on earth.

Planning the future has helped Kerala take many relevant steps. Kerala today is the first state government and the second sub-national economy in the world to have conducted Tourism Satellite Accounting Research (TSA). Done by the World Tourism Trade Council/Oxford Economic Forecasting (WTTC/OEF) in 2002, the findings of the study are more than impressive[5].

It stated that the Kerala travel and tourism demand was expected to grow by 11.6 percent per annum over the coming decade. This was the highest recorded growth rate in the world, eclipsing WTTC's fastest growing country, Turkey (10.2 percent) as well as India (9.7 percent), which was the second highest in the world. These figures show high levels of consumption of the tourism product in the state by both domestic and foreign tourists. Even more remarkable was the fact that Kerala was expected to register a record growth of 23.5 percent in terms of visitor exports or external account earnings from travel and tourism over the next ten years. India's estimates for this period are 14.3 percent, while the world average was only 6.5 percent.

Significantly, in 2001, while India's visitor exports suffered a decline of 4.8 percent as a result of 9/11, Kerala's visitor exports actually increased by eleven percent over the 2000 results. This was a clear

Box F

The millennium's most acclaimed destination

One of the ten paradises in the world
National Geographic Traveller

Voyage of enchanting hours
Conde Nast Traveller

Seductive
Financial Times, London

Truly God's own country
Sir Paul McCartney

Kerala's real pull lies in the rich masala of its cities and its milder backwaters
The Guardian

Mecca of the oldest holistic health system – ayurveda
Geo Saison, Germany

A country within a country
Richard Branson

Paresh Maitey's Kerala

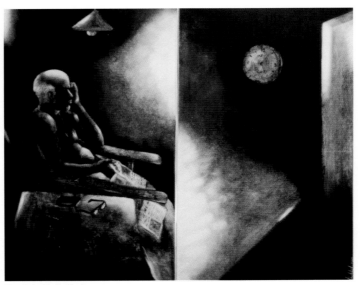

Yusuf Arakkal's Kerala

pointer to the fact that visitors felt more secure in Kerala than in other parts of the country. Over the next ten years, the WTTC/OEF forecasts suggested that Kerala would nearly triple its current level of travel and tourism economy employment from 0.7 million to 2 million.

At the behest of the government of India, CRISIL (Credit Rating Information Services of India Limited) conducted a study on Kerala's approach to tourism development. Its analysis revealed that 'Kerala has built on its strengths; it has forged partnerships and engineered positive approaches necessary to achieve a quantum growth in the tourism sector. Critical among these has been the state's success in bringing private sector participation, in bringing together the various stakeholders on a developmental platform, in encouraging committed professionals and bureaucrats who have been with the state for a decade or more and in achieving a clear positioning for Kerala on all international platforms.'[6]

Kerala also received high ratings from both domestic and international tourists on several parameters of evaluation (for a snapshot of the result, see Box G).

To ensure planned development, Kerala Tourism created the Conservation and Preservation Act in 2005.[7] A path-breaking achievement, the Act lays down clear guidelines that will ensure the preservation of tourist areas in the state by empowering the Department of Tourism to directly regulate the growth and impact of tourism in select areas.

The Tourism Vision 2025, the most recent state tourism policy document, will also go a long way 'to make Kerala an upmarket high-quality tourist destination through rational utilization of resources with focus on integrated development of the infrastructure sector, conserving and preserving the heritage and environment and enhancing productivity, income, creating employment opportunities, alleviating poverty thereby making tourism the most important sector for the socio-economic development and environment protection of the state. The focus will be on fostering sustainable development to attract quality tourists by developing quality tourism infrastructure with private sector participation.'[8]

Kerala Tourism is all set to make another paradigm shift that will make sustainability more practical and viable. So from addressing the affluent traveller, Kerala will move towards addressing the Alert

Homestays: A New Niche

The breed of Alert Independent Travellers is slowly, but surely, on the rise – these are travellers who seek authentic experiences that enable them to be part of the fabric of the land, both culturally and emotionally, in addition to striving to leave a destination better than they found it.

This, in every way, is the perfect environment for homestays to grow and flourish. And that is exactly what is happening in Kerala. From a handful of homestays a few years ago, there are 400 approved homestays today, spread across this vibrant green state.

There is nothing that captures the Kerala experience as much as a homestay does. How else can one revel in the simple delights of the land and its people, experience the beauty of the Keralite lifestyle, the richness of the cuisine, the magic of the local temple festival and the charm of a quiet village tucked far away from the regular tourist circuit?

Homestays provide a personal touch and a remarkable sense of informality that is absent or minimal in other means of accommodation. Here, the studied detachment of hotels is replaced with an unparalleled friendliness and intimacy. Where else will you find hosts who cajole you to have a second helping, lend an ear to your stories and regale you with their own?

Take for instance, Philipkutty's Farm in the backwaters of Kumarakom in Kottayam. Far from the madding crowd and surrounded by lush greenery, it opens up for the traveller not just the enchanting beauty of Kerala, but its fascinating way of life as well. Fishing, canoe rides, dips in the backwaters, walks through paddy fields, visits to quaint churches and temples, bird watching, organic farming, cooking classes, painting sessions, ayurveda.

For me, what makes the homestay an absolute winner is the whole new world of opportunity that it opens up – not just for the traveller and the host, but also for the destination. Homestays are more than just an affordable accommodation option and an employment generator. They also address the larger issue of tourism becoming a participatory process involving the local community and play a key role in effectively dispersing the benefits of tourism to the rural areas. What's more, homestays are an important tool in sustaining the cultural ethos and social fabric of the land. Kerala's homestays are rapidly heralding tourism development that is perfectly in harmony with the tenets of 'responsible tourism'.

Kerala Tourism has gone all out to foster and promote homestays by facilitating loans from financial institutions, offering technical guidance, assisting in capacity-building, ensuring marketing support, lending the Kerala Tourism branding to approved homestays and so on. An exclusive society – the Kerala Homestay and Tourism Society – solely devoted to coordinating the activities of the homestays and a new website – www.homestaykerala.org – provides complete district-wise information on the homestay service-providers in the state. With a dramatic increase in the number of homestays, Kerala Tourism has also launched a classification scheme that clearly spells out guidelines on mandatory facilities, service standards etc.

In a destination like Kerala that is heavily dependent on natural attractions, sustenance is of prime importance – and this is where homestays play a larger-than-life role. To begin with, the natural environment becomes the centre of attraction; ordinary people turn hosts and entrepreneurs, bringing them closer to the concept of tourism and its riches – both cultural and financial; and most importantly, it attracts the sensitive traveller who treasures the land, its traditions and its people, thus ensuring that the destination is sustained in more ways than one.

The success of homestays in Kerala is a perfect case study of how tourism can inspire social change and economic development in a destination. The rest of India can take a leaf out of Kerala's book to make more room for a development that respects our land, its culture and values and truly upholds the spirit of 'Atithi Devo Bhavah'.

Increase in Domestic Tourist Arrivals 1995-2006

Increase in Foreign Tourist Arrivals 1990-2006

Foreign Exchange (Rs. In Crores)

39.15.66

4403.00

4953.40

4481.71

4888.29

5013.22

525.3

416.07

302.08

273.23

196.38

158.76

142.97

176.86

182.94

189.94

202.17

209.93

95   96   97   98   99   2000

87

Source: Kerala Tourism

6271.72

6642.94

5946.42

5871.23

59.72.18

5568.26

2640.9

1998.4

1552.31

1266.77

983.37

705.67

515.80

428.53

346.50

345.55

294.62

232.56

02   03   04   05   06   2007

88

Independent Travellers (AIT) – people who believe in leaving the destination better than they found it and those who travel to make the world a better place. With groups becoming smaller and smaller and with AITs on the rise, it will slowly become easier to be more responsible for the environment and the community. In sync with this move, the focus has been on creating partnerships for 'responsible tourism'. 'Responsible tourism' will contribute by maintaining both the natural and cultural heritage of the destination, conserving the living culture of the people and attracting the right kind of visitor.

Kerala has set an example for other Indian states by pursuing a visionary approach in tourism; by pushing doors open rather than waiting for doors to open; by being truly authentic in the experiences it offers; by building relationships worldwide; and by thinking globally and acting locally. Where does Kerala Tourism go from here? It needs to constantly evolve, innovate, create local authentic experiences and retain the native charm of its tourism products while contributing to the sustainable development of the state.

Box G

5

Hospitality — Overall Experience — Information Provided — Tour Operators — Basic Amenities — Hygiene Factors — Safety — Quality of Destinations — Cooperations — Helpfulness — Accommodations — Connectivity

Source: CRISIL - AC Nielson ORG-Marg Survey 2004

91

'Travel & tourism has important indirect positive development effects. It encourages infrastructure improvements such as better roads, electricity, telephone and public transport networks, which, as well as facilitating tourism, improve the economy's overall development prospects and the quality of life for its residents.' World Economic Forum

Infrastructure: propping up the fundamentals

Soon after joining the ministry of tourism in 2001, my first official visit was to the Buddhist Circuit of Bodhgaya, Rajgir and Nalanda in Bihar. We took the Rajdhani train from Delhi to Gaya and drove down from there. The national highway stretch was probably the worst in the world – the entire distance of 96 kilometres was full of large potholes. It was a bone-rattling nightmare – a journey that should have taken an-hour-and-a-half took us almost five hours. No wonder the Japanese and Southeast Asian tourists, who should have flocked to visit the Mecca of Buddhism, had been driven away. It took all our persuasive skills to get additional funds sanctioned to mend these roads and bring them up to international standards, but the agreement was only on the condition that the work would be directly executed by central agencies. The roads have since been done up, the integrated development of Bodhgaya, Rajgir and Nalanda implemented, and better conservation, preservation and lighting undertaken.Similarly, in Agra, in close proximity to India's most visited World Heritage Site – the Taj Mahal – we were welcomed by accumulated garbage, ugly hanging wires, a stinking cowshed, terrible commercial hoardings and touts attempting to fleece the foreign tourists. Since then, a project has been implemented to improve the quality of the roads and hoardings, relocate shops and increase parking space near the Taj.

These experiences confirmed our belief that any marketing of India without a simultaneous focus on infrastructure improvement would be a disaster. For essentially, a brand is what a brand does. The 'Incredible India' campaign could not be sustained if the quality of experience offered to tourists did not remain credible. In the long run, a branding campaign which does not match with the actual experience does damage to the destination rather than promote it. Infrastructure development and destination management, therefore, hold the key to India's sustained growth in the tourism sector.

International Image

Infrastructure in India has been seen as a problem area in various surveys as well. The Gallup Poll Organization had, at the behest of

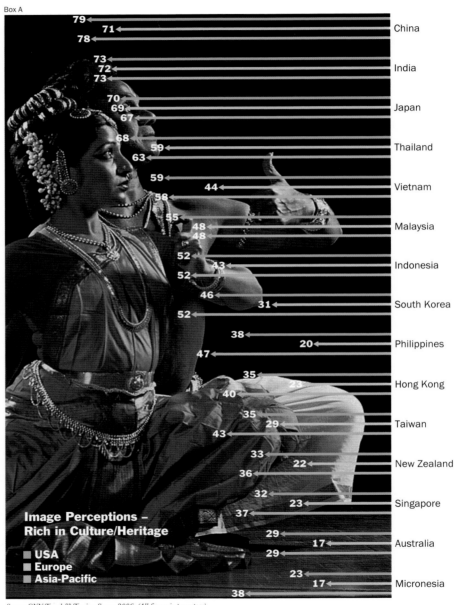

**Image Perceptions –
Rich in Culture/Heritage**

■ USA
■ Europe
■ Asia-Pacific

China — 79 / 71 / 78
India — 73 / 72 / 73
Japan — 70 / 69 / 67
Thailand — 68 / 59 / 63
Vietnam — 59 / 58 / 44
Malaysia — 55 / 48 / 48
Indonesia — 52 / 52 / 43
South Korea — 46 / 52 / 31
Philippines — 38 / 47 / 20
Hong Kong — 35 / 40 / 23
Taiwan — 35 / 43 / 29
New Zealand — 33 / 36 / 22
Singapore — 32 / 37 / 23
Australia — 29 / 29 / 17
Micronesia — 23 / 38 / 17

Source: CNN Travel & Tourism Survey 2006. (All figures in percentage)

93

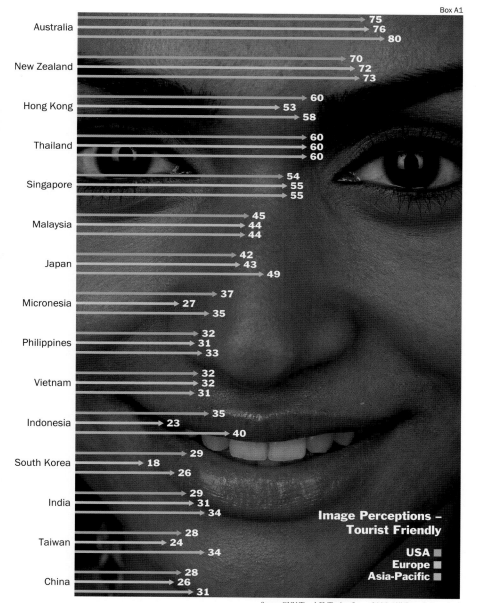

Australia 75
76
80

New Zealand 70
72
73

Hong Kong 60
53
58

Thailand 60
60
60

Singapore 54
55
55

Malaysia 45
44
44

Japan 42
43
49

Micronesia 37
27
35

Philippines 32
31
33

Vietnam 32
32
31

Indonesia 35
23
40

South Korea 29
18
26

India 29
31
34

Taiwan 28
24
34

China 28
26
31

**Image Perceptions –
Tourist Friendly**

USA ■
Europe ■
Asia-Pacific ■

94

Source: CNN Travel & Tourism Survey 2006. (All figures in percentage)

Indian tourism, conducted a survey[1] in October-November 2006 in thirteen major source markets. According to the survey, the key concerns of the market relating to travel in India in order of importance were:

1. Cleanliness and hygiene;
2. Safety and security;
3. Transportation;
4. Promotional support;
5. Affordability.

Again, a survey conducted by Synovate on behalf of CNN in December 2006[2] demonstrated that while the image-perception of India across respondents in Asia, Europe and North America was extremely positive, with the country being seen as immensely rich in culture and heritage (see Boxes A and A1), it figured extremely low as a destination in terms of tourist friendliness. This was a consequence of the low quality of experience undergone by tourists visiting India.

The World Economic Forum based in Geneva has been engaged in studying issues relating to national competitiveness, with the objective of understanding the factors that have an impact on growth and prosperity. In the process, it has developed the first Travel and Tourism Competitiveness Index (TTCI).[3] The aim of the TTCI, which covered 124 economies, was to provide a comprehensive strategic gauge to measure what it termed as 'the factors and policies that make it attractive to develop the travel and tourism sector in different countries'. Switzerland takes the leading position in the TTCI rankings, followed closely by Austria and Germany. India figures extremely low at the sixty-fifth position (see Box B).

Box B

	Overall Index		Regulatory Framework		Business Environment and Infrastructure		Human Culture, Natural Resource	
	Rank	Score	Rank	Score	Rank	Score	Rank	Score
Switzerland	1	5.66	2	5.80	2	5.36	2	5.81
Austria	2	5.54	3	5.79	12	4.97	1	5.86
Germany	3	5.48	6	5.62	3	5.23	6	5.61
Iceland	4	5.45	5	5.69	8	5.04	5	5.61
United States	5	5.43	33	5.06	1	5.74	12	5.50
India	65	4.14	62	4.24	55	3.64	81	4.55

Source: Travel and Tourism Competitiveness Report 2007, World Economic Forum

Tourism Infrastructure Deficiencies

A recent report by the Asian Development Bank (ADB) points out:

The provision, operation and maintenance of utilities such as water, electricity, sanitation, waste water, solid waste infrastructure at key tourism destination cities, towns and resorts continue to be problematic in most of the main tourist destinations in India. The issue is especially critical in high volume centres such as domestic pilgrimage sites, cities and towns that are important starting points for international and domestic tourist activity such as Jaipur in Rajasthan, resort centres such as Goa, and hill resort centres such as Manali in Himachal Pradesh. At the same time, specific tourism support infrastructure such as information centres, public toilets, directional signage, interpretation facilities, street lighting and environmental landscaping at key destination cities, towns and resorts, and those at the public areas of the main cultural heritage sites of tourism importance is inadequate relative to world-class standards. Most of the complaints and concerns expressed by tourists and by the service-providers in India and in the source markets concern the poor quality of sanitation, lack of cleanliness and hygiene, problems with transportation, safety and security, poor condition of access to key tourist sites and inadequate support facilities in public areas at major cultural attractions such as parking, public toilets, visitor information, signage and interpretation, trained guides, etc. These tourism infrastructure deficiencies threaten to derail India's thrust to become a world-class global destination within the next decade.[4]

Infrastructure Policy

Infrastructure has been widely defined as an investment made in creating an asset with a view to deriving long-term benefit from it, depending upon the quality and nature of the asset. The main feature of any infrastructure is that it is capital-intensive, with a long gestation period, and becomes economically and commercially viable after a considerably long period of time. Infrastructure projects are a prerequisite for enabling the user industry to expand and create large-scale employment opportunities and in turn, have an indirect multiplier effect on the economy as a whole.

What Tourism Means To Me

This is the Age of Tourism, Not Travel – J. Cartwright

Asavari Singh

Paul Theroux put it aptly when he said in a recent interview with the Guardian, *'Imagine just going up and down India on a train. Fantastic!' But anyone who's been on a narrow gauge train to dusty Muzaffarnagar in a three-tier berth filled with smelly babies and scraps of grease-smeared tin foil will probably snort in derision at this. India, a wonderful country though it may well be, is not, let's face it, always a very pleasant place to travel in. Theroux, as is well documented, revels in his plight as he misses train after train in platforms teeming with touts and thugs. His writer's masochism aside, the part of his quote that I want to focus on, is 'fantastic'.*

I don't mean this in the highly literal sense (as in 'He writhed feverishly in bed, delirious with unrelenting Delhi Belly, seeing fantastical visions of gol gappas out to eat him.') but in its most colloquial sense. The synonyms for 'fantastic' in the Oxford English Dictionary *are 'incredible; great; extraordinary; excellent'. In short, tourism is all about a transcendence of the ordinary. An experience that doesn't always characterize travel. Travel, more often than not, is goal-oriented. But to be a tourist is to be willing to pick out, even shop, for a truly unforgettable, pleasurable experience. As I say this, I get a palpable sense of the accusing fingers of ravaged backpackers pointing at me, 'But what about authenticity?'*

I got this reproachful response most recently when I signed up for a sublime 'three-day/four-night' package tour to Goa. As it happens, I am all for authenticity! Except that I don't cling to the fanatical belief that what is authentic must necessarily be painful. An organized tourism industry does not attempt to disguise truth. It's not using the secret service or extra-terrestrial intelligence to camouflage what's out there. It simply distills the best for you to savour. Why wait to feel the breathless relief of the mauled survivor when you can enjoy the breathtaking expanse of the ocean, secure in the knowledge that you have a comfortable bed and a well-planned itinerary waiting (and you can still wear that backpack and trek all you want!)?

In other words, I don't want to confound my subjective experience of India's remarkable natural and cultural bounty with a nagging awareness of physical discomfort, or worry about whom to trust and where to go. Most of us live lives that are almost always marked by mundane preoccupations that blind us to India's staggering wealth of visual, sensory, and yes, spiritual offerings. Tourism to me is about escaping the ordinary enough to be able to fully appreciate how extraordinary India is. It's about reminding myself that there is more to life here than heat, dust, and traffic jams. And thanks to the tourism industry, it's just a brochure and a phone call away.

(This essay won the 1st prize in a nationwide contest)

Tourism sector projects that are capital-intensive, such as destination development (roads, signages, relocation of commercial establishments, lighting, guest facilities etc.), remain commercially non-viable and require government funding. It is, however, necessary that such infrastructure is created utilizing the professional expertise of architects and landscaping experts and is then privately managed through a transparent process. Other infrastructure projects, such as the setting up of convention centres and golf courses and running tourist trains, normally have substantial gestation periods and become economically viable over periods exceeding twelve to fifteen years. In order to attract tourists, sufficient facilities must be created through private initiative, with the government acting as a facilitator and catalyst. (See Box C for UNWTO's approach to defining tourism infrastructure).

The national tourism policy, formulated and approved in 2002, had alluded to the tourism revolution that had been sweeping the world. However, on account of the low prominence given to tourism and the inability to comprehend its potential to create employment, the state tourism outlays were extremely meagre. The ministry of tourism's outlay itself was extremely minimal till 2001 (end of the ninth Five-Year Plan) and hovered around just Rs100 crore per annum. This was very thinly distributed through a vast array of schemes. The average sanction per project was in the region of only Rs 10-15 lakhs. As a consequence, the Central Financial Assistance (CFA) for infrastructure hardly made any impact at the ground level.

Box C

Approach to Defining 'Tourism' Infrastructure

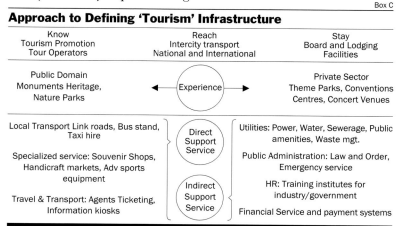

Know Tourism Promotion Tour Operators	Reach Intercity transport National and International	Stay Board and Lodging Facilities
Public Domain Monuments Heritage, Nature Parks	←—(Experience)—→	Private Sector Theme Parks, Conventions Centres, Concert Venues
Local Transport Link roads, Bus stand, Taxi hire Specialized service: Souvenir Shops, Handicraft markets, Adv sports equipment	Direct Support Service	Utilities: Power, Water, Sewerage, Public amenities, Waste mgt. Public Administration: Law and Order, Emergency service
Travel & Transport: Agents Ticketing, Information kiosks	Indirect Support Service	HR: Training institutes for industry/government Financial Service and payment systems

Source: UN World Tourism Organization

With the objective of ensuring focused attention, the wide-ranging schemes were merged into just two: integrated development of tourist circuits and product/infrastructure and destination development. The outlay for destination development was raised to Rs 5 crore and was limited to Rs 8 crore for circuits (linking three or more destinations). For key destinations, where focused development is being undertaken, projects upto Rs 50 crore can now be sanctioned. For rural tourism projects, the outlay is Rs 50 lakhs for the hardware (infrastructure component) and Rs 20 lakhs for community participation.

Resources are, however, still being spread thinly across states, as seen in the year-wise statistics of the sanctioned number of destinations and circuits (see Box D). The table demonstrates that far too many projects with too few resources are still being taken up for implementation. It is vital that world-class experiences are created at a few tourism sites to instil a sense of pride and ownership among the local population and to serve as demonstration projects for other heritage and cultural projects.

Towards this objective, tourist sites and destinations need to be carefully selected on the basis of their tourism potential. The aim should be to provide all infrastructure facilities required by the tourist within such destinations and circuits. Master planning of these destinations and circuits will then enable their development in an integrated holistic manner. The objective should be to achieve convergence of resources and expertise through coordinated action with state governments and the private sector. The master plan for these destinations and circuits needs to be prepared with sensitivity regarding conservation and preservation and their project implementation constantly monitored by state governments. In fact, the government should select only ten major destinations and six circuits cutting across the geographical boundaries of the states (north, south, east, west, central and northeast) on an annual basis and convert them into centres of excellence. These projects should be centrally driven and constantly reviewed and monitored.

The success of this approach is visible, for example, in the Ajanta Ellora Conservation and Tourism

		Box D
Year	Destination	Circuit
2002-03	78	10
2003-04	71	25
2004-05	66	26
2005-06	97	45
2006-07	54	45

	Public	**Private**
Large Scale	Cleanup & Restorations Transport Infrastructure Tourism Training Power/Water IT STA	Convention Centres Star Hotels, Resorts & Spas Amusement, Theme Parks, Water Sports Adventure Telecom
Small Scale	Arts/Crafts & Museums Jungle Camps Signage Other Amenities Information	Sports Specialty Restaurants Motels & Smaller Hotels Tourist Vehicles Internet

Source: *ADB report on 'The study to prepare a road map for tourism infrastructure development in India'*

Infrastructure Development Project (See Box E) and Humayun Tomb Garden Restoration project, undertaken in a private-public partnership (see Box F).

In my view, the tourism departments should focus on regulatory and infrastructure functions, while promotional and marketing activities need to be organized through the tourism board with private-public partnerships. Private players should bring in both expertise and resources and become active stakeholders in the professional marketing and branding of India. The tourism board should be professionally managed and assigned the task of marketing India internationally and within India in partnership with state governments and with the private sector.

100

Tourism – A Multi-Sectoral Activity

Since tourism cannot be the business of the tourism department alone, it is essentially multi-sectoral in character. For a destination to succeed, it needs to be everyone's business and its ownership must transcend the tourism sector, allowing ownership by several stake-holders (its multidimensional nature is best demonstrated by the diagram in Box G).

As the implementation of tourism infrastructure projects has to be through multiple government departments at the state level, coordination is often a casualty, leading to cost and time overruns. Experience in the successful implementation of the Ajanta-Ellora project, financed by the Japanese Bank for International Cooperation, and the ADB-assisted Rajasthan Urban Infrastructure Development Project has demonstrated

Ajanta-Ellora – A Case Study

In 1819, a party of British Army officers on a tiger hunt in the Western Deccan forests, suddenly spotted their prey on the far side of the loop in the Waghora river. The tiger was silhouetted against the carved facade of a cave, and when the officers investigated, they discovered a series of carved caves, each more dramatic than the other. The cave complex had been continuously inhabited from 2000 BC to about AD 650. There are thirty caves in all, including some unfinished ones. Of the Ajanta caves, five are chaityas or prayer halls and the rest are viharas or monasteries. The Ajanta caves resolve themselves into two phases, separated from each by about four hundred years. These architectural phases coincide with the two schools of Buddhist thought: the older Hinayana school, in which the Buddha was represented only in symbols like the stupa, and the later Mahayana sect, which did not shy away from giving the Lord a human form.

The sculptures and paintings in the caves detail the Buddha's life as well as his previous birth, as related in the Jataka tales. The caves illuminate the history of the times through vivid court scenes, street scenes, cameos of domestic life and even animal and bird studies.

101

Unlike the caves of Ajanta, the Ellora caves were never lost. Largely because it lay on a more frequented route, Ellora always remained in the public eye. In fact, Kailasa Temple remained a shrine frequented by worshippers until the nineteenth century. Several travellers to India, including the tenth-century Arab geographer, Ali Masudi, and Niccolao Manucci in the early seventeenth century mentioned the caves in their accounts. There are thirty-four caves, of which twelve are Buddhist, seventeen Hindu and five Jain. Although not too far removed from the Ajanta caves in terms of both space and time, the chaityas and viharas of Ellora are architecturally and sculpturally different. Compared to the Ajanta paintings and sculptures, the Ellora representations are more earthly, drawing elements from the Vajayana School of Buddhism, which is permeated with ideas of magic and mysticism. It is the architectural skill rather than sculptural aesthetics that Ellora is noted for. What stuns visitors at Ajanta and Ellora is the realization that all the beauty that one beholds was fashioned by human hands, more than a millennium ago.

The ministry of tourism implemented the Ajanta-Ellora Conservation and Tourism Development Project based on an integrated project financed through a loan agreement by the JBIC. The project implementation comprised the following:

1. Monument Conservation by the ASI: Improvement of approach paths to the caves and approach roads inside the Ellora cave complex, procurement of conservation and logistic equipment and a wireless network, geological

investigation of the caves to formulate a conservation plan;

2. Afforestation by the Forest Department: Afforestation of 730 hectares of forestland near the cave. Out of this, 500 acres are at Ajanta and 230 at Ellora;
3. Roads by the Public Works Department: Upgradation of almost 162 kilometres of roads in the Ajanta and Ellora region;
4. Water supply by Maharashtra Jeevan Pradheekaran: Raising the height of the Tondapur Dam, installing filtration plants and water supply system at Ajanta;
5. Visitor Circulation Plan at Ajanta-Ellora: This is based on the carrying capacity of the caves and splitting the total number of tourists arriving here so that there is no double circulation;
6. Fibre-optic Illumination of the Caves: To ensure that the paintings do not get affected by the existing lighting systems, the most modern technology has been used;
7. Visitors Management System: this involves –
a) Development of an alternative junction site for the resettlement of shops,
b) Landscaping at the foothills of the Ajanta and Ellora caves,
c) Training of tourism planners and guides.
8. Procurement of Electric Buses: The entire traffic movement from the junction to the Ajanta caves will be through eco-friendly buses and the area has been declared a No-Pollution Zone.

The entire integrated project was completed by 2003 and the JBIC was so impressed with its implementation that it sanctioned a Phase II project costing Rs 400 crore.

The Ajanta-Ellora project is a unique conservation and preservation project at a World Heritage Site. It encompasses heritage preservation, involvement of the local community, visitor management and ensuring that the destination is conserved and managed based on its carrying capacity (see the before-and-after visuals in the adjacent page).

It was Jagmohan's drive, determination and conviction that made the implementation of this project feasible. I recall how the 250 shop-owners based at the foothill of the Ajanta caves brought immense political pressure not to shift them. It required forty-two rounds of meetings to convince them that new shops at the centralized point, where all the buses would bring tourists, would enhance their earnings. Eventually it led to their earnings going up by almost 310 percent within two years. At the field level, it was the dynamism and coordination ability of Ashish Singh, the then managing director of MTDC, that enabled the implementation without cost and time overruns. Singh was energetic and enthusiastic about improving the quality of infrastructure. He drove the project with clockwork precision. In fact, the project is a great example of coordination between the central and state governments.

Ajanta – Ellora Caves

Before

After

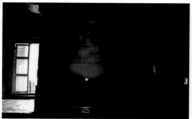

Virtual invisibility and viewing through hand-held lamps and torches

New lighting arrangement in the caves

Before

After

Ajanta Caves(10) conservation

Paintings, under fiber optic lighting

Eco-friendly buses

Afforestation at Ajanta

Kumbhalgarh

Before

After

Mahabalipuram

Before

After

Before

After

Hardwar

Before

After

Before

After

104

Humayun's Tomb Garden Restoration: A Private-Public Partnership Initiative

The restoration of the gardens in the Humayun's Tomb in Delhi was the first private-public funded restoration of a World Heritage Site in India. The objective of the project was to revitalize the gardens, pathways, fountains and water channels of the charbagh (four-part paradise garden) surrounding Humayun's Tomb.

Over the period 1997-2004, the Aga Khan Trust for Culture (AKTC) funded and collaborated with the ASI in implementing the garden restoration of the Humayun's Tomb World Heritage Site under the aegis of the National Culture Fund. In addition to this fund and the implementing organizations – ASI and the Trust – two other parties also played a role: the Indo-British Fiftieth Anniversary Trust and the Oberoi Group of Hotels.

The US$ 650,000 project was based on systematic archival research and the archaeological excavations included, among other conservation work, the following main elements:

- Reinstating the walkways and conserving the edging stones,
- Repairing, extending and reactivating the irrigation system,
- Establishing water sources for the water channels and irrigation system, including a pump station for a water-recycling system,
- Conserving, repairing and rebuilding the water channel system,
- Re-levelling the planted zones and revitalizing them with species and arrangements that conform to the customs and patterns of Mughal sources, and
- Supporting research that informs the conservation and restoration process, contributes to the development of educational materials for use in schools of architecture, conservation and heritage management, as well as for visitors to the Tomb.

More specifically, hundreds of craftsmen worked with a multidisciplinary team of professionals to carry out the following works:

- Removal of 3,000 truckloads of earth (12,000 cubic metres),
- Planting of 12 hectares (thirty acres) of lawn,
- Re-setting and alignment of over 3,500 kilometres of path kerbstones,
- Preparation of 3,000 metres of hand-dressed red sandstone channel edging by some sixty stonecutters,
- De-silting of 128 historic wells as part of the largest rainwater harvesting system scheme in any heritage site in India,
- Creation of a site exhibition,

- Planning and installation of a new water-circulation system for the walkway channels,
- Planting of 2,500 trees and plants, including mango, lemon, neem, pomegranate, hibiscus and jasmine favoured by the Mughals,
- Restoration of fountains,
- Provision of wheelchair access to parts of the site,
- Conservation of numerous minor structures.

Following the completion of the garden restoration project, ASI carried out major interventions in the environs of the World Heritage Site such as creating parking space in the entrance zone. Visitor numbers to the Humayun's Tomb have seen a ten-fold increase since the project commenced, as a major public space in the heart of the capital city has been restored to its Mughal grandeur and serenity.

Public and official endorsement of the results of the collaborative project work by the ASI and the AKTC in the rehabilitation of the Humayun's Tomb gardens (1997–2004) in Delhi has prompted the Government of India and the Aga Khan Development Network (AKDN), of which AKTC is a part, to consider further possible partnerships aiming at the integrated physical and socio-economic development of cultural heritage sites in India.

106

After research into a number of possible sites, suggested by the ministries of tourism and culture, government of India, AKTC recommended an area development project in the vicinity of the Humayun's Tomb, focusing on the Nizamuddin Basti and the Sundar Nursery site, which, together with their unique cultural assets and heritage, would unify these three zones into an urban conservation district of considerable breadth and significance for the city of Delhi.

This Area Development Project will combine conservation and urban environmental rehabilitation work with a series of community-based socio-economic development initiatives designed to improve the quality of life and the environment for the well-established communities within the project area. The project, the MoU for which was signed in July 2007, is a public-private partnership initiative with the ASI, CPWD and the Municipal Corporation of Delhi as public partners, with the Aga Khan Development Network as the private partner agency.

A public-private partnership framework is the best basis for this form of integrated community-based development, which will need to rely on the coordination and cooperation between public, private and NGO organizations for the creation of a layer of community groups for the governance of projects after their inception.

Humayun's Tomb in 2000

that when multiple agencies are involved, it is imperative to have a project management unit with a project director to oversee the project and an empowered committee headed by the chief secretary of the state to ensure close coordination, constant review and monitoring.

Tourism and its Impact on the Economy – The Tourism Satellite Account and its Findings

Tourism in India has always been viewed as an elitist sector and its significance as a driver of growth and employment creation has only just begun to be recognized. The ministry of tourism commissioned the National Council of Applied Economic Research (NCAER) to develop the Tourism Satellite Account (TSA) and provide a consistent and reliable source of information on the economic dimensions of tourism. The major problem with measuring the impact of tourism spending is quite simply that tourism does not exist as a distinct sector in any system of national accounts. Systems of national accounts are the main mechanism for tracking what is produced and sold in the economy and what happens to expenditure – they are structured around what is produced (clothing, hotels, electrical goods, air transport etc.).

Humayun's Tomb after restoration in 2003

In contrast, tourism is an activity that is defined by the consumers at the point of consumption. Anything that tourists buy and any form of expenditure they incur is a contribution to the income that is generated by tourism. A significant component of tourist expenditure goes into identified tourism sectors such as transport and hotels, but tourists also spend a substantial component on other sectors, such as food and petrol. In Canada, for instance, research has revealed that almost twenty-five percent of tourism expenditure is on non-tourism sectors. The economic contribution of tourism is, therefore, far beyond only the tourism-related sectors of hotels and transport. Since the contribution of tourism is spread across several sectors, its impact cannot be assessed by utilizing standard national accounts.

On account of this lacuna in the existing accounting system, a large number of countries like Canada, the US and New Zealand have developed the Tourism Satellite Accounts. This new set of accounts is linked to the existing system of national accounts and enables the tracking of tourism expenditure across a wide range of both tourism and non-tourism characteristic sectors. The UN World Tourism

Tourism (Multi-Sectoral Activity)

Urban Development
• Land for hotels - 150,000 rooms in 3 years • Lease, not auction for budget hotels • Commercial utilization for budget hotels to be increased • FSI for hotels to be increased • Include civic services • Promote land use • Change in transport modes

Rural Development
Road for Tourism sites under PMGRY • Integration with road schemes • Panchayats to undertake tourism schemes / community stay homes / management of tourism sites

Culture
• Opening Heritage Sites to private & public management • Toilets & ramp for handicapped • Creating experiences around World Heritage Sites • Improve museums, art galleries, open air theatres • Promote dance, music and other soft culture items at destinations

Road & Highways
• Linking up all World Heritage Sites to National Highways • Wayside amenities on Highways

Textiles
• Handicrafts - Souvenirs Development • Shops at all tourism sites • Product development for tourists • Undertaking a massive handicrafts / souvenirs scheme for tourists

Shipping
• Develop India as a cruise destination • Dedicated cruise terminals in Mumbai / Cochin • Opening inland waterways & backwaters for cruise

Home
• Visa on arrival / Long terms visa • E-visa • RAP / PAP / inner Line Permit to be revisewed • Training for immigration officers • High value opening of Andamans / Lakshadweep

Health
• Medical Tourism • Accreditation of hospitals • Price banding of similar treatments • Insurance regime • Improve medical facilities at tourist destinations

Railways
• 100 sites to be opened for private sector hotels • Joint air and rail booking • Approved tour operators to be permitted to do booking on railways for tourists • Run tourist trains for char dhams and pilgrimage sites • Improve stations at tourist destinations through PPP

Environment & Forests
• Open up wildlife / beach destinations based on carrying capacities • Andamans & Lakshadweep to be opened in sensitive manner

Civil Aviation
• Open sky for next 5 years from 15 key source markets • Modernizing Delhi - Mumbai & other metro airports • Promote hotels / tourism projects at surplus land • Declare more international airports

109

Organization has been encouraging countries to adopt TSAs, arguing that it is the only way to measure tourism's economic contribution in a manner that is consistent with the measurement of other sectors in the economy. Policy-makers in countries where TSAs have been adopted and implemented have gained a clear perspective of the impact of tourism on the economy and have been able to evaluate the benefits that tourism brings.

So what did the TSA based on vigorous international and domestic surveys reveal? It established that in 2002-03, the direct and indirect contribution of tourism to GDP was 5.83 percent and that the employment in the tourism sector was 38.6 million, amounting to 8.27 percent of the total employment in the Indian economy. By 2005-06, this had risen significantly to 10.6 percent.

Domestic Tourism

On account of it being a long haul destination, the inflow of inbound foreign tourists is seasonal for India (tourists come after substantial planning and preparation during peak holiday period). Domestic tourism is essential to balance this seasonality. It can enable investment in the infrastructure to be viable over a much shorter period. The strategy necessitates creating awareness among the rising Indian middle classes about new experiences (such as chasing the monsoon), new attractions (such as plantation holidays) and the variety of new resorts that have come up in several states of India. There is also a need to highlight domestic products like pilgrim circuits, heritage sites and monuments in order to fully tap the potential of domestic tourism.

110

One of the key findings of the TSA was that domestic tourism was an impetus for economic growth. Also, taking into consideration people who visited different parts of the country for social purposes, such as weddings, the average number of persons (tourists) per trip undertaken by tourism-generating households was 2.6, indicating that the total volume of domestic tourists was 549.4 million – of which 157 million were urban residents and 392.4 million were rural residents (in 2002-03, the year of survey). This reveals that the accommodation data as collected by the states and compiled by the ministry of tourism is an understatement. This is largely on account of states not including visits for social purposes (see Box H).

The average growth in domestic tourism visits was about 15 percent between 2002 and 2006. This establishes that one of the major beneficiaries of sustained economic growth in the Indian economy has been the tourism sector. After fulfilling their basic requirements, Indians have been travelling from one part of the country to another, discovering its unexplored facets. According to projections by Euromonitor International, domestic visits in India are expected to more than double by 2011 to 970 million. The fact that sustained economic growth has a positive effect on domestic tourism is adequately established by China, where domestic visits in 2006 reached 1.2 billion, up by 15 percent from a year earlier, and by 2011 the annual domestic trips in China will almost double to around 2 billion.

Domestic tourist visits to all states/UT's in India

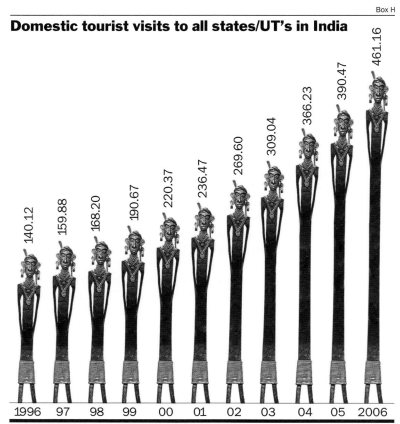

140.12   159.88   168.20   190.67   220.37   236.47   269.60   309.04   366.23   390.47   461.16

1996   97   98   99   00   01   02   03   04   05   2006

Source: Ministry of Tourism

As India's economy continues to grow and expand, domestic travel will witness phenomenal momentum. States like Kerala have emerged as 365-days-a year destinations on the strength of domestic tourism (foreign tourists come for only six months). They have vigorously promoted their own special attractions – for instance, the monsoon season and ayurveda in Kerala – to attract long-staying and adventurous domestic tourists. A similar dynamism is now seen in Madhya Pradesh – a state which advertises its presence in commercials on television networks in the most vibrant, creative and energetic manner, inspiring the potential visitor to take the next flight to Madhya Pradesh. The success of the states in attracting domestic traffic will become the springboard for providing an impetus to key international source markets. This only highlights the fact that states should focus on improving the quality of the infrastructure at major tourism sites.

Throughout the world, there are now more people choosing from a more diverse range of destinations, and leisure traveller preferences are evolving away from packaged tours to individually bundled options. Anticipating this, Indian tourism had identified six niche tourism products for development – rural, medical, cruise, MICE (Meetings, Incentives, Conventions, Exhibitions), Buddhist trails and adventure tourism. The selection was based not only on international travel trends but on India's innate strengths as well. Of these, Indian medical tourism is catching up worldwide and the Buddhist trail has found many fascinated customers in Japan and South Asian countries. In later chapters, I have dealt at length on rural and medical value tourism. Let me briefly dwell here on the MICE market, the potential of the Buddhism circuit, the future of cruises and the untapped market of adventure tourism in India.

112

MICE (Meetings, Incentives, Conventions, Exhibitions)

The fastest growing segment of the tourism market, the MICE holiday is an important economic contributor, with a high multiplier impact. It stimulates tourism and generates revenues for airlines, convention centres, hotels, restaurants, ground transportation and entertainment spots. The multiplier for the US MICE industry has been estimated to be eight – for every dollar spent on the event directly, seven dollars flow into the economy indirectly.

The global MICE industry is estimated at around US$ 280 billion with around 400,000 major conferences held around the world annually.

Insights on Domestic Tourism

The NCAER survey (2003) on domestic tourism provided some fascinating insights regarding the main places visited by pilgrims, who combine religion with leisure, and the percentage of total tourist visits generated by them. The key findings were:

- Tirupati in Andhra Pradesh, Bangalore in Karnataka and Sabrimala in Kerala in the south accounted for 18.77 percent of all domestic visits;
- Vaishno Devi in Jammu & Kashmir, Haridwar in Uttarakhand and Delhi in the north accounted for almost 17 percent of tourist visits;
- Puri in Orissa, Bodhgaya in Bihar and Darjeeling in West Bengal in the east accounted for 10.7 percent of domestic visits;
- Ajmer Sharif in Rajasthan, Shirdi and Mumbai in Maharashtra in the west accounted for 7.9 percent of all domestic tourist visits.

These sites are essentially religious pilgrimage sites. However, visits to hill stations and monuments have also been extremely significant. The domestic survey findings established that domestic travel patterns are characterized by:

- Travel to pilgrimage sites for religious reasons and worship;
- Travel to cultural sites and monuments;
- Travel to hill stations for winter leisure and beaches for summer vacations;
- Travel to friends and relatives to participate in weddings, social functions and festivals.

The NCAER survey also concluded that the major tourist-generating states were Delhi, Rajasthan, Andhra Pradesh, Karnataka and Uttar Pradesh. The tourist-generating households had undertaken 230 million trips, of which 61 million were undertaken by urban residents and 169 million by rural ones.

This implies an average of 2.64 trips per tourist-generating household, with urban households generating a higher rate at 2.8 trips. The main purposes of these trips as emerged from the survey were:

- 59 percent for social reasons such as visiting friends and relatives, attending weddings and other functions;
- 14 percent for religious, pilgrimage purposes;
- 6 percent for leisure and recreation;
- 8 percent for business purposes; and
- 14 percent for other purposes.

    Some of the other discernable trends that emerged were:

- South India accounted for 39 percent of domestic tourism (leisure and holiday) and 36 percent of the religious pilgrimage market segments, while the north accounted for 26 percent and 24 percent respectively. This was a function of better connectivity, access, and the high levels of economic growth that south India was registering. With increased emphasis on improving the quality of road, rail and airport infrastructure in south India, an increase in the flow of domestic tourists to south India was likely.

- The average expenditure per trip was Rs 1389 with trips originating in urban India averaging Rs 2043. The average expenditure on leisure and holiday travel was significantly above the average among urban travellers (Rs 3700 compared to Rs 2700), but lower for the rural traveller (Rs 2200 compared to Rs 2700).
- Only 1.7 percent of the tourist trips in India are arranged as packaged tours. This demonstrates the immense potential for well-structured value-for-money packages in the domestic market.

Europe is the leader with a 58 percent share of all international meetings and conventions held. Asia-Pacific and North America trail behind Europe with shares of 16 percent and 15 percent respectively, while the total value generated by the Asia-Pacific region is around US$ 60 billion. Within the Asia-Pacific region, Australia has performed extremely well and leads in the market share, followed by Japan, South Korea and China.

Singapore, Sydney, Bangkok, Shanghai and Hong Kong have emerged as key destinations and, in consequence, have established a number of world-class convention centres. Most of them are integrated facilities with options for staying, entertainment, shopping and business centres being provided as an ancillary to the convention centre complex. The convention centres are highly flexible and can handle different kinds of events, from exhibitions to conferences to concerts and meetings. Most convention centres have positioned themselves as different from the other – the Sydney Convention and Exhibition Centre leverages its natural advantage of being located on the Diamond Harbour; the Beachside Convention Centre in Bali markets itself as a facility with golf, beach and entertainment on offer; the QSNCC in Bangkok markets itself as one of the largest repositories of Thai art; while SUNTEC in Singapore highlights its efficiency and technical expertise.

India is a small player in the Asia-Pacific region with a share of a mere seven percent. India's share of the market for hosting international conventions has been increasing at the rate of nine percent per annum, but the present low market share is on account of the unavailability of integrated facilities offering state-of-the-art facilities. The only such facility available is the 5000-seat International Convention Centre in Hyderabad, created by EMAAR of Dubai and operated by ACCOR, with exhibition facilities in close proximity at HITEX. There is also an excellent exhibition facility created by textile exporters at Greater NOIDA, which enables them to hold regular exhibitions and permanent displays to interact with buyers. Several new projects of international size and standards are underway –the Bandra Kurla Complex Convention Centre in Mumbai; the Dwarka Convention and Exhibition Centre by the DLF in Delhi and a convention centre by the Rahejas in Trivandrum. Such convention centres are also planned at Kolkata, Pune, Chandigarh and Bangalore.

With the creation of these large integrated facilities, India is likely to emerge as a significant MICE destination in the coming years.

Buddhism

India is not taking sufficient advantage of its treasure of holy sites relating to the life and times of Lord Buddha. India is home to the Mahabodhi Temple Complex in Gaya (where the Buddha attained supreme and perfect insight), Sarnath (where he gave his first sermons) and Kushinagar (where he achieved salvation), in addition to seventy-five to eighty Buddhist sites spread across the country, out of which twenty-two sites are prominent.

The improvement of connectivity, development of infrastructure, availability of decent accommodation facilities and provision of adequate information can lead to India's emergence as a Mecca for Buddhist tourists and a significant growth in the inflow of short-haul tourists from the neighbouring Southeast Asian countries.

Indian tourism has made some attempts to improve the quality of infrastructure and showcase these sites to the international community. Substantial external funding from Japan through the Japanese Bank for International Cooperation (JBIC) has been mobilized for development of the infrastructure at major Buddhist sites.

The first project for the development of a tourism-related infrastructure was taken up for the important Buddhist circuits in 1998

'Walk with the Buddha' Campaign

in Uttar Pradesh and Bihar (covering Sarnath, Kushinagar, Piprawaha and Srawasti in Uttar Pradesh and Bodhgaya, Nalanda, Rajgir, Vaishali in Bihar), then the OECF (Overseas Economic Cooperation Fund of Japan). The total expenditure on this project was Rs 251 crore. Under this project, Rs 105.93 crore were spent in Uttar Pradesh and Rs 143.15 crore in Bihar. The works undertaken related to roads, wayside amenities, landscaping, water supply and electricity and the project was completed in 1998. While it was reasonably well implemented in Uttar Pradesh, it was a disaster in Bihar – as I mentioned earlier, the roads leading to Bodhgaya and Rajgir were in a terrible condition. It was only in 2002, with central government funding, that these roads were redone.

JBIC has recently entered into an agreement with the Government of India to extend loan assistance for Phase II of this project covering important Buddhist sites in Uttar Pradesh. It includes development of the infrastructure at Buddhist sites in Sarnath, Kushinagar, Kapivastu, Sravasti and Sankisa. JBIC envisages a loan amount of 9495 million JPY (Rs 395.63 crore) spread over a period of seven years from 2005 to 2012. The work includes strengthening and widening of national and state highways, roadside plantations, conserving monuments, landscaping, construction of visitor centres, maintaining museums, upgrading of meditation centres, ensuring electric and water supply, and developing tourist villages and wayside amenities.

In Maharashtra, the Ajanta Ellora Conservation and Tourism Infrastructure Development Project was undertaken with the assistance of JBIC. The project was completed at a cost of Rs127.5 crore in March 2002. Under Phase I of this project, the major components completed were monument conservation, afforestation, extension of the Aurangabad airport, roads, water supply and sewage, power supply and visitor management system. The project was so well implemented that it led to the conceptualization and sanction of a Phase II project by JBIC for Maharashtra.

Phase II of this project is being implemented with the objective of conservation and preservation of monuments and natural resources in the Ajanta-Ellora region and also to further improve the quality of life of the local people. The places being covered are Ajanta, Ellora, Aurangabad, Daulatabad, Patnadevi, Lonar, Nasik, Pune, the Elephanta caves, Bhaja and Bedsa, Shivneri, Malshej and Kolvan in Maharashtra.

The newly created meditation park at Bodhgaya.

Bodhgaya after revitalization.

In this project, JBIC has agreed to provide a loan assistance of 7331 million JPY (approximately Rs 299 crore). The project implementation is nearing completion.

India has also been pursuing the integrated promotion of Buddhist sites of South Asia and BIMSTEC (Bangladesh, India, Myanmar, Sri Lanka, Thailand-Economy Cooperation) region as a whole for attracting tourists to these sites. The South Asia Sub-regional Economic Cooperation (SASEC) initiative taken up by ADB has identified Buddhism as a theme for tourism development in Bangladesh, Bhutan, India and Nepal.

Cruise Tourism

Cruise tourism is a major area of growth with unexploited potential. Despite its position in the South Pacific international sea route, comprising 7516 kilometres of coastline, and several natural ports and breathtaking destinations, India has missed out on its cruise tourism potential.

The cruise shipping industry annually generates $4 billion worldwide with a passenger base of over 10 million and is growing by 15-20 percent each year. Despite twelve major ports and 185 minor ports along the coastline, India's share of this market is negligible. A new cruise policy announced by the government of India in June 2008 aims at making India internationally competitive by providing tax exemptions, enabling smooth immigration facilities and creating a dedicated infrastructure. Four cruise ports have initially been singled out for improvement – Chennai, Mumbai, Goa and Cochin, followed by ports in Mangalore, Marmugao, Kolkata, Andaman and Nicobar and Tuticurin in the next four years. The objective is to develop cruise terminals in public-private partnership. In Mumbai, a dedicated cruise terminal is planned for completion in late 2010 and work has begun on a new terminal in Cochin.

Globally, the cruise industry is a horizontally concentrated market with four players (Carnival, Royal Caribbean, P&O Princess and Star Cruises) holding more than eighty-one percent of the world supply of operators, more than seventeen brands and 114 ships. It is a supply-driven market because cruise liners are always in search of new markets, itineraries and destinations. If India provides adequate facilities, services and infrastructure, it will be able to attract global cruise operators. While several major cruise liners have been visiting Indian ports for short stops, it is necessary to fully tap the potential of India's coastlines.

Port infrastructure constitutes a major requirement of the cruise sector. International cruise terminals have facilities and services similar to those provided to tourists at the airports. It is, therefore, necessary to develop attractive cruise services targeted at different segments, identify cruise ports, provide a world-class port infrastructure and passenger services, make cruise terminals into destinations by themselves and develop the required infrastructure at more exotic Indian locales like Lakshadweep and the Andaman and Nicobar Islands.

Adventure Tourism

The unique potential of India as an adventure tourism destination was best summed up by Subhash Goyal, president of the Indian Association of Tour Operators, at the World Travel and Tourism Council Summit in New Delhi in 2005, when he said, 'We tour operators look after everything – hotel accommodation, transport etc. – and take the hassle out of the trip for consumers. And when we find that the roads are bumpy or that the taxis are not airconditioned, we simply sell the Indian tour as an adventure trip.'

Goyal's comments aside, India has immense potential in a wide range of products. The Himalayas have some of the toughest and most exciting river runs in the world. Trout fishing in the rivers and ice-fed mountain streams make India a great angling destination – the mahseer, for instance, attracts anglers from all over the world. Indian rivers, especially those in north India, represent the best white water in the world within a small geographical location. The Ganges, with its upper tributaries (Alaknanda, Bhagirathi and other small tributaries), is often hailed as the queen of white water rafting. The Indian Himalayas offer the opportunity to climb some of the longest and highest peaks with more than 100 peaks above 6000 metres. There are also jeep safaris in the Thar Desert and the Manali-Leh route, the unmatched elephant safaris in the Corbett National Park and horse safaris in the Marwar region. There is skiing in Jammu & Kashmir, Kumaon and Himachal Pradesh. There are also aero sports – ballooning, hang-gliding and para-gliding in several regions of India. Another popular sport is speleology (caving) and with around 780 caves near Cherrapunji and Shillong and in the Garo and Jaintia Hills, there are exciting opportunities for people to explore it in northeast India. Adventure tourism is expected to generate US$ 20 billion by 2010. According to industry estimates, domestic adventure tourism is witnessing an annual growth of about thirty percent while inbound adventure tourism is increasing by up to eight to ten percent annually. According to the Adventure Tour Operators Association of India, we have over one million adventure tourists in India every year.

Extensive tours to Ladakh have also made me realize that in far-flung regions of the country, adventure tourism promotes a more equitable distribution of the economic benefits while ensuring that such regions get integrated into the mainstream. The youth of these regions can also be trained as guides in adventure activities.

Several initiatives have been taken in recent times – the opening up of 113 peaks for expeditions, showcasing of Indian adventure tourism in the world arena with a marketing campaign, finalization of specific guidelines in adventure tourism and, more recently, the issuing of Sikkim permits in Delhi itself for the convenience of tourists. Several drawbacks still remain – adventure expeditions are not permitted to use the Global Positioning System, walky-talkies or satellite phones; contour maps for adventure areas are not available; and there is a lack of synergy between the tourism and forest departments at the state level. There are also not enough trained professionals to work for the industry.

One person who has played a major role in creating awareness

Make India your summer retreat

Come experience the sheer fascination of an Indian Summer. The misty or the mystical. The serene or the sensual. The steamy or the frozen. The stark or the vibrant. Always enchanting. Always incredible.

Incredible India

Summer Campaign

about the potential of adventure tourism in India is Ajeet Bajaj. He is not just a dynamic president of the Adventure Tour Operators Association of India, but is the first Indian to ski in both the North and South Poles. He has also earned the distinction of being the first Asian to have rafted and kayaked on some of the most challenging rivers on the planet, spanning six continents. Adventure tourism is his passion and India needs people like him to emerge as a premier destination in this area.

Human Resource Development – A Key Issue

The rapid rate of growth in the tourism sector and the enhanced expansion in infrastructure facilities will confront the key constraint of shortage of trained human resources in the coming years.

A study conducted by Market Pulse at the behest of the tourism ministry had forecast that by 2020, the total qualified manpower requirement in the travel and tourism sector would be around 6,472,000 persons, of which 3,500,000 would be needed in the hotel sub-sector, 2,730,000 in the restaurant sub-sector and 242,000 in travel operations.[5] The study had highlighted the imperative need to not merely expand the number of hospitality management and tourism education and training institutions, but also to substantially expand the capacity of existing institutes.

To my mind, the Market Pulse study is both outdated (it was undertaken in 2004) and has underestimated the requirement. Since 2004, the hospitality and travel and tourism sectors have expanded at a phenomenal pace and the size, scale and dimension of investments by the private sector in the hotel sector is increasing rapidly. Both FICCI and the ministry of tourism have forecast the requirement of 150,000 rooms in the country by 2010 itself.

At present, the demand for human resources is being met by the 175 institutes operating in India. These comprise 24 institutes affiliated to the National Council of Hotel Management and Catering Technology (NCHMCT), 26 government-approved food craft institutes, and 125 private institutes affiliated to various universities/boards. Only 180,000 students graduate from these institutes each year with degrees and diplomas, Of these, about thirty-five percent of trained people join call centres, airlines and other sectors on account of better remuneration. Thus, only 111,700 formally trained personnel are available each year for the tourism sector.

An analysis of manpower requirements for the 150,000 approved hotel rooms by 2010 undertaken by the ministry of tourism has concluded that 609,000 personnel would be required for the hotel sector (see the break-up in Box J). In addition to this, the restaurant sector would require another 1,55,998 hospitality-trained people by 2010.

The Indian tourism ministry's analysis projects the hospitality-trained manpower requirement to be approximately 3.03 lakhs a year. In sharp contrast, as stated earlier, after attrition only 111,700 formally trained candidates are presently available. So the demand-supply imbalance is to an extent of 1.91 lakhs personnel per year.

A critical issue is that thirty-four percent of the manpower training is required for managerial positions whereas sixty-six percent is required at the skills and operational level. In reality, at present the supply of management personnel is seventy-eight percent while the skilled personnel supply is only twenty-two percent.

125

'Air transport is a driver of economic development. The economic stimuli of airlines, airports and their direct affiliates beyond their direct impact can be expressed using output and employment multipliers. Every $100 of output produced and every 100 jobs generated by air transport triggers additional demand of $325 and 610 jobs in other industries throughout the global economy. For every job saved by protectionist air transport policies upto four can be lost in the economy through reduced tourism spending.'

International Civil Aviation Organisation (ICAO)

Air transport – piloting the growth of tourism

Clark, a leading travel writer, woke me up frantically at 1 a.m. a week before Christmas in 2001. He was just a week away from checking into Coconut Lagoon in Kumarakom for a two-week holiday in Kerala – but there were no tickets available for India from London. All flights were choc-a-bloc. Sounding a bit sheepish, he asked if I could talk to the chairman of Air India and swing two tickets for him. I was now wide awake. Though a few tour operators at the World Travel Market in London had cribbed to me about insufficient flights just about a month ago, I had no idea that it was so difficult to get seats to India from the UK. I assured him that I would try my level best – and I did – but Clark ended up travelling five days after his scheduled departure date.

Just eight years down the line, things have changed dramatically, with even Indian carriers like Jet and Kingfisher flying in to Heathrow.

For years, India's growth in the tourism sector was severely retarded by the civil aviation sector. India is a long-haul destination for most of the key and emerging source markets, and almost 97.2 percent of its inbound traffic arrives by air (see Box A). Therefore, air access is the basic infrastructure required for the growth of tourism in India.

The ministry of tourism had repeatedly emphasized that GDP and tourism growth should not be constrained by insufficient international seat capacity to and from the country. A study conducted for the ministry on 'the impact of civil aviation policies on tourism in India'[1] highlighted the drawbacks of protectionist aviation in terms of GDP, tax revenues and jobs. The WTTC, in its report 'The Way Forward', made a strong argument for liberalization, focusing on the elimination

Box A

Modes of transport to India

 97.2%

 1.1%

 1.8%

Source: Tourist Statistics 2007, Department of Tourism, GOI. (Bangladesh & Pakistan not included.)

of market control, privatization, cross-border ownership, end to subsidies and fair competitive opportunities.

However, the Indian aviation sector, pursuing a protectionist policy, remained deep in slumber, and as stated in 2004 by the committee constituted to prepare a road map for the civil aviation sector, 'India lost out in aviation; it has missed the travel boom of the nineties, ceded its national geographic and economic advantages as a cargo and courier hub to other countries and air travel still remains confined to a tiny section of the domestic population. The share of India in the total world aviation continues to remain miniscule.'

The Centre for Asia Pacific Aviation (CAPA) had alluded to the restrictive and controlled regime in the following manner, 'We need to account for the loss that this caused for India and for its economy. In a different 1990s climate, Mumbai and Delhi, for example, would today have developed into aviation crossroads between Europe and Asia. Imagine the jobs and other national economic benefits that this would have brought! Instead, to "protect" a national flag carrier (which actually involved starving it of funds and driving it to the edge of oblivion) and its employees, India turned its back on the global trend of liberalization and privatization. It is a mistake that India cannot afford to make again.'[2]

There is a high correlation between growth in world air traffic and world economic growth. Analysis reveals that

Box B

Growth in air seat capacity
(Per week/Each direction)

	1989	2000	% Change
China	47725	279404	485%
Spain	189390	656596	247%
Germany	479208	1367185	185%
Turkey	68679	175869	156%
Portugal	61123	143063	134%
Ireland	88375	200998	127%
Italy	269287	602903	124%
Sweden	95975	212870	122%
UK	743460	1493371	101%
France	489027	887427	81%
Japan	370134	931507	71%
Canada	289111	481182	66%
USA	1238904	1989339	61%
India	111277	155693	40%

Source: AOG, 2000

historically, for every one percent growth in GDP, revenue passenger kilometres (RPKs) and available seat kilometres (ASKs) have grown at double the rate. The converse is that for every two percent growth in RPKs/ASKs, the GDP has grown at one percent. This relationship has been well established by the International Air Transport Association (IATA).

From a tourism viewpoint, the argument was that the growth potential for seat capacity was huge and that the trip per capita remained extremely low. In its presentation before the committee constituted to prepare the above-mentioned road map for the civil aviation sector, the ministry of tourism pointed out that between 1989 and 2000, the seat capacity on all international routes to India had registered a growth of 40 percent. In comparison, China saw a growth of 485 percent and even countries like the UK and US, with a relatively higher base than India, recorded a higher growth rate at 101 percent and 61 percent respectively (see Box B).

We had also demonstrated the marked discrepancy in air connectivity from Indian destinations to other countries. An example of this was the air connectivity of Mumbai as compared with that of Hong Kong, relative to their respective key source markets (see Box C).

In its report submitted to the government in 2004, the committee laid down the road map for the civil aviation sector and recommended private participation and competition in air transport services in order to reduce fares and enhance affordability. It also recommended lowering of entry barriers, liberalization of investment norms for foreign equity and foreign airlines and further liberalization of the international

Box C

Hong Kong Vs Mumbai – Connectivity comparison

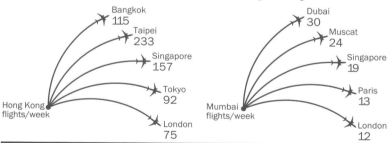

Source: CRISIL/M&A survey

air transport segment, starting with permission for domestic private airlines to operate international air services.

One of the most remarkable changes in India in recent times has been the new and refreshing mindset of the civil aviation ministry. It started with the permission to ASEAN carriers to operate services to seven Indian metros, permitting a low-cost carrier like Deccan to launch its operations, liberalization of the charter policy, the opening of the Indo-UK bilateral agreement, granting government approval to new airlines and permitting private airlines to operate on international routes. The measures were both radical and revolutionary. The most closed sector of the Indian economy had suddenly opened up and it unleashed a huge growth process in both GDP growth and tourism.

The magnitude of liberalization and enhancement in capacity can be seen from the extent of increase in air traffic (see Box D).

Low-cost Carriers

As the PATA Total Tourism study undertaken in 2007 states, 'all the key stakeholders are bullish about the country's prospects. India is seen as the newest air transport giant in Asia, alongside China and Japan. The country could even surpass Japan in terms of passenger traffic over the next decade'.[3] The phenomenal growth in traffic can be assessed from the fact that by the end of March 2008 Indian airports had handled more then 116.88 million passengers (see Box E).

Probably the biggest revolution in the Indian skies has been the accessibility provided to the first-time air traveller by low-cost carriers (LCCs). These carriers have a market share of almost thirty-seven percent, up from a nil share in August 2003. CAPA research indicates that this will rise upto almost seventy percent by 2010 – one of the highest in the world. This is feasible because of India's large population base, its poor rail and road infrastructure and on account of it being

Box D

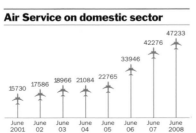

Air Service on domestic sector

15730 — June 2001
17586 — June 02
18966 — June 03
21084 — June 04
22765 — June 05
33946 — June 06
42276 — June 07
47233 — June 2008

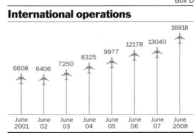

International operations

6608 — June 2001
6406 — June 02
7250 — June 03
8325 — June 04
9977 — June 05
12178 — June 06
13040 — June 07
16918 — June 2008

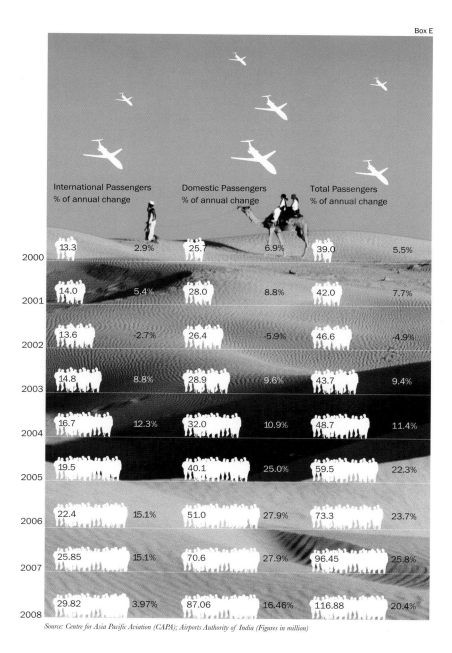

	International Passengers % of annual change		Domestic Passengers % of annual change		Total Passengers % of annual change	
2000	13.3	2.9%	25.7	6.9%	39.0	5.5%
2001	14.0	5.4%	28.0	8.8%	42.0	7.7%
2002	13.6	-2.7%	26.4	-5.9%	46.6	-4.9%
2003	14.8	8.8%	28.9	9.6%	43.7	9.4%
2004	16.7	12.3%	32.0	10.9%	48.7	11.4%
2005	19.5		40.1	25.0%	59.5	22.3%
2006	22.4	15.1%	51.0	27.9%	73.3	23.7%
2007	25.85	15.1%	70.6	27.9%	96.45	25.8%
2008	29.82	3.97%	87.06	16.46%	116.88	20.4%

Source: Centre for Asia Pacific Aviation (CAPA); Airports Authority of India (Figures in million)

a highly price-sensitive market. However, for LCCs to penetrate and enhance their market share at a rapid pace, it is essential that the internet revolution spreads to non-metros and relief is provided from a high-cost operating environment by reduced sales tax on aviation turbine fuel, lower airport charges and separate terminals so that there are savings in equipment commonality and maintenance, with lower landing and user charges. Enhanced efficiency of airports is a critical factor for these airlines as, at present, Indian airports, despite their poor-quality infrastructure, cost almost 60-70 percent higher than other countries. Quick turnarounds of aircraft are not feasible, taking at least forty-five to fifty minutes, and fuel costs account for thirty percent of the airlines cost structure. This is almost 2.5 times more than in Southeast Asian countries.

Captain G. R. Gopinath had the passion and determination to build India's first low-fare, no-frills airline – Air Deccan. Gopinath's story was the story of a new India, the India of possibilities. He started with one helicopter and turned Air Deccan into India's second largest airline with forty aircraft flying to almost sixty destinations. Air Deccan was India's first airline to establish web-based reservations and issue e-tickets backed by twenty-four-hour multilingual call centres. Its tickets were available at an unprecedented network of seven thousand distribution outlets varying from petrol bunks to post offices.

While LCCs increased their market share significantly, most of them, on account of huge price wars in the domestic market, were charging unrealistically low fares. This led to a wave of consolidation. In fact, the period 2007-08 can be characterized as the year of mergers and acquisitions. The first major deal was when Jet Airways acquired Air Sahara for Rs1450 crores in April 2007. Soon after this, Jet's rival, Kingfisher Airlines, acquired a twenty-six percent stake in Air Deccan in a deal valued at around Rs 550 crores. Shortly thereafter, Kingfisher's stake was raised to forty-six percent and two months later, a merger of the two companies was announced. A little later the government of India got its act together and merged the two national carriers, Air India and Indian Airlines. The new airline, called the National Aviation Corporation of India Ltd., now flies as Air India.

This consolidation exercise has eased the price wars, and enhanced yield improvement, cost reduction and capacity rationalization. Integration and mergers are, however, extremely complex issues involving skilled human resource management and enhanced capital inflows. Unless well managed with vision, clarity and firmness, integration can also turn into a nightmare with a huge negative impact on performance. Moreover, globally, there are hardly any successful models of airline groups running both a full-service and a low-cost airline. The only successful model that comes to mind is the Qantas-Jet Star model. Therefore, the process needs to be calibrated and requires careful management.

Potential for Growth

The enormous potential for growth can be assessed from the fact that India's annual domestic passenger traffic is only one fifth that of China and less than four percent of that of the US. As shown below in Box F, airline trips in India at present are only 0.02 per capita compared with 0.09 per capita in China and 2.2 per capita in the USA. India's large population base, its growing and vibrant economy, and the inability of the inadequate rail and road infrastructure to meet the growing demand are likely to catalyze further growth.

This realization has led to Indian carriers placing orders for delivery of almost 480 aircraft till 2012 against an existing fleet size of 310 operating in June 2007. During the last two years alone, almost 150 aircraft have been added for scheduled services with another fifty private aircraft in the general category. Airbus Industries has estimated that India would need 935 aircraft over the next twenty years.[4] Boeing, in its 2006-07 outlook has, in its twenty years' market forecast,

Box F

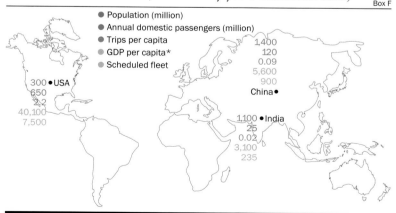

- Population (million)
- Annual domestic passengers (million)
- Trips per capita
- GDP per capita*
- Scheduled fleet

1,400
120
0.09
5,600
900
China●

300 ●USA
650
2.2
40,100
7,500

1,100 ●India
25
0.02
3,100
235

Source: CAPA

stated that India would need 856 commercial airplanes at a value of US$ 72 billion. Later, it revised its outlook for the Indian aviation industry and said that it would require 911 new commercial planes worth more than $ 86 billion. It stated that if the aviation infrastructure improved, demand would cross the 911 unit mark.[5]

There has been a radical movement from the objective of merely protecting the national carrier, Air India, at a huge cost to the Indian economy to a realization that air connectivity is a key driver for trade and tourism. The 2003 agreement between India and ASEAN led to the opening of India's secondary destinations and enhanced connectivity between the two regions. Singapore, Malaysia and Thailand have strong carriers which have opened up new markets such as Trivandrum, Cochin, Hyderabad, Kolkata, Ahmedabad, Gaya, and Varanasi (see Box G).

Enhanced Air Connectivity

One of the first key initiatives was the granting of liberal traffic rights for airlines within SAARC member countries. The major beneficiary has been the Sri Lankan Airline, which has access to fifteen Indian destinations under a bilateral agreement. Today it operates to ten Indian destinations with over a hundred weekly flights, the airline being the foreign carrier with the largest number of frequencies to India.

Nine carriers from the Gulf region are operating on a daily basis to over twenty Indian cities, most of them servicing the expatriate Indian workers in the Gulf region. It is unbelievable but true that a city like Calicut (Kozhikode) is linked to fourteen cities in the Arabian Peninsula, benefiting the large community of Indian workers from the Malabar region. The Calicut airport itself is a good example of public-private-partnership. During my tenure as district collector of Calicut, a Malabar International Development Society (MIADS) was constituted and the airport, on a hilltop, was expanded and its runway extended to enable the operation of large-bodied jets. The entire development was undertaken with local participation through the concept of a User's Fee. For the first time in India, a User's Fee of Rs 500 was levied on every international user to repay a loan of Rs 70 crore provided by the financial institution Hudco (Housing and Urban Development Corporation Limited).

In this way, the expansion of the airport was facilitated without utilizing any funding from the Airport Authority of India (AAI) or

South Asia: shortcut to India. New airline routes are opening up some of the country's most intriguing cities Stan Sesser

Getting to smaller cities in India used to be a nightmare, literally. Travelers would have to stop in New Delhi or Mumbai, where overseas flights often arrive and depart in the middle of the night. But during the past three years, several foreign airlines have launched nonstop flights from Bangkok, Singapore, Dubai and other cities to more than a dozen second-tier destinations in India.

This means a tourist or business traveler in Asia can now take a long weekend or easy side trip, bypassing India's modernized cities and going straight to parts of the country that haven't yet been as transformed by the booming economy.

Travellers can spend a long weekend visiting Varanasi, one of India's holiest cities, where Hindus come to wash away their sins in the Ganges river. In the south, flights are open to Kochi in Kerala state, a gateway to lavish resorts with traditional ayurvedic massage and treatments. Or they can take a trip to Ahmedabad, the bustling capital of Gujarat known for its handicrafts, museums and 15th-century mosques.

All of this is a boon for travelers. It's also marking a new phase in the changes shaping India. The country's biggest cities are becoming accustomed to the influx of westerners. Now, places that have been more insulated may be forced to adapt – albeit at a much slower pace due to the lack of infrastructure.

Source: Wall Street Journal

government sources. With private airlines now being given the permission to operate in the Gulf sector, it is likely that low-cost carriers will emerge even more emphatically, on account of price sensitivity and the changing profile of travellers.

The UK, which had always witnessed immense imbalances in demand and supply, has witnessed a quantum jump. Between August 2004 and 2006, the weekly seat capacity between India and the UK has grown by 235 percent – from 34 flights a week to 114. London is linked to seven cities in India. This growth has seen the emergence of airports like Birmingham and Manchester, which are linked to Indian cities such as Amritsar. Between the summers of 2003 and 2006, frequency entitlements between India and Europe, including the UK, have increased from 70 flights a week to 204.

The American market, which was slow to respond due to the financial difficulties of American carriers after 9/11, has started moving in vigorously. An open sky agreement has replaced the 1956 agreement, which placed restrictions on frequency, destination and pricing. Air India operates to four US destinations – Chicago, Los Angeles, New York and Newark – with a stopover in Paris. It has now started direct flights from Mumbai and New Delhi to New York, utilizing its new aircraft, and will shortly extend direct flights on the Mumbai-San Francisco sector. Jet Airways has linked up New Delhi and Mumbai to New York via Brussels, with its Boeing C777-300 ER (long-range) aircraft. Continental now flies non-stop from Newark to Delhi and Mumbai, and American Airlines from Chicago to Delhi. Northwest Airlines operates a daily flight from Minneapolis to Mumbai via Amsterdam, and Delta is operating New York to Mumbai and Atlanta to Mumbai via Paris. The next big growth will be carriers flying from different regions of America to regional hubs such as Bangalore and Hyderabad. In November 2003, airlines on the India-USA route offered a weekly capacity of 3948 seats; in November 2006, this increased to 11,144. With the arrival of non-stop flights between India and the US, the impact is being felt by Singapore, Emirates and Qatar Airlines, which were carrying substantial Indian traffic to the East Coast cities of the US.

The charter policy has also been fully liberalized, permitting Indian passport holders and allowing ITP (Inclusive Tour Package) charter flights to transport tourists brought into the country on domestic sectors in India as part of the package. The pressure to liberalize the charter policy came at a time when there was an acute shortage of scheduled services. Charters have their own limitations as they are based on low-cost traffic and in the long run do more harm than good to a destination. A high-value, upmarket business and leisure traveller always likes to travel as he wants and when he wants on scheduled airlines. This is the traffic India needs to target and focus on in the long run.

While the Indian skies have radically opened up, 2007 witnessed the return to profit of several international carriers. The boom was, however, short-lived on account of the escalating oil prices. This forced leading Indian carriers to curtail service frequency and air routes to cut losses. Most airlines have initiated measures to rationalize operations which are not earning profits. The aviation tribune fuel in India accounts for more than forty-five percent of the airlines' cost. Its prices have now fallen and the government has scrapped the five percent import duty. Excise duty and state sales tax continue to be extremely high and need to be substituted by a central sales tax of four percent by granting declared goods status to aviation turbine fuel.

The high-cost environment is forcing airlines to reduce meal choices, introduce kiosk check-ins, have common ground-handling services and synergize engineering and maintenance services. These components form thirty-seven percent of the operating costs and provide room for some manoeuvres, unlike fuel, which constitutes forty percent and employees, who constitute twenty-three percent of the cost component.

Will the rising fuel prices lead to low-cost carriers becoming history? The underpinning of cheap air travel in India was a price-driven search for more volume in passengers. The combination of low fares and rising incomes led to a spurt in air travel and passenger traffic grew at a CAGR of 25.5 percent through three years to 2006-07.

For low-cost carriers to survive and flourish, they must have low-cost operations leading to low-priced tickets. This necessitates the use of secondary airports or, in off-peak times, increased frequency of movements from main airports so that landing, parking and airport charges are low. There has to be lower aviation tax on fuel and the route dispersal policy of operating on unviable routes needs to be avoided. Southwest Airlines, the world's largest low-cost carrier, is ending 2008 with cash in hand despite oil prices at $150. My view is that as in past downturns, the best airlines, large or small, legacy or low cost, will adjust. But this will require resolve and efficient management.

The present economic downturn has led to oversupply in a shrinking market. Airlines are facing a scenario where they need to cut down their flights and increase prices to achieve breakeven levels. However, cut-throat competition is ensuring that unserviced routes are quickly filled up. Thus overcapacity remains. The downfall in traffic has also severely impacted revenues of the Airport Authority of India.

Airport Infrastructure

With this flurry of activity in the Indian skies, the airports have been bursting at the seams. There is just no space available and it is a near miracle that despite severe traffic jams and 'near hits', no major untoward incident has taken place. According to one source, airlines are losing close to Rs 320 crore on account of the high level of congestion, which has led to additional fuel consumption and employee overtime work periods and higher maintenance costs. This inadequacy of physical infrastructure was therefore responsible for almost sixteen percent of the airline industry's loss of Rs 2000 crore in 2006-07.

India's number of passengers has already reached 120 million in terms of the numbers of air travellers. Its traffic growth has been the highest in the world for the second year running.

India's ambitious plans of growth and expansion in the civil aviation

Box H

Airport Development Programme

Particulars	Airport	Indicative Cost (in cr)
Restructuring/Modernization for world-class airports	Delhi & Mumbai Chennai & Kolkata	15,000 5,000
Greenfield airports	Bangalore, Hyderabad, Goa, Pune, Navi Mumbai, Nagpur (hub) & Greater NOIDA	10,000
Upgradation	25 selected airports	7,000
Modernization / Improvement	55 airports	3,000
Total investment		40,000

Source: Report of the Task Force on Airport Infrastructure, Planning Commission.

sector are entirely dependent on the upgradation and modernization of its airport infrastructure. As the report of the Planning Commission's task force on financing plan for airports states, 'The quality of airport infrastructure contributes directly to the country's international competitiveness and economic growth by the smooth movement of people and high-value cargo, spurring trade and tourism. In the past, airport development has not kept pace with the growth of the Indian economy, specially the quantum jump in passenger and cargo air traffic since 2002. As a result, several major airports are congested and offer inefficient services.' [6] The report has envisaged an investment of about Rs 40,000 crore during the period 2006–07 to 2013–14, of which approximately Rs 31,000 crore is expected from private-public partnership (see Box H).

Delhi and Mumbai airports account for almost 44.3 percent of India's total air traffic. After an arduous bidding process, joint venture companies with seventy-four percent private sector participation were finalized in January 2006 to modernize and upgrade airports in New Delhi (GMR and Frankfurt Airport Authority – Fraport) and Mumbai (GVK and Airport Company of South Africa – ASCA). In Delhi, Terminal 3 is being constructed for a pre-Commonwealth Games launch, which will give it the ability to handle 40 million passengers every year. A new domestic terminal and parallel runways, both of which will be operational by 2008, are also being built.

138

In Mumbai, the major issue is that the total area available is less than 600 hectares compared with over 2000 hectares in Delhi. A second runway can be implemented only when the urban slums in the encroached areas are cleared. Without a new runway, Mumbai's passenger capacity can only be expanded to 27 million passengers a year. With another runway, the airport will be able to accommodate over 40 million passengers a year. The existing plan envisages development in three phases: the first phase aims to improve existing facilities as an interim measure; the second phase aims at enlarging the facilities in the existing infrastructure, while the third phase will see the construction of a new terminal building integrating both domestic and international traffic. The current terminal will thereafter be utilized for low-cost airlines. The government has, therefore, proceeded with the development of a new greenfield airport at Navi Mumbai, the opening of which is targeted for mid-2013.

Box I

Kerala's 3 Airports and One More on the Anvil

The major drive for Kerala tourism came from the establishment of the Kochi airport. Kochi international airport was the first joint sector airport. Its establishment owes substantially to the dynamism of a young IAS officer, V. J. Kurien, and non-resident Keralites. Kochi International Airport Limited (CIAL) has shown such robust growth in such a short time that it was able to declare a dividend of eight percent in 2004, a rare occurrence of its kind in the infrastructure. Considering that the airport became operational in only 1999, the declaration of the dividend just five years later should give airport companies anywhere in the world food for thought.

In addition to Kochi, non-resident Keralites have also funded the development and expansion of Calicut airport into an international airport. The catalyst for the development of this airport was the Malabar International Airport Development Society (MIADS). The society mobilized the resources for its expansion, which were repaid through the User's Development Fee (UDF). This was the first time that such a concept was introduced in India at the request of the local people, who wanted Calicut airport to become the driver of economic growth in the Malabar region of Kerala.

In addition, Kerala has an international airport in Thiruvananthapuram. This is being further developed and expanded by the Airport Authority of India. Not satisfied with the three airports, the government and the people of Kerala have got a fourth airport sanctioned in Kannur. This will cater to the northern region of Kerala and lead to the development of Bekal as a leading tourism destination.

The new Hyderabad airport, now operational, has been constructed at a cost of US$ 390 million by the GMR Hyderabad International Airport Ltd. (GHIAL), which is a private-public joint venture comprising the GMR group, Malaysia Airports Holdings Bhd (MAHB), the government of Andhra Pradesh and the Airport Authority of India. GMR has sixty-three percent equity while Andhra Pradesh and AAI have twenty-six percent and MAHB has eleven percent. This airport will be handling 7 million passengers and 100,000 tonnes of cargo at the end of its first phase.

The new Bangalore airport has also become operational at a total cost of US$ 449 million. It has been built by the Bangalore International Airport Consortium (BIAL), with Siemens holding forty percent and Zurich Airport seventeen percent of the equity. The balance is being held by the state of Karnataka and the Airport Authority of India (AAI). At the end of its first phase, the airport will be handling 11 million passengers with an airport city complex comprising duty-free shopping centres, offices, business centres and a terminal for the proposed rail link.

The Kolkata and Chennai Metro airports are also being upgraded and modernized, a task is being undertaken by the Airport Authority of India. The investment earmarked for both airports is around US$ 900 million, with its completion planned by March 2010.

A unique example of the public-private partnership has been demonstrated by Kerala, which has three airports, and a fourth has just been sanctioned (see Box I).

Each of the new airports being developed is envisaged as an aerotropolis, with townships being developed around them. Non-aeronautical activities will provide revenue streams as real estate development plans are implemented. In Hyderabad, the airport has 5495 acres of land while in Bangalore the new airport has 4050 acres. Real estate development with hotels, township, entertainment hubs, convention centres and a range of economic undertakings will be the feature of these airports.

Airports will be the key drivers of economic growth. They will evolve into multifaceted commercial operations containing hotels, conference centres, duty free shops, shopping malls and entertainment facilities. In a sense, they will be the hubs of a multi-model transport network that will serve as host to a myriad economic activities. The southern states of India have rapidly moved forward to create and develop international standard airports. These will, in the coming years, be the impetus for both trade and traffic to south India. The government is actively promoting the development of services at regional airports to reduce the concentration of traffic at the primary gateways. The major beneficiaries will be the southern states, which will emerge as the regional hubs.

There are several challenges as India's aviation industry moves into the twenty-first century. The issue of human resources is of critical concern. CAPA has estimated that an additional 2000 pilots will be required by 2010, but this necessity cannot be met by locally trained resources. Almost 600 foreign pilots are flying in India. A long-term solution requires substantial investments for training academics in various regions of India and it may be worthwhile for state governments to take the initiative in this field.

The economic and financial downturn, the terrorist attack in Mumbai and the slowing down of commercial opportunities have all impacted airlines. The managements have taken action to reduce excess capacity, abolish irrationally low ticket prices, bring down wage structure and cancel orders for yet more aircraft. Jet Airways and Kingfisher, which have been bitter rivals in the past, have announced an alliance in order to survive these difficult times. The scope of this alliance includes cross-utilization of crews, cross-selling of flights, common ground-handling, joint fuel management to reduce fuel costs, code sharing on both domestic and international flights and leveraging of a joint network deploying the 189 aircraft of the two airlines. The two airlines hold close to sixty percent of the market share and critics fear that this could lead to cartelization at the expense of the consumer.

What does the future scenario look like? It took China almost two decades to transform its air transport industry into one of the largest in the world. India is likely to achieve the same result in less then a decade. This would, however, require coordinated action to ensure adequate infrastructure, a competitive cost structure, rational taxes and growing and expanding commercial and tourism opportunities. As CAPA states, 'The growth of the Indian aviation sector has the potential to absorb up to US$ 120 million in investment by 2020 and create 2-3 million jobs, which would be further supplemented by an indirect growth in the tourist related industries.'[7]

'Extraordinary as it is, the rise of India and China is nothing more than a return to the ancient equilibrium of world trade, with Europeans no longer appearing as gun toting, gun boat-riding colonial masters but instead reverting to their traditional role: that of eager consumers of the much celebrated manufactures, luxuries and services of the east.' William Dalrymple

143

Hotels: creating room for growth

In mid-2006, the *International Herald Tribune*, in a lead story headlined 'In Gold Rush India hotel rooms are scarce and expensive', had highlighted how the imbalance in demand and supply of rooms had led to escalating prices, and the immense damage that this was likely to cause to the growth of tourism in India. 'Yet for all these travellers, India offers only 110,000 hotel rooms. China has ten times more rooms. The New York metropolitan region alone has about as many rooms as all of India. The shortage is pushing peak season rates for basic rooms into the stratosphere, by Indian standards.'

Land development authorities in major metros have never viewed tourism as a factor that has an impact on growth, and hotels, in particular, were seen as symbols of elitism. A classic example of this is the Delhi Development Authority (DDA), which failed to auction even a single site for hotels during 2004-06. Propelled by the Commonwealth Games scheduled for 2010 and the severe paucity of tourist accommodation in the capital, it has gone on to auction almost thirty-six hotel sites since March 2006. The huge appetite for hotels in Delhi can be seen from the successful bid of the Leela hotel for a mere three acres at Rs 611 crore. Most analysts forecast that to operate a commercially viable entity, the hotel will have to sell rooms at US$ 1200 a night when it becomes operational.

144

As I write this, I am reminded of the *Times of India* article in November 2007 headlined '5 star room rates in Delhi hit the roof'. The article quoted the director of the Delhi Taj Hotel as saying that the average room rate in Delhi was US$ 400 and that tourists could get almost similar accommodation at half the price in Southeast Asian cities like Bangkok, Singapore and Kuala Lumpur.

Over the last few years, tour operators had complained that Delhi being the entry point, the lack of rooms and the consequential high prices had led to neighbouring destinations like Rajasthan, Agra and Varanasi getting adversely affected, despite the availability of rooms there.

India's economic buoyancy with a growth rate of over 8.5 percent, its focus on improving its infrastructure, the rapid opening up of its skies, the removal of restrictions on foreign investment, and the 'Incredible India' campaign in traditional as well as emerging markets had all contributed to the spiralling demand for hotel rooms. Domestic tourism, presently at 460 million, is also acting as a major catalyst in creating this demand. As India gets younger and richer, its middle class will grow and expand with increased disposable incomes. Almost sixty-five percent of India's population (about 700 million) is below the age of thirty-five and fifty percent of the population is below twenty-five. They will want to discover new and exciting spots within the country. The ministry of tourism's own estimate of additional hotel rooms required by 2010, based on the present rate of growth of international and domestic tourism, is around 150,000 rooms, with the National Capital Region itself requiring an additional 30,000 rooms to cater to the Commonwealth Games.

Given India's geographical size and dimension (it is bigger than the twenty-three countries of Europe plus another 23,000 kilometres), the total number of classified and approved hotels is extremely minimal. India has only around 2000 approved hotels with a total room capacity of 120,000 rooms. This despite the fact that apart from the four major metros, India has thirty-five other cities with a population of more than one million. A study[1] conducted in 2004 by the tourism ministry to look at the manpower requirements of the hospitality and travel operations sector had estimated that the licensed and classified rooms in India represented only seven percent of the total estimated room capacity. According to PATA's Total Tourism study, 'Of the total room count only about eight percent are approved. It is interesting to note by way of comparison that the city of Shanghai alone has 135,000 rooms.'[2] Hotels approved by the ministry of tourism, therefore, constitute a very small fraction of the total hotel inventory currently being used in India. Cities such as Bangalore and Gurgaon have guest houses, service apartments, youth hostels and hotels which fall outside the purview of ministry of tourism. The challenge is to invoke the existing building laws / licensing rules to bring these within the purview of the organized sector so that they are considered safe and secure and are effectively promoted and marketed.

Capacity Constraints

What have been the major constraints in the creation of adequate hotel accommodation capacity?

First and foremost, there has been an inadequate provision of land for hotels in the land-use plans in major metros and tourist destinations; land is also being sold with extremely high reserve prices rather than being auctioned on long-term leases by land-owning agencies; and the floor area ratio (FAR) available for construction of hotel properties has been fairly low, not taking into consideration the investment return required from the project. In fact, the prices at which hotel sites are being sold in public auctions in Indian metros (land prices accounting for 40-50 percent of project costs) can only lead to the creation of five-star deluxe hotels. Most states across the country have not granted hotels an industry status and the central government has not accorded hotels infrastructure status under the provisions of the Income Tax Act. Thus, there is a lack of adequate fiscal incentives for entrepreneurs to invest in a capital intensive industry like hotels. In most cities across the world, hotels are situated in the central business districts so that travel over long distances can be avoided. These properties are based on excellent mixed-use development – very high floor space index (FSIs) ranging between twelve and eighteen, but with surrounding greenery, underground parking, exhibition space, solid waste and sewage facilities. Good scientific urban planning ensures that hotels enable the destination to compete globally. In contrast, in India, hotel sites are far-flung and FSIs are extremely low. This has resulted in very high tariffs.

Absence of Budget Hotels

More significantly, it has led to an almost total absence of budget category two- to four-star hotels in metro cities of India, leading to India's inability to penetrate large-volume markets such as China, tourists from where spend less on accommodation but more on shopping. The price competitiveness of Indian hotels is reduced vis-à-vis competing destinations in the neighbourhood, such as Thailand, Malaysia, Singapore and China. In fact, hotel room rates in the Indian gateways are among the top ten highest in the world.[3] A study by HVS Global Hospitality Services of 'Hotels in India: Trends and Opportunities 2007' has revealed that key markets such as Bangalore, Chennai, Delhi and Hyderabad are showing a decline in occupancy, but increased average room rates (ARR) on account of better yield management and their ability to sell rooms at rack rates to high paying consumers. In fact, the all-India occupancy of hotels during 2006–07 has risen only marginally by 0.7 percent as compared to 2.6 percent in the previous year.

Why did this happen despite the growth in international arrivals and the explosion in domestic tourism? The high rates have led to leading companies, such as Infosys, starting their own guest houses and companies (see Box A).

In Bangalore, Chennai and Delhi, there has been the emergence of a totally new regime of unregulated hotels and guest houses at reasonable rates with decent services, including meals. This trend is likely to extend to other major cities. An analysis by HVS Global Hospitality Services points out that Bangalore has a base of approximately 2000 rooms in the unbranded category, which is higher than in the branded and approved category. Most of these establishments are charging between Rs 3000 and Rs 7000 a day. There is an imperative need to bring them within the fold of the organized sector.

Leading chains which have invested in hotels have reaped major gains on account of the tourism boom. Almost all of them are reinvesting

Box A

Infosys Venture in Hospitality Sector

Perennial traffic problems in Bangalore and high tariffs have prompted some software companies to open their own hotels. Infosys has set up an in-house 500-room hotel complex called Le Terrace, equivalent to a four-star hotel, for its visitors and clients.

The five-storeyed Rs 40-crore project has come up on a 275,000 sq. ft. area in the electronic city complex. All the rooms have wireless connectivity and plasma TVs.

Infosys has 36,000 employees worldwide, a number of whom need to travel to Bangalore for training, meetings, client visits and presentations. Hotel occupancy being always high in Bangalore, it was becoming difficult for Infosys to get rooms, and the commute from the hotels to the campus was long because of traffic congestion. Apart from Bangalore, Infosys now also has its own hotel set-up in Mysore.

heavily in new projects. A welcome trend has been the arrival of leading real estate companies in the hospitality section in collaboration with hotel chains – for instance, DLF with Hilton and MGF Emaar with Accor and Marriott. This is likely to be a major driving force in the creation of the hotel infrastructure in the coming years. Hilton Hotels has created a joint venture with DLF to develop and own seventy-five hotels and service apartments in India over the next seven years. High returns have led to new hotels on the horizon – as many as 566 projects with 43,484 rooms have been approved by the tourism ministry. A study by Lodging Econometric has concluded that China has around 222,000 hotel rooms in the development pipeline with another 88,000 completed by the 2008 Olympic Games in Beijing. In contrast, India has nearly 48,000 rooms under construction or on the drawing board, the second largest in the Asia Pacific region.[4]

The focus for creating additional capacity to meet the demand-supply imbalance has also led to increased emphasis on budget-category hotels. There have been some unique initiatives like the Ginger chain from the Tatas, who have started hotels in places like Haridwar, Agartala, Pant Nagar, Nasik, and Bhubaneshwar, and the Sarovar chain with hotels in destinations like Badrinath, Durgapur, Gangtok, Indore and Shirdi. Realizing the importance of providing incentives for creating capacity in this segment, the government has announced a tax holiday for new hotel properties up to four-star categories in the National Capital Region, subject to their being operational before the Commonwealth Games in 2010. A remarkable initiative in the finance minister's budget proposal for the financial year 2008-09 is the announcement of a five-year income tax holiday for two-, three- and four-star hotels established in districts that have a UNESCO-declared World Heritage Site. This is likely to provide a huge impetus to the growth of mid-segment hotels in Indian cities.

148

Patels and Motels in USA

A few years ago, I was the keynote speaker at the annual convention of the Asian American Hotel Owners Association (AHOA) in Dallas, USA. I was amazed at the size, scale and dimension of this immense gathering. The hall was packed with young, vibrant and dynamic 'Patels' who had created wealth in America by establishing 'motels' on the highways. Of the 53,000 motels and hotels in the US, more than

22,000 are owned by AAHOA mentors. AAHOA has over 9,300 members with over $60 billion in property value.

The rising interest of the 'Patels' in establishing motels in India coincides with the vast opportunities arising with the development of the Golden Quadrilateral and the National Highway Network. As Hugh and Colleen Gantzer in an article entitled 'Highways to Prosperity' write, 'NHAI must build "lay-bys" and the feeder roads to serve them. Alternatively, they should facilitate the setting-up of "lay-bys" just after the exit from the toll plaza when cars have already decelerated. They should also encourage the private sector and the oil companies to set-up appropriate facilities in these "lay-bys" making sure that small stalls are reserved for local artisans, traders and farmers to market their products directly to the highway users.' Their analysis is that 58,000 kilometres of National Highways make up for only two percent of the total traffic. There are another 20,000 kilometres of two-lane highways which are being upgraded and converted into toll highways. Thus, there will be at least 78,000 kilometres of toll highways. 'Even if toll plazas are created at a distance of 100 kilometres, almost 780 hotels can be created on the National Highway network. This is absolutely essential to enable tourists driving and discovering India on these toll highways to rest, relax and unwind.'[5] Here lies a huge opportunity for the Patels to replicate the American 'motels' model in India. As the Indian economy grows and expands, Non-Resident Indians (NRIs) and People of Indian Origin (PIOs) are looking for opportunities in several states of India.

The tourism ministry has also brought out guidelines for the classification of apartment hotels, time share resorts, guest houses and bed-and-breakfast establishments. An exceptional initiative has been taken to build up an inventory of budget-category rooms through recognition of spare rooms available with home-owners under the 'Bed-and-Breakfast Scheme'.[6] The ministry will provide capacity-building training on hospitality to house-owners and promote them through the e-commerce platform. While there is huge potential in this segment, the scheme needs to be carried out vigorously with private sector tour operators as active players. An example of this enterprise is the Clark Group's Jaipur Pride project, where guests stay with select, like-minded families.

The Indian hospitality sector has a Foreign Direct Investment (FDI) of hundred percent foreign equity through the automatic route. This, along with the vast potential of tapping the burgeoning market, has led to the entry in India of almost all the leading international hotel chains – Four Seasons, Accor, Marriot, Hilton, Hyatt and Shangri-La. Most of these chains had initially focused their attention on the upscale premium segment in the major metros and on leisure destinations. We now see a major trend of international chains moving in to fill the vacuum in the mid-market and budget sector.

A remarkable feature of Indian tourism is how the major Indian hotel chains have established a reputation for redefining luxury (see Box B).

What will be the impact of the global meltdown on the hotel industry? As corporate travel slows down, the hospitality sector will feel the heat. There will be increased efforts at cutting costs leading to a higher demand for budget-category hotels, which are sorely lacking in India.

Creating World-Class Luxury

The Taj Group remains India's greatest chain of hotels with its tradition of fine hospitality, world-class luxury and the collection of some of the finest hotels and authentic palaces in the world. It has grown its brand internationally with the expansion of its presence in key gateway cities of the world. It acquired the Pierre in New York, unveiled the Taj in Boston, operates the Blue Woolloomooloo Bay and the Taj Exotica Resort & Spa in the Maldives and is launching the Taj Exotica Resort & Spa in Dubai. Focusing on the emerging domestic travel market, it has created a new chain of low-cost and smart Ginger Hotels.

The Oberoi properties – Udaivilas in Udaipur, Amarvilas in Agra and Rajvilas in Jaipur – have constantly been rated by readers of *Travel & Leisure* and *CondeNast* as amongst the finest hotels in the world. These hotels, along with Wildflower Hall in the Himalayas and Vanyavilas in Ranthambore, are major landmarks and have taken Indian tourism to another level. The credit goes entirely to the vision of P.R.S. Oberoi, whose entire life has been devoted to the pursuit of excellence in hospitality.

151

The ITC, which started with the Chola Sheraton in 1975, is a fairly young hotel chain, but already boasts of eighty hotels in over seventy destinations. Several of its hotels are part of the world-renowned luxury collection from Sherwood Hotels & Resorts. It has always reflected a deep understanding of the Indian ethos in each of its hotels – The Grand Maratha, Mumbai, presents the glory of the Marathas; the Windsor Bangalore recreates the elegance of the colonial age; the Maurya New Delhi has an iconic image among world leaders, especially on account of its famous 'Bukhara' restaurant; the Sonar Bangla revived the business spirit of Kolkata; and the architecture and unique spa in Mughal Sheraton, Agra represents the history, character and dynamism of the Mughal era. The ITC group also operates the Fortune brand for hotels at business locations and the Welcome heritage brand spreads across palaces, forts, havelis and jungle lodges.

A remarkable story has been that of Captain Krishnan Nair, who has provided the Indian hospitality experience at its best through the Leela Hotels & Resorts. He created a unique business opportunity at the Leela, Mumbai, in the backyard of the Mumbai International Airport, and tied up with Kempinski, which brought in the best of marketing, technical assistance and its worldwide clientelle. He has gone on to create unique properties at Goa, Bangalore and Kovalam, and his expansion plans envisage New Delhi, Madras, Hyderabad and Udaipur. Captain Nair's story has been one of vision, foresight and business acumen, with him winning against all odds in a highly competitive industry.

When the government-owned ITDC (India Tourism Development Corporation) hotels were being disinvestment in 2002 -2003, most of them were acquired by Lalit Suri. He also successfully bid for the 168-year-old Great Eastern Kolkata hotel. Soon, his hotel company was India's largest and fastest-growing. Suri was aggressive, politically astute and in his capacity as the chairman of the India initiative of the World Travel and Tourism Council (WTTC), became a spokesperson of the Indian tourism industry. His untimely demise in 2006 let to his dynamic wife, Jyotsna, driving the chain with even greater vigour and enthusiasm under the rechristened brand entity 'The Lalit'.

There is also the dynamic Priya Paul, who has created a niche for Park Hotels by estabilishing India's first chain of boutique hotels. Her hotels are classy, contemporary and chic with stylish bars and nightclubs. Priya is an amazing entrepreneur with tremendous energy, whose vision of 'Leadership through differentiation' is clearly visible in her products and services.

And then there is India's unique tourism product – royal homes and ancestral states converted into heritage hotels and resorts. It started with the Maharajas of Udaipur and Jaipur converting their palaces into hotels and giving them to the Taj Group to manage them on professional lines. Later, the maharajas refurbished and converted the other palaces and hunting lodges and started running them as their own chain. Their success led to the Maharajas of Jodhpur, Bikaner, Kota, and Bharatpur, followed by nobles across Rajasthan, converting their ancestral havelis and castles into heritage properties. These have been conserved, preserved, revived and furnished with carpets, family photographs and traditional furniture, presenting a slice of India's rich historical past. There is also innovation – Devigarh, for instance, has a contemporary, classy interior in a well-preserved fort in the midst of a village in Udaipur. This heritage property has been widely appreciated by leading travel and tourism journals from across the world and has won numerous awards.

These properties are classified and approved by India's tourism ministry as heritage classic and heritage brand. They have played host to the rich and famous – Elton John, Angelina Jolie and Brad Pitt, Julia Roberts and Bill Clinton, amongst others – and are today magnificent venues for hosting 'royal weddings'.

'Citizens of the information society will enjoy new opportunities for productivity, learning and entertainment. Countries that move boldly and in concert with each other will enjoy economic rewards. Whole new markets will emerge and a myriad new opportunities for employment will be created.'

Bill Gates

E-business: making travel & tourism click

Ashwin Damera is a young entrepreneur whose business plan for an online travel website won him second place at the Harvard Business School. Within a year of the launch of his e-commerce portal 'Travel Guru', it seized 12.5 percent of the Online Travel Agencies' (OTA) market share. Similarly, Sandeep Murthy of Cleartrip is an MBA from Wharton. Prior to establishing and operating Cleartrip with three other co-founders, Stuart Crighton, Mathew Spacie and Hrush Bhatt, he worked at Interactive Corp, a firm behind the online travel major, Expedia. Cleartrip has now grown into a 350-person business, attracting around 100,000 people on the site on a daily basis and converting almost 5.5 percent of them into customers. Cleartrip averages almost 7500 air bookings, around 2000 hotel reservations and its daily revenue earnings are close to Rs 2.2 crore. Likewise, Deep Kalra and Sachin Bhatia of Makemytrip.com are today selling close to 10,000 domestic tickets online and have captured thirty-one percent of the OTA's total market (see Box A).

The Rise of the Online Travel Market

The online travel market surpassed US$ 2 billion (Rs 8000 crore) by 2008 – an almost seven-fold increase from the US$ 300 million market in 2005 (Box B). This is expected to grow to US$ 6 billion (Rs 24,000 crore) by 2010. This unprecedented growth has been made possible by a new generation of urban Indians researching and booking travel on the internet and the partnership between the low-cost carriers (LCCs)and the online travel agencies. LCCs account for close to 40 percent of India's domestic travel market. In addition to Air Deccan (now Kingfisher Red Airlines), which has been the pioneer, and Jet Lite (earlier Air Sahara), the opening of the

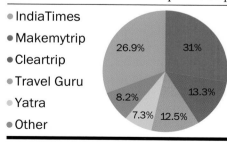

- IndiaTimes
- Makemytrip
- Cleartrip
- Travel Guru
- Yatra
- Other

26.9% 31% 8.2% 13.3% 7.3% 12.5%

Source: Eyefortravel research   Box A

India Online Leisure/Unmanaged Business Travel Presentation (USSM)

Year	Online	Total
2005	295	13,500
2006	796	15,466
2007	1,325	17,467
2008	2,004	19,493

■ Online ☐ Total

Source: PhoCusWright Inc.

sector has seen the emergence of six new airlines (Go Air, Spice Jet, Paramount Airways, Indigo, Indus Air and MDLR). These LCCs offer short-haul, point-to-point services on a no-frills basis. Most of them have single seating arrangements (all economy, no business or first), their fleet consists of a single aircraft model, and they do not pamper their clients with fancy cuisine. Their objective has been to reduce their cost by 35 to 40 percent as compared to legacy carriers. With reduced operational costs, high passenger loads and low staffing, LCCs have aimed to break even within two to three years of their operation. On account of their emphasis on cost-optimization, these carriers have vigorously embraced the internet and made online travel agencies their logical partners.

Several demand and supply side factors propel this growth. On the demand side, India's sustained economic growth has resulted in an expanding middle class and a cultural disposition attuned to travel. On the supply side, travel-supplier partnerships with the banking industry have promoted online payment; the information technology sector has allowed homegrown online solutions; the immense growth of online bookings of Indian railways and now the low-cost carriers have acted as a catalyst and the influx of venture capital in the online travel agency sector has given it greater momentum.

Young Entrepreneurs Tap Venture Funds

One of the biggest contributory factors has been India's leadership in information technology and business process outsourcing. This has enabled online travel agencies and LCCs to host solutions, build technology platforms and customer service capabilities and provide secure booking engines. Another critical factor has been the huge opportunity available in the internet space, where permission from government agencies is not required. This has led to young entrepreneurs raising resources from venture funds and launching operations. For instance, Makemytrip.com has had three rounds of funding amounting to almost US$ 39 million from Tiger Fund, Gabriel Venture Partners,

Sierra Ventures etc. ClearTrip.com has recently received its third round of funding, bringing the total investment to US$ 30.2 million from venture funds such as Draper Fisher Jurvetson, Sherpalo Ventures, Kleiner Perkins, Caufield & Byers (KPCB) and Gund Investment. Travel Guru has raised a seed investment of US$ 25 million from Battery Ventures and Sequoia Capital India. Other leading players are Travel.Indiatimes.com backed by Bennett and Coleman, Ezeego1.com driven by Cox and Kings and Travelocity India with Sabre as the key investor. These travel portals are aiming for profitability in 2010 with an initial public offering in the next two years.

The trend was earlier set by the Indian Railways, which runs the country's largest e-commerce platform. It sells Rs 1,700 crore worth of online tickets per year and almost 78,000 tickets on a daily basis every day. Its online sales are growing at over two hundred percent on a year-to-year basis. The railways have tied up with petrol pumps and Sify's cyber cafes to make online railways ticketing services available across their networks. The use of technology by the Indian Railways has been responsible for radically reducing queues at railway stations.

The Indian online market is likely to expand to US$ 6 billion by 2010. Its potential can be gauged from the fact that the US-based Expedia, the world's largest online travel company, recorded transactions worth US$ 19.6 billion in 2007, earning US$ 2.67 billion in revenues and US$ 296 million in net profit. As Expedia and Travelocity set up shop in India, the market is likely to explode.

156

At present, the OTA's business model relies heavily on air bookings. This is similar to matured markets like the UK and US, with their high online penetration and competition between airlines. It is quite unlike other APAC markets, where a duopoly of airlines exists and the intermediaries have largely been hotel consolidators. The classic examples are those of Mytrip.net in Japan, Ctrip in China and Wotif.com in Australia. A recent study by PhoCusWright has termed India as 'the most dynamic APAC aviation market in terms of consumer choice. For example, the Indian traveller has options among eight airlines on high traffic routes like Mumbai-Delhi. The tendency towards price wars in markets with multiple competitive routes provides a major opening for online travel agencies to add value. The lack of a competitive air offering in more sophisticated markets such as Australia, Japan and Korea has prevented online travel agencies from achieving traction.'[1]

This is, however, likely to undergo a radical change as air booking margins and commissions get squeezed. The next major opportunity will be for consolidation in the lodging industry and enhancing yield management by booking hotel rooms online. Travel Guru, which markets itself as 'hotel ka guru', has tied up with more than 4000 hotels across the country with an inventory of over 2000 rooms. It is today booking over 1000 rooms a day.

This dynamic growth in the Indian travel and tourism industry has to be viewed in the background of various innovative trends (see Box C).

The PhoCusWright study has projected the idea that online channels would continue to outpace the total travel market growth and online penetration would surpass twenty-three percent in the total travel market by 2010. The supplier direct channel would dominate the online distribution with a market share of sixty-five percent in 2008, while online travel agencies would have increased their share to twenty-five percent from the present level of seven percent. This growth would be at the expense of the traditional travel agencies, whose share would declined from thirty-two percent in 2005 to a mere ten percent in 2008. According to the report, traditional agencies would 'neither have the scale and financing, nor the brand equity and knowhow to compete with the venture fund backed startups and subsidiaries of multi-billion dollar international conglomerates.'[2]

Internet as a Medium of Marketing

Now let me turn to the role played by information technology in promoting and marketing India. The ministry of tourism's outlays for information technology were being utilized as Central Financial Assistance (CFA) to assist state tourism departments in computerizing and procuring hardware. Most states prepared project reports for installing Hark systems and kiosks. These were never updated and upgraded and in most states, the equipment lay collecting dust. In many ways, this was a classic case of poor utilization of assistance provided by the central government.

In 2002, with the launch of the 'Incredible India' campaign, this radically changed. Since then, outlays for information technology have been utilized for branding, positioning and marketing India as a destination of choice on the worldwide web.

Box C

Innovative Trends

• By March 2007, internet penetration in India rose to 42 million ever users with 28 million active users. By March 2008 this will rise to 54 million ever users and 43 million active users. An 'active user' is defined as someone who has used the internet at least once in the last thirty days, while an 'ever user' is someone who has used the internet at least once.

• India is at fourth place in the list of the top fifteen countries in internet usage:

a) In the next decade, most internet users will be supplementing PC internet usage with smart phone and mobile device internet usage. India's total mobile subscriber base in February 2009, stands close to 365 million in comparison with China's 534 million, USA's 262 million and Russia's 172 million. India is adding 15 million subscribers per month and is expected to have 737 million subscribers by the turn of the decade. This implies that every third Indian will have his/her own mobile phone by 2010.

b) India is among the fastest growing credit card markets in the world with around 45 million credit cards in circulation (13 million credit and 32 million debit) and a forty percent year-on-year growth. As per forecasts, credit purchase volumes in the country are likely to triple to US$ 21 billion by 2010. The higher disposable incomes of a relatively young workforce is fuelling this growth.

c) Broadband reaches only 4 million users in India. This translates into a mere 0.2 percent broadband penetration compared to 9.6 percent in the US, 20 percent in the UK and 32 percent in smaller countries like Denmark and Iceland. China adds 3.2 million broadband connections in a quarter, whereas India adds just 8000. The reasons for the slow take-off of the broadband are several – the high cost of personal computers and problems in establishing last mile internet connections, poor infrastructure and the failure to make BSNL share its copper infrastructure with others. Once broadband connectivity becomes the norm, we will find Indians indulging heavily in online transactions. The gains are so enormous that we need to seriously think of driving a broadband penetration revolution. The digital vision for India by 2012 is to have 500 million of its population connected to the internet with more than 100 million broadband connections and 100 million broadband connected devices. This is feasible if broadband connectivity utilizes wireless technology just as telephony growth has been driven by wireless.

158

d) In 2008, while nearly 100 million people in India had activated GPRS (General Packet Radio Service) on their mobile, only 30 million were active mobile internet users. For internet via mobile to have deeper penetration we need handsets that are GPRS friendly, aggressive promotion and better services and content. The 3G (3G is the third generation of tele standards and technology for mobile networking, superseding 2.5G) is likely to trigger a mobile internet revolution. 3G will ensure better and higher GPRS speed and service, taking internet on mobile to another level.

What has led to this radical restructuring and enhanced emphasis on utilizing the internet as a medium of marketing? An E-Forecasts analysis in July 2001 had forecast that by 2006 there would be 1333 million internet users.[3] Travel and tourism has already become the single largest category of products sold over the internet – almost close to thirty-five percent of the total sale by websites. It was forecast that the US online travel industry sale would be close to US $ 63 billion in 2006. Various studies showed that travellers both in the US and in Europe were increasingly using the net to buy airline tickets, make hotel reservations and rent cars.

The internet has had a major impact, relative to other channels, as a source of information for choosing and planning holidays and other forms of travel, and increasing importance as a booking channel.

As a study on Marketing Tourism Destination Online[4] stated, 'it is now clear that within a few years, the internet will become an important medium for travel planning and purchasing, affecting the role of Destination Marketing Organizations (DMOs) and of equal importance is the fact that this new marketplace allows DMOs to communicate directly with end-users and with intermediaries as well.'

Towards the end of September 2001, www.incredibleindia.org was created. As a strategy, the entire work was outsourced to Grey Worldwide to ensure that the content was current, accurate and relevant to the target audience. An immense amount of work was put in to create a lively design, which maintained interest and differentiated India as a tourist destination. Our objective was to create a content-rich site so that awareness was raised and information provided. Later, different language versions for key markets were created for the site – French, Spanish, Italian and recently, Chinese and Japanese. Since then, several net advertising campaigns have been undertaken to encourage traffic from key source markets, outlays have been enhanced and the results constantly reviewed and monitored. The internet as a medium allowed competitive bidding and selection on the basis of the lowest-cost bidder. Media plans based on substantial research and inputs received from various agencies were prepared. Intense competitive pressure among agencies led to the ministry of tourism getting highly discounted rates.

The website aimed at creating a meaningful experience – the branding process would work only if we were able to utilize the web as a building tool. As David Aaker, the leading brand expert says, 'the brand is the one thing that cannot be copied. So, the trick then is to build the brand and create an experience that people associate with the brand. The experience can be created by using the unique qualities of the web and keeping up with changing technologies in order to realize the opportunities that it represents.'[5]

Several innovations were carried out. The ministry of tourism moved from super floating ads to monsters to road blocks (different sizes and value-added advertisements on the net), promotional newsletters, chats with eminent celebrities on various aspects of India to advertorials on featured destinations. Website visits, page views and click throughs were constantly monitored to assess the efficacy of the campaigns.

The internet being a highly dynamic medium, it was feasible to assess the performance and persist only with the creatives that were effective. Several contests were launched and every single contestant was tracked. This enabled the ministry of tourism to measure the response to the print ads and pursue only those print collaterals which had shown a favourable response. It was also feasible to identify the geographical regions where excitement and interest were being created by the campaign.

For the campaign undertaken during February to July 2007, the media efficiency in terms of the CTR (Click Through Rate) is demonstrated in Box D.

Our experience has revealed that advertising on the net requires building relationships with consumers and feeding constant information, not merely selling products and services. Continuous innovation and introduction of new concepts are required as technology is constantly moving to higher levels. At Indian tourism, we had to regularly evolve, learn and adapt in an arena that was entirely knowledge-driven. This necessitated cutting several layers within the organizational structure. State governments that wished to aggressively drive online tourism advertising had to reorganize their structure, culture, strategies and business process.

An article entitled 'Contextual Marketing – the real business of the internet' rightly states that organizations need to discard the notion that a website equals an internet strategy.[6] It concludes that instead of trying to create destinations that people will come to, we need to use the power and reach of the internet to provide information to customers when they need it. According to the authors, organizations need to become contextual marketeers. They define the phenomenon as the ubiquitous internet – where the internet will be accessible from almost everywhere. Consumers will be linked to the net via wireless telephones, interactive television, personal digital assistants or laptops with wireless connections. Consumers will constantly be in a digital environment. As the internet becomes ubiquitous, a traveller would be able to change plans mid-journey through an internet-enabled mobile device while he is still on a flight or a computer terminal, or while he is in the departure lounge or in an airline club. The passenger may also modify his requirements of hotel reservations and ground transportation as his plans change. This is getting reflected in the advancement of mobile commerce technology being pushed by global distribution companies like Amadeus and Abacus. The technology is equipped to provide flight and destination information round the clock, even when passengers are travelling.

The dilemma we faced at Indian tourism was whether we should be merely a content and information provider to the consumer or move beyond that. In the initial years, the consumer accessing incredibleindia.org was seeking information online. Soon, he or she started expecting more. The demand was to transact online booking and reserve the varied tourism products that fascinated him or her.

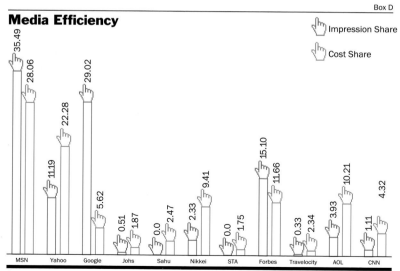

Media Efficiency

Box D

 Impression Share

Cost Share

MSN: 35.49, 28.06
Yahoo: 11.19, 22.28
Google: 29.02, 5.62
Johs: 0.51, 1.87
Sahu: 0.0, 2.47
Nikkei: 2.33, 9.41
STA: 0.0, 1.75
Forbes: 15.10, 11.66
Travelocity: 0.33, 2.34
AOL: 3.93, 10.21
CNN: 1.11, 4.32

Source: Group M

Having invested and vigorously promoted and marketed incredibleindia.org, there was a need to carry consumer demands to their logical stage of fulfilling specific requirements. There was an immense demand to create a 'bazaar' – a market place where consumers could interact and deal with a range of service-providers, who were registered and provided quality services. We also needed to bring a range of small-scale service-providers, particularly bed-and-breakfast establishments, which did not have an online presence. There was also a need to build a reservation system that could be utilized by small businesses providing tourism services in addition to accommodation.

However, Indian tourism was definitely not equipped to transact business and operate in the e-commerce situation by itself. The answer lay in outsourcing e-commerce and building on a private-public partnership to promote and market India as a destination. This has been done, but will require courage, conviction and determination to sustain it in the long run.

As Martin McClanan, the internet guru, has rightly stated, 'the web represents the convergence of media and commerce in a way that may fundamentally destabilize existing communication channels.'[7]

The Shift Towards New Media

For Indian tourism, the Incredible India website cannot merely be an e-commerce platform but has to build and evolve its brand through creating unique experiences. It will increasingly need to harness the speed and spread of information dissemination that the net makes possible. This was hitherto restricted to pop-ups and banners whose impact was limited. With the dramatic use of social networks, Web 2.0 and user-generated content destinations have found new ways of penetrating the minds of travellers. The traditional media will increasingly be under threat as the internet will eat into time spent on the print medium, and to a lesser extent, television. A recent report has alluded to Google reporting a forty-two percent increase in its revenue in the first quarter of 2008 over the same period of 2007. In contrast, a leading US newspaper witnessed its advertising revenue fall by 9.2 percent. This demonstrates the likelihood of a major shift by travel destinations towards online advertising.

165

'With hospitals abroad offering hundreds of treatment procedures and super-specialties it pays the healthcare consumer to be informed – the savings often far outweigh the rigours of travel abroad.'

Josef Woodman, Author, *Patients Beyond Border*

Healthcare: holistic healing in India

My experience of tourism in Kerala has shown me that marketing of tourism requires constant innovation. It necessitates bringing to the marketplace new products that differentiate the destination. For instance, in Kerala, ayurveda and holistic healthcare were vigorously promoted and emerged as key positive influences on tourism growth.

Around the beginning of this decade, Indian doctors who had developed an outstanding reputation in the West for delivering quality medical care were returning home to explore opportunities in India. The reverse brain drain was in full flow. Several of these enterprising medical experts teamed up with leading Indian entrepreneurs to establish centres of excellence that offered a wide range of medical procedures at standards comparable to the best in the world. In 2002, the Indian national health policy had stated, 'To capitalize on the competitive cost advantage enjoyed by domestic health facilities in the secondary and tertiary sectors, the policy will encourage the supply of services to patients of foreign origin on payment of foreign exchange. The rendering of such services on payment of foreign exchange will be treated as "deemed exports" and will be made eligible for fiscal incentives extended to export earnings.'[1]

The CII McKinsey study 'Healthcare in India - The Road Ahead' (2002) had projected that medical tourism in India had the potential to generate close to US$ 2 billion by 2012.

Crisis in Healthcare Systems of Advanced Countries

The healthcare system in developed countries, particularly the US and UK, was already in a deep crisis. In the US, the cost of healthcare was being highlighted as a major concern in several Fortune 100 companies. The US spends almost US$ 2.3 trillion for healthcare – a sum equivalent to the entire GDP of China. Despite this, almost 50 million people are unable to buy health insurance. In terms of the percentage of GDP, this cost had risen to almost fifteen percent in 2003 (see Box A). This was almost double the average for the twenty-nine economically advanced nations in the Organization for Economic Cooperation and Development (OECD).

US National Healthcare Expenditure

	1960	1990	2003
Total Expenditure (billion US$)	26.7	696	1553
Expenditure as a % of GDP	5.1	12	14.9
Per Capita Health Expenditures	14.3	2738	5440

Source: U.S. Department of Health and Human Service, HealthUS 2004

By 2006, the US spending on healthcare had risen to sixteen percent of its GDP. Most of this was private, but even the amount that the government spent exceeded, in per capita dollars, all of Britain's outlays (national health service and private spending combined). In addition to the high cost of medical care, it is estimated that in the US, 43,000,00 people do not have medical insurance and 120,000,000 people have no dental coverage. The 2003 average corporate health benefit cost for full-time employees was almost fifteen percent of the total compensation and almost twenty percent of the total cost of retiree benefits. Most US corporations were in the process of curtailing or eliminating healthcare benefits of retirees. The classic example of this was General Motors. Its North American unit was the largest private provider of healthcare and its president, Bob Lutz, had gone on record to state that the company must dramatically cut health-related costs or be forced to cut the production of two of its six US car lines, namely, Pontiac and Buick. The calculation was that General Motors had spent almost US$ 5.9 billion on healthcare costs in 2002, or about US$ 1400 for every car produced for the American market.[2] By October 2005, General Motors had announced plans to radically cut retiree healthcare costs by almost twenty-five percent. It was a similar story with most US airlines, where health care costs were severely impacting their margins. It was only in 2007 that General Motors and the United Auto Worker's Union agreed to a four-year contract, which created a giant union-managed healthcare fund known as the Voluntary Employees Beneficiary Association or VEBA. This allows companies to offload healthcare liabilities from their balance sheets and eliminate the continuing costs of providing these benefits. General Motors has healthcare liabilities of more than US$ 50 billion. It is expected that General Motors' contribution to the fund will be around US$ 30-35 billion. Several other US companies, including Good Year Tyre, Navi Star, the truck and engine-maker, and Dana, an automatic part supplier, have also introduced VEBA, though on a much smaller scale than General Motors.

A similar crisis exists for over 45 million uninsured individual Americans as well. Many American families are only one major medical event away from bankruptcy. Retired families with no health insurance end up spending a substantial component of their retirement savings on medical procedures. Many retired people go through lives of pain and agony simply because they cannot afford a life-saving medical procedure. Healthcare remains one of the most explosive issues in American politics. The US government estimates that healthcare spending will grow at an average of 6.9 percent a year until 2016, when the US$ 4,100 billion expenditure on health will represent about twenty percent of the GDP.

In recent times, employers have increasingly turned towards healthcare plans where the patient pays a component of his care cost out of his own pocket. These out-of-pocket costs vary, depending on the insurance plans. However, patients can end up paying thousands of dollars before the insurer takes over the cost of treatment. Several of these bills are not paid and end up as bad debts. According to one report, bad debts for hospitals in USA in 2004 were estimated to be between US$ 26 billion and US$ 30 billion, representing about twelve percent of the hospital's revenue.[3] This is triggering deep and growing problems within the US healthcare system.

The national health scheme in the UK is characterized by its inability to cope with rising patient loads, reporting a severe shortage of doctors and hospital beds. Waiting lines for procedures such as hip replacements or liver transplants are excessively long and patients have to wait for almost two years for a liver transplant. Several studies carried out in the UK[4] reveal that while the waiting list period has declined over the last few years, a substantial number of people still have to wait for over six months for specialist programmes. According to a study, reported in the British Medical Journal, while the number of patients waiting for more than six months for surgery fell by almost 8.5 percent between 1999 and 2005, the average waiting period for patients on waiting lists in 1999 was the same as that for 2004, stable at eighty-seven days.[5] In this scenario, the alternative available for residents is the very expensive private clinic, or to seek medical treatment at reasonable prices abroad. The last alternative is increasingly being explored by patients.

Thus, several key factors had combined around 2005-2006 to help market India as a global healthcare destination: the desire to look for an alternate tourism product; the emergence of centres of excellence attracting the best Indian doctors with significant experience abroad; and the decline and decay in the healthcare systems in the US and UK. The time was ripe. The private sector had taken the initiative to constitute the Indian Health Care Foundation. On our part, in the ministry of tourism, the concerns were two-fold: firstly, to ensure that the public healthcare system catering to the vast population should not be adversely affected. Only a few hospitals that went through the entire process of meeting the requirements of the Indian Health Care Foundation and were vetted by the ministry of health would be taken up for promotion and marketing. These hospitals would function within a defined price-banding. Secondly, there would be a process of accreditation of hospitals through the National Accreditation Board of Hospitals under the Quality Council of India. The objective was to develop measurable criteria and standards for all hospitals so that there were transparent parameters for internal and external evaluation of the healthcare delivery system. This would also encourage hospitals to develop and sustain a continuous quality-improvement process of patient care.

India as a Global Healthcare Destination

What is India's core competency to emerge as a global healthcare destination? To my mind, the most significant feature is that Indians view the human being in totality. Treatment in India is based on the physical, social, nutritional and spiritual needs of each individual. India is the only country which has integrated medicare with holistic therapies like ayurveda, homeopathy and yoga to hasten the healing process. In contrast to the Western approach to medicine, ayurveda works to remove the cause of illness, not just treat the disease by suggesting lifestyle and nutritional guidelines. The constraints of modern medicine have led to a growing interest in the five thousand-year-old ancient healing system of ayurveda. It teaches a new way of life, one of optimum health and well-being, and has become popular in leading spas of the world. Yoga and meditation also have their roots in India. Thus, when it comes to health care that goes beyond medical treatment, to connecting the body, mind and soul, there is no place like India. Secondly, of course, India presents significant cost advantages to foreign customers.

Optamin Medical Services was set up in the US to promote and facilitate the travel of US and Canadian patients for medical treatment to India. The name Optamin was derived from 'Opportunities for

Box B

Cost Comparison Analysis for Selected Medical Procedures

Procedure	US	India	Savings
Bone Marrow Transplant	250000	69000	181000
Liver Transplant	300000	69000	231000
Heart Surgery	100000	10000	90000
Orthopaedic Surgery	40000	6000	34000
Cataract Surgery	5000	1250	3750

Cost in US$

Hypothetical Savings for 50000 Procedures

Procedure	Savings ($000)	Count (000)	Total ($million)
Bone Marrow Transplant	181	5	905
Liver Transplant	231	1	231
Heart Surgery	90	15	1350
Orthopaedic Surgery	34	15	510
Cataract Surgery	4	14	53
		50	$3049

Source: Estimates based on various articles and published reports

Americans in India'. Based on its detailed study, the cost comparison analysis for selected medical procedures between India and the US has been made (see Box B). The hypothetical savings for 50,000 procedures have also been calculated.

Optamin's contention was that General Motors had approximately one million individuals in its healthcare programme. The target was that almost 50,000 medical procedures could be undergone by this population each year in India. This would lead to General Motors saving up to US$ 3 billion a year.

In addition, the clinical outcomes in India are at par with the world's best centres due to internationally qualified and experienced specialists and super-specialists and state-of-the-art hospitals. For instance, the Escorts Health Institute Research Centre in Delhi boasts a death rate for coronary bypass patients of 0.8 percent. This compares favourably with 2.5 percent for the same procedure in New York.[6] India also has one of the largest pharmaceutical industries in the world and exports pharmaceuticals to more than 180 countries.

Cost Differential

In 2006, a leading US newspaper ran a lead story titled 'First Class Treatment at Third World Prices'. The difference in costs in India was so large that certain procedures cost one-fifth or one-tenth of what they would in developed countries. A recent report released by India's Planning Commission has alluded that while a heart bypass surgery would cost a patient US$ 600 in India, the same surgery would cost the person $ 7894 in Thailand, $ 10,417 in Singapore, $ 23,938 in the US and $ 19,700 in the UK.[7] A heart valve replacement surgery would cost a patient $ 10,000 in Thailand, $ 12,500 in Singapore, $ 20,000 in the US and $ 90,000 in the UK. In India it would cost a mere $ 8000. While a bone marrow transplant would cost $30,000 in India, doctors in the US would charge anywhere between $ 250,000 and $ 400,000, while those in the UK would charge $150,000. A cosmetic surgery would cost $ 3,500 in Thailand, $ 20,000 in the US and $10,000 in Britain. But in India, it costs only $ 2000.

However, it was clear to us that it would neither be appropriate nor sustainable to market India as a cheap medical tourism destination. India was leveraging a tremendous pool of highly qualified doctors and nurses in every field of healthcare. A majority of the doctors practising in India had been trained in the US or UK. This, combined with world-class medical facilities, made it an attractive healthcare destination. India also has a culture of warmth and care for the elderly, which in many ways is reflected in the care given to patients in the hospitals. Thus, after substantial debate, the positioning and branding of India was that of a 'global healthcare destination'. In 2005-06, this concept of medical value tourism was given an impetus by the ministry of tourism in partnership with the Indian Healthcare Federation through brochures, CDs, publicity material, TV commercials, participation in the World Travel Mart (WTM), International Tourism Bourse (ITB) and also with the introduction of a new category of medical visas (M-visa) and a medical attendant visa known as an 'MX' visa.

Since then, several case studies of foreign patients having undergone treatment in India have appeared on the net and in the international media. The US News and World Report in its cover story entitled 'Under the Knife in Bangalore' quotes the case of Brad Barnum, a fifty-three-year-old building contractor in the US, who underwent surgery for a new knee and hips at the Wockhardt Hospital in Bangalore.[8] It states that he had been able to afford the otherwise prohibitively expensive operation because he had to pay only $ 23,000. Even after adding $ 5000 for the airfare, passport, visa and incidentals, the total was nearly eighty percent less than the $ 125,000 or more he could easily have been charged by a US hospital – and that bill would not have included physician fees and auxiliary charges.

The major contributory factor for the development of medical tourism has been the rising health needs of an ageing population in the US and Europe. Several studies have estimated that by 2015, the American Baby Boom generation's health demands will rise and approximately 220 million people in North America, Europe, Australia and New Zealand may seek medical treatment outside the boundaries of their own countries. This is inevitable when we take into consideration the fact that 8000 Americans are retiring every day. These baby boomers are creating a new trend of medical tourism.

A report published by the Singapore-based air ticketing firm Abacus International has projected that Asia's medical tourism industry is expected to generate more than US$ 4.4 billion a year by 2012 with India, Thailand, Singapore and Malaysia as the top destinations.[9] Based on government research, it states that 'a medical tourist spends

172

an average of US$ 362 a day compared with an average traveller spend of US$ 144 a day'. According to Abacus International president and CEO, Don Birch, 'the lure of low cost, high quality health care in Asia is estimated to be attracting more than 1.3 million tourists a year.... There is a new breed of travellers. They have particular needs, they are going to these locations for a specific reason, and reports are showing that their daily spend is more than double that of other tourists.'

In the business of medical value tourism, quality is the key because inferior medical care would not be worth having at any price. The hospitals and clinics that cater to the tourist markets have to be among the best in the world and be staffed by physicians trained at major medical centres in the US and Europe. Futurist Marvin Cetron, founder and president of Forecasting International and co-author of a book on tourism trends, says, 'Escorts Heart Institute and Research Centre in India performs around 15,000 heart operations every year and the death rate is less than half that of most major hospitals in United States...India is among the world's leading countries for bio-technology research, while both India and South Korea are pushing ahead with stem cell research at a level approached only in Britain.'[10]

Paradigm Shift

In reality, there is a paradigm shift taking place and the primary healthcare doctors have only just begun to realize that there is good quality treatment available outside the US. In these formative years, it will require professionals like Tom Keesling[11] (founder and president of INDUS Health, USA) to act as a facilitator and catalyst. Keesling, whom I met at the Indian Health Summit in Delhi in 2007, told me that economics makes it a highly attractive option to send patients from the US to India. According to his calculation, the savings are of almost US$ 1000 per flying hour – almost US$ 30,000 for the thirty-hour return flying time from the US to India and back. According to him, the economics are obvious to chief financial officers (CFOs), but it is important to convince CEOs and the patients about the quality of healthcare in India being at par with the best in the US.

Keesling is recognized as a pioneer in making safe and affordable healthcare available to individuals and companies in the US. Speaking at the health summit, Keesling said that more than incurring expenditure on promotion and marketing, it is essential that Indian hospitals have independent studies on medical outcomes of patients and get them regularly published in international journals to establish that they can match the world's best – Mayo and Johns Hopkins. The approach has to be similar to that of Indian hotels, which figure prominently amongst the finest in the world. Indian hospitals like Max, Escorts, Apollo and Wockhardt and ARTEMIS (a phenomenal new hospital in Gurgaon) need to figure in the list of the best hospitals in terms of their medical performance. This will give them enhanced credibility for referral purposes. Dr Naresh Trehan, who has aggressively driven the Indian Health Care Foundation, aims to achieve this excellence through the establishment of his Medicity in Gurgaon.

In the UK, the Taj Medical Group provides fully inclusive treatment packages, a clinical back-up and seamless follow-up. It has been responsible for the huge interest there in India as a medical value destination. This started with the case of fourteen-year-old Elliot Knott from Dorchester, who hurt his back in an ice-skating accident and urgently required a spinal operation. He was in constant pain, could not sit, stand or walk properly and had not been to school for three months. Nevertheless, the local hospital said that they were unable to help him for at least ten months. Then the Taj Medical Group stepped in and arranged to have his spinal surgery in New Delhi. He had a highly successful operation and when he was examined back home, Elliot's consultants at Southampton told the Knott family that the surgery in India was of an extremely high standard.

Ivy Teh and Calvn Chu of Synovate Business Consulting write that medical tourists expect the highest possible quality of care, having travelled great distances to seek world-class doctors and hospitals.[12] This clearly extends from the initial point of secondary referrals, through the time spent in an overseas hospital and well into the after-care stage. Many leading hospitals have expounded on this by extending their medical expertise into super-specialization. Medical quality is also supported by hardware and software investments.

Becca Hutchinson, in an article entitled, 'Looking ahead, are there any medical technologies and procedures in which particular countries excel?' writes that India has top-notch centres for open heart and paediatric heart surgery, hip and knee replacement, cosmetic surgery, dentistry, bone marrow transplants and cancer therapy, and virtually all of India's clinics are equipped with the latest electronic and diagnostic equipment.[13] She states that unlike many of its competitors in medical tourism, India also has the technological sophistication and infrastructure to maintain its market niche and that India's pharmaceutical expertise meets the stringent requirements of the US Food and Drug Administration. Additionally, India's quality of care is up to US standards and some Indian medical centres even provide services that are uncommon elsewhere. For example, hip surgery patients in India can opt for a hip resurfacing procedure, in which damaged bone is scraped away and replaced with chrome-alloy – an operation that costs less and causes less post-operative trauma than the traditional replacement procedure performed in the US.

Swiss Reinsurance has recently published its sigma report on 'Global Trends in Private Medical Insurance', forecasting that in view of the significant savings, potential health insurance plans covering medical tourism will eventually become available and revolutionize healthcare delivery. It states, 'The globalization of healthcare is expected to have a significant impact on the strategy of health insurance companies. Even if one-tenth of US patients travel abroad for treatment, savings of US$ 1.4 billion could be realized after taking into account the cost of travel.'[14]

Medical Value Tourism – Downside Factors

Medical value tourism has to be seen in an overall perspective and there are several downside factors which need to be taken into consideration:

First, governments have to be sensitive to their primary role of providing health services for their citizens and should not be perceived as being interested only in generating revenue from public resources sold to foreigners. For instance, India has only four doctors for every 10,000 people; the UK, by contrast, has eighteen. In rural India, state hospitals have very little funds for basic medical equipment and for maintenance of buildings. In fact, India has less than one hospital bed and one physician for every 1000 people. It is therefore necessary that only a few hospitals that meet stringent quality norms and have been through a strict, rigid process of due diligence and have agreed to price banding are taken up for promotion and marketing of medical tourism. Keeping this in mind, the Indian Health Care Federation has enlisted only forty-two hospitals for medical value.

Second, the hospitals undertaking medical value tourism should be accredited. Unlike in the US, it is still not mandatory for hospitals to get accreditation in India. The Joint Commission for Accreditation of Healthcare Organizations (JCAHO) is responsible for giving accreditation for hospitals in America. It has 1300 parameters of quality, based on which a hospital is provided accreditation. It created a body called Joint Commission International (JCI) for taking the same standards to other parts of the world. Several leading Indian hospitals like Apollo have gone in for JCI accreditation while the Quality Council of India has established the National Accreditation Board for Hospitals and Healthcare Providers (NABH) to run accreditation programmes for healthcare organizations in India. I would not like to get into a debate about which one is the better of the two systems. It is for individual hospitals to take a considered view, but it is imperative that hospitals providing medical value tourism should get accredited so that service quality standards are transparent and well established.

Third, there is growing criticism that profitable private sector medical tourism is drawing the best medical resources and personnel away from the local population. This is an area of concern and needs to be addressed.

Fourth, concern has been voiced about there being little follow-up care in medical tourism. The patient is in hospital for a few days and then either goes on a vacation or returns home. In case of any complication or side-effects, post-operative care becomes the responsibility of the medical care system in the patient's home country.

Fifth, medico-legal cases in India are on the increase, particularly after the enactment of the Consumer Protection Act, 1986. Doctors and hospitals are increasingly being sued in the consumer forums and in the civil courts for medical negligence. However, medical councils are ineffective and there is hardly any case where a medical council has taken punitive action against a doctor in the form of suspension or cancellation of his or her licence to practise. In consumer forums, complaints are on the increase and in a large number of cases the verdicts are against the medical profession. There can be huge liabilities in cases of medical negligence or deficiency of service in the treatment of overseas patients and the costs of defending claims can be prohibitive. Therefore, care has to be taken in the contracts to retain Indian law as applicable and within the jurisdiction of Indian courts.

Sixth, for patients travelling to India for medical treatment, there have to be clear and precise agreements or contracts in which hospitals providing medical treatment have to be a party. Apart from providing details of the payments to be made by the patients, these agreements have to spell out the obligation of doctors and hospitals to the patients. An overseas patient has to be fully aware of his rights, entitlements as well as the obligations of the treating doctor in the concerned hospital.

And lastly, private hospitals in Indian metros are viewed as islands of excellence with outstanding facilities of staff and medical care. However, the moment the patient steps out of the hospital he faces issues of hygiene – disease-spreading mosquitoes, unsafe drinking water, accumulated garbage – aspects that undo all the efforts that have gone into making the patient well enough to go back home. The British national health service and the US department of health have listed 'destination associated risks' such as the patient's vulnerability to heat and dust, poor public hygiene and exposure to malaria-transmitting mosquitoes. Long hours of air travel also complicate matters for post-operative patients. This is a reminder of the fact that we need to bring our infrastructure in urban cities – roads, solid waste, sewage etc. – to world-class standards. Jeffrey S. Schult, author of a book on medical tourism, *Beauty from Afar,* states, 'People who cannot afford health care in USA and then find they can get what they want or need elsewhere at a price they can afford, are profoundly grateful that the option exists.'[15] He recalls that he was watching Michael Moore's *Sicko* and remembers the part where he brought the sick 9/11 rescue workers to Cuba for healthcare. It was a stunt but it was medical tourism and he was moved by how thankful the patients were.

Tilman Ehrbeck, in a 2008 article in *Business Standard* entitled 'Medical Tourism Can be a Marvel', states, 'Given the price differences between procedures in the United States and in developing markets, it might seem that US health insurers in particular stand to gain substantially by including treatment abroad in their coverage.... If payers covered medical travel, the potential US market would more likely range from 500,000-700,000 patients a year compared to 5,000-10,000 today. This represents an estimated US$ 15 billion opportunity for receiving countries.'[16]

Medical value tourism will continue to grow steadily and will be integrated in the healthcare system of India. Once international consumers have a choice of providers and the private hospitals in India are transparent about their outcomes, and the transparent data is readily available, the global consumers will choose the best value-for-money hospitals for medical care. What we are witnessing at this moment is just the tip of the iceberg. As insurers and professional health companies get involved, medical value tourism will grow and expand. Realistically, however, it will remain only a miniscule component of India's total medical system.

'Responsible tourism is about enabling local communities to enjoy a better quality of life, through increased socio-economic benefits and an improved environment. It is also about providing better holiday experiences for guests and good business opportunities for tourism enterprises.'

Responsible Tourism Guidelines – South Africa

Sustainability : the itinerary for the future

Kovalam was India's first planned beach development project. The plans were initiated and developed in the early 1960s and it was here that the Indian Tourism Development Corporation's first beach resort, designed by India's renowned architect Charles Correa, was established in 1968. By 2000, Kovalam had emerged as a classic example of high-mass, low-value tourism, flooded by charters from the UK and Germany. This led to unplanned development, illegal constructions and a rapid decline in its natural beauty on account of litter and garbage. The waste disposal method being followed was that of dumping, burying and open burning – practices that were environmentally unfriendly.

In 2001, Thanal, a voluntary organization based in Thiruvananthapuram, initiated a unique movement of 'Zero Waste Kovalam', with the objective of involving the local people and building up a sustainable tourism movement. The initiative led to the clearing of dumped waste and removal of 72,000 plastic bottles from the beach. Following this, plastic bags were replaced by paper bags made by local women groups. Bio-degradable discard from fifteen hotels was collected and a bio-gas plant was established to convert them and generate around 2.5 kilowatts of electricity. 'Zero Waste Kovalam' involved the community, and children played a major role in the movement. Toxic-free workshops and a variety of creative programmes were organized by the Zero Waste Centre for children to raise awareness. The involvement of the local people led to a change in the mindset of the people and slowly but gradually led to the re-emergence of Kovalam as a tourism destination of choice for the discerning traveller.

The concept of Zero Waste was first documented by the Australian city of Canberra, which planned to get rid of waste by 2010. The 'Zero' was the ultimate goal. The concept is designed to reduce consumption, increase efficiency, eliminate toxic inputs, maximize recycling and ensure that products are safely reused, repaired or recycled back to nature or the market place. The concept has emerged as a total quality management term, where management aims at proper resource utilization. As stated by Robin Murray in the book *Zero Waste: Creating Wealth from Waste*, 'For those at the bottom of the Zero Waste Mountain, it is hard to believe it can be climbed. There is no simple model, no one set way. But a broad pattern is emerging which makes it easier for those still looking up from below.'[1]

The critical issue is that tourism development has a significant impact on the natural world and quite frequently, it ends up destroying it. For instance, Australia's tourism demand causes the production of fifty mega tonnes of greenhouse gases per year (twelve percent of the total). Tourism units which fail to protect their environment surroundings adversely impact the attractions that their success is dependent on, while those that adopt good environmental practices significantly contribute to enhancing the experience of their guests and improving the living standards of local communities. In fact, the entire focus today has shifted to sustainable tourism development. As the WTO guidebook on indicators for such development succinctly puts it, 'The management of tourism affects the conditions of destinations and host communities, and more broadly, the future of ecosystems, regions and nations. Informed decisions at all scales are needed so that tourism can be a positive contributor to sustainable development in keeping with its role as a significant source of both benefits and potential stress.'[2]

Sustainable Tourism

Sustainable tourism development aims at a balance between the environmental, economic and socio-cultural aspects. For tourism development to be sustainable, there must be optimal use of environmental resources and the sector must help conserve natural heritage and biodiversity, respect the socio-cultural authenticity of host communities, and provide socio-economic benefits to all stakeholders. Sustainable tourism should also maintain a high level of tourist satisfaction and ensure a meaningful experience for the tourists, raising their awareness about sustainability issues and promoting sustainable tourism practices amongst them. J. Swarbrooke has defined sustainable tourism as 'mass tourism which is economically viable but does not destroy the resources on which the future of tourism will depend, notably the physical, environmental, and the social fabric of the host community.'[3]

The concept of sustainability emerged from the Brundtland Report (Our Common Future, World Commission on Environment and

Development) in 1987. It defined sustainability as 'meeting the needs of the present without compromising the ability of the future generations to meet their need'. The subject was further discussed and debated at the United Nations Conference on Environment and Development in Rio de Janeiro in June 1992. It spelt out the strategies and measures required to halt and reverse the effects of environmental degradation and usher in an era of sustainable and environmentally sound development. The World Travel and Tourism Council has laid down the framework for sustainable development to be established by the travel and tourism industry based on the Rio de Janeiro declaration on the environment and development (see Box A).

There have been several initiatives to lay down standards for good practices, such as WTO's sustainability indicators or WTTC's Green Globe Corporate Destination and certification criteria. The Global Reporting Initiative (GRI) provides guidance for organizations to disclose their sustainability performance. It facilitates transparency and accountability by organizations and provides stakeholders a universally applicable, comparable framework from which to understand disclosed information. It attempts to set world standards on environmental reporting for public and private organizations. Based on the GRI, the Tour Operators Initiative – a network of tour operators committed to sustainable development – has elaborated guidelines for sustainability reporting through performance indicators for tour operators.[4] WTO's guidebook, entitled 'Indicators of Sustainable Development for Tourism Destinations' focuses on the use of indicators for improved planning and management in a manner that leads to better decision-making.

182

The philosophy of sustainability has been an essential component of the ancient Indian civilization where man and nature were viewed not as two separate entities but as part of the same organic entity, the same divine spirit. It was best summed up in one of the earliest Vedic hymns:
'Whatever I dig of you, O Earth,
May you of that have quick replenishment
O purifying one, may your thrust never
Reach right into your vital points, your heart!'

In India, the basic elements of nature constituted the Cosmic Being – the mountains His Bones, the earth His Flesh, the sea His Blood, the air His Breath and the fire His Energy. The earth was viewed as our

Guiding Principles for Sustainable Tourism

The guiding principles for sustainable tourism based on the Rio de Janeiro Declaration on Environment and Development, 1992 are:
- Travel and tourism should assist people in leading healthy and productive lives in harmony with nature;
- Travel and tourism should contribute to the conservation, protection and restoration of the earth's ecosystem;
- Travel and tourism should be based upon sustainable patterns of production and consumption;
- Travel and tourism, peace, development and environmental protection are independent;
- Protectionism in trade in travel and tourism services should be halted or reversed;
- Environmental protection should constitute an integral part of the tourism development process;
- Tourism development issues should be handled with the participation of concerned citizens, with planning decisions being adopted at the local level;
- Nations should warn one another of natural disasters that could affect tourists or tourist areas;

- Travel and tourism should use its capacity to create employment for women and indigenous people to fullest extent;
- Tourism development should recognize and support the identity, culture and interests of indigenous people;
- International laws protecting the environment should be respected by the travel and tourism industry.

For travel and tourism companies, the main aim is to establish systems and procedures to incorporate sustainable development issues as part of the core management function and to identify actions needed to bring sustainable tourism into being. The ten areas for action are:
- Waste minimization, reuse and recycling;
- Energy efficiency, conservation and management;
- Management of fresh water resources;
- Waste water management;
- Hazardous substances;
- Transport;
- Land-use planning and management;
- Involving staff, customers, communities in environmental issues;
- Design for sustainability;
- Partnerships for sustainable development.

mother and we were its children. This was best expressed in the following Sanskrit shloka:

'Moola Bramharoopaya Madhyalo Vishnuroopaiae Agarato Shivaroopay Vraksharayay te Namah.'

('From root to stem to crown/Thou art the incarnation of Brahma/ Vishnu and Shiva/ My Salutations to thee/ Oh noble tree.')

India is richly endowed by nature in terms of diversity. Myriad climatic situations have given rise to countless habitats across the length and breadth of the country. These rich ecosystems not only harbour a rich biodiversity, including a stunning variety of plant and animal forms, but also form the cradle of our rivers and soil, which assure our food security. The geographical diversity of India is the wealth of the ecosystem. There are seven biosphere reserves (the Nilgiris, Nanda Devi, Nokrahs, Nicobar, Gulf of Mannar, Manas and Sunderbans), which are multipurpose protected areas for preserving the diversity and integrity of plants, animals and macro-organisms in representative ecosystems. India also boasts mangroves, coral reefs, deserts, mountains and forests, flora and fauna, sea, lakes and rivers and caves.

Traditionally, India has sought to protect its biodiversity through a network consisting of 572 protected areas, including 89 national parks and 482 wildlife sanctuaries spread over 4.68 percent of the geographical area. Various agencies, including the private sector, have participated in preserving India's cultural and natural heritage.

At the same time, eco-tourism activities occur not only in and around national parks and wildlife sanctuaries but also in other natural and forest areas with varied attractions. Adventure activities such as hiking, river rafting and snorkeling are becoming a part of the Indian experience. Again, India has a vast stretch of mountain ranges and coastal areas in which eco-tourism can play a significant role.

However, the pressure of overpopulation and industrial development often takes a heavy toll on the natural areas, causing pronounced shrinkage and degradation. As a result, many ecosystems and species of flora and fauna have come to be endangered. Most communities living in and around the protected areas are among the most disadvantaged due to inadequate and inappropriate support in rural development and welfare programmes. Their dependence on natural bio-resources is substantial, which is why India's tourism strategy needs to factor them in.

Bhutan's Policy of Sustainable Tourism – Gross National Happiness (GNH)

The Himalayan kingdom of Bhutan, pursuing its policy of sustainable tourism, has long asserted its preference for the concept of gross national happiness (GNH) over that of gross domestic product (GDP). The concept was enunciated by Jigme Singye Waugchuk when he was crowned king of Bhutan in 1972. His contention was that economic growth was not an end in itself but a means to achieve other aims such as greater well-being and happiness. While the GDP-based economic model promoted limitless material growth for excessive comfort, GNH offered a holistic paradigm within which the mind received equal attention. Bhutan, therefore, focused on the four pillars of GNH: economic self-reliance, a positive environment, the preservation and promotion of culture, and good governance.

This new agenda has gained ground in the developed world, too. The London-based think tank, New Economics Foundation, is pushing for the implementation of a set of natural well-being accounts that would focus on life satisfaction and personal development. The accounts would also include liabilities, such as stress and depression. The Philippines has also made progress in this direction. A Philippine Happiness Index (PHI) strives to measure happiness by combining it with conventional economic indicators to come up with a more relevant measure of the progress of a society. Its guiding principle is that economic progress and happiness are not synonymous.

As Imtiaz Muqbil, executive editor of *Travel Impact Newswire*, states, 'The GNH theory has several implications for travel and tourism. Taking a holiday will be viewed as a means of seeking happiness. The tourism industry will also have to find alternative ways of measuring success rather than just tabulating visitor arrivals, foreign exchange earnings and length of stay. An analysis of visitor happiness quotients will become imperative.'

Eco-tourism

Sustainability and eco-tourism are complementary to each other because the basic components of eco-tourism demand the implementation of sustainability principles. The concept of eco-tourism basically comprises four fundamental components.[5] Travel has to be restricted to relatively undisturbed or protected natural areas; it has to be nature-based; it has to be conservation-led; and it must have an educative role – which implies that eco-tourists must have a desire to learn about nature on their trips. Eco-tourism is, therefore, a logical component of sustainable development, requiring a multidisciplinary approach, careful planning (both physical and managerial) and strict guidelines and regulations which will guarantee sustainable operations.[6] Broadly, eco-tourism can be defined as responsible travel to natural areas that conserves the environment and sustains the well-being of the people.[7]

Research by the US travel industry has revealed that eighty-three percent of travellers are inclined to support Green Travel companies, which focus on low environmental impact and energy use and respect for the culture and well-being of the local population. A UK survey revealed that fifty-two percent of people are prepared to pay an average of Aus$ 18 more to each of the tour operators, transport companies, accommodation providers, caterers or retailers to ensure their commitment to environment protection. The Tearfund Research 2000 has shown that 'over half would be willing to pay more for their overseas holiday if they were guaranteed that the money goes towards preservation of the local environment, workers in the destinations are guaranteed good wages and working conditions, or the money goes to support a local charity. Of those who were willing to pay more, the average increase they would accept was five percent i.e. £ 25 on a holiday of Aus$ 500.' Tourists are not always simply looking for the lowest price: they are willing to pay for principles. The World Tourism Organization has estimated that all nature-related forms of tourism accounted for about twenty percent of total international travel and that nature tourism, in particular, generated seven percent of global travel expenditure. Eco-tourism experts like Fillion have identified, through an analysis of motivation of tourists, that forty to sixty percent of all international tourists are nature tourists and that twenty to forty percent are wildlife related tourists.[8] No wonder there has been a dramatic shift towards defining economic performance in terms of the 'triple bottom line' – growth that is economically, socially and environmentally sustainable. Corporates, like ITC in India, have advocated this philosophy vigorously. Tourists themselves have become vigilant consumers wanting to learn about local destinations and the host communities. In fact, today tourists want to contribute to the destination and therefore destinations with good eco-practices enjoy an immense market advantage.

This has led to destinations laying down specific guidelines for 'Responsible Tourism'. The best example of this is South Africa Tourism, which in 2002 published such guidelines, reflecting its vision to manage tourism in a way that contributes to the quality of life of all South Africans.[9] The guidelines set the standards for accommodation and transport operators, tourism associations and custodians of cultural and natural heritage. The objective was to gain market advantage while practising responsible tourism. In India, the movement for Responsible Tourism has just begun, with Kerala taking the lead and getting the Pacific Asia Travel Association (PATA) Grand award for environment endeavours.

The Thenmala Experience

In the context of a country like India, eco-tourism cannot and should not be viewed as nature tourism alone. It should have a much wider dimension. It should be a catalyst in eliminating poverty, in creating rural livelihood, in enhancing new skills, in preserving and conserving natural heritage and in improving the overall environment.

My own experience of implementing an eco-tourism project was in the process of developing Thenmala in Kerala as an eco-tourism destination. A small village at the foothills of the Western Ghats and predominantly a forest area, Thenmala is located about 72 kilometres from Thiruvananthpuram, the capital of Kerala.

Thenmala was the first planned eco-tourism project in the country. The most important eco-tourism resource of this project is Shendurruney Wildlife Sanctuary, which was established for the conservation of a most important endemic and endangered tree species called *Gluta travancorica* (locally known as 'Chenkurinji'). The tree has high medicinal properties, which can control arthritis and blood pressure, and even has aphrodisiac qualities. Conservation of this tree was the focus of the Thenmala project.

Eco-friendly general tourism was planned as an operation only in the periphery of the sanctuary, so that the pressure of tourism would not affect it. Only tourists committed to conserving the environment were encouraged to take part in this experience. Others could enjoy eco-friendly features such as short nature trails, elevated walkways through canopies and mountain biking, which gave them an inkling of what awaited the visitor as eco-tourism in the sanctuary area. Facilities such as boating in the sanctuary reservoir, a boardwalk, a sculpture garden, an amphitheatre and a musical dancing fountain were also provided at Thenmala.

The sustainability issues were addressed through the conduct of environmental impact assessment, regular monitoring and practising wormi-composting techniques (which involves the cultivation of worms to break down waste; the worm casts contain recovered nutrients which can then be used for fertilizer or soil conditioning), battery-powered vehicles, use of solar lamps, zoning sites, use of site hardening techniques and promoting tree planting through the concept of astro forest based on vastu sastra.

Apart from educating the people, local community participation was envisaged through supporting the local women self-help groups in opening shops and cafeterias within the project area, training local youth for utilizing opportunities for self-employment, supporting community-led eco-tourism aspects like management of waterfalls within the forest area, conduct of bird-watching trails, trekking programmes and butterfly identification.

A conservation project of this nature required cooperation and coordination among stakeholders. In its implementation, it institutionalized the coordination of tourism, forest and wildlife, irrigation departments and local bodies. The local community support for eco-tourism products was organized through the committees of the local dependent community.

The project also envisaged an active synergy among the government, private sector and the local community. There were opportunities for the private sector in the areas of accommodation and transport for the local community, in eco-tourism product management, local traditional transport, handicrafts and art within the overall regulatory and supportive framework provided by the government.

Thenmala eco-tourism was a unique learning experience. The novelty of the planning process adopted and its implementation conformed to the accepted principles of eco-tourism and the operational results achieved so far suggest that it can become a viable model both environmentally and economically. Through all these initiatives, Thenmala has today become Kerala's leading eco-tourism destination.

Thenmala eco-tourism won the prestigious PATA Gold award for 2003-04, the national tourism award for the most eco-friendly organization (2001-02) and the best eco-tourism practices award (2003-04).

Andaman Islands – The Last Frontier

The Andamans have the potential to emerge as the world's most exotic and high-end holiday destination for eco-tourism (rainforests and backwater retreats), for adventure tourism (scuba diving, water sports) and sun, sand and sea holidays. This potential needs to be fulfilled with sensitivity, ensuring minimum disturbance to indigenous tribes and environment, and in a manner designed to ensure local community participation.

A Supreme Court ruling on sustainable development of the Andaman and Nicobar islands (following the Professor Shekhar Singh commission report recommending the closure of exploitative industries) is welcome from an anthropological and ecological perspective. It, however, entails a loss of livelihood for a large number of residents. In fact, no new jobs are being created in the islands. The employment issue, therefore, needs to be tackled vigorously. Tourism is a large employment creator, and has a huge multiplier effect. The continuance of environmentally exploitative industries is not a suitable long-term option for the development of the islands. Alternative employment opportunities need to be tapped in order to safeguard the balanced and equitable development of the islands. Keeping in view the fragility, ecology and limited carrying capacity of the islands, the objective should be to strike a balance between the environment and economic development through eco-tourism.

In an island economy, eco-tourism represents one of the few available means of sustainable development. Globally, there are examples of economies built around high-value tourism – the Maldives, Seychelles and Mauritius draw rich and famous tourists from around the world and derive a major proportion of their revenues and employment from the tourism sector. Galagapos (Ecuador) and Hawaii (USA) are examples of island states within the federal structure which have identified tourism as their core competency sector and reaped major economic benefits.

Despite its unique natural wealth, the Andaman islands have been attracting meagre tourist traffic – about 90,000 per annum. Almost ninety percent of the tourists are domestic and eighty percent are day tourists. Most foreign tourists are low-spending ones, while the majority of domestic tourists are government officials on a Leave Travel Concession (LTC) who arrive with a limited budget. There are constraining factors relating to connectivity – non-availability of direct

189

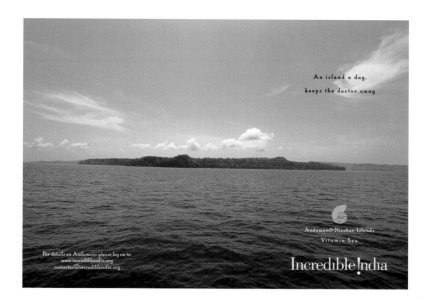

An island a day,

keeps the doctor away

Andaman & Nicobar Islands
Vitamin Sea

Incredible !ndia

For details on Andamans please log on to:
www.incredibleindia.org
contactus@incredibleindia.org

190

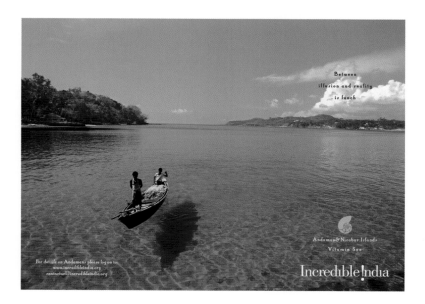

Between

illusion and reality

is lunch

Andaman & Nicobar Islands
Vitamin Sea

Incredible !ndia

For details on Andamans please log on to:
www.incredibleindia.org
contactus@incredibleindia.org

Tradition at a Premium

The Casino group, which was rechristened CGH Earth in 2000, pioneered a unique concept in 1993 with Coconut Lagoon, situated on the famed Kerala backwaters in Kumarakom. Motivated by a philosophy of environment-friendliness, it was keen to avoid adulterating the ten-acre area, which is crisscrossed by canals. So, instead of building a road to make the resort accessible, it arranged for guests to be taken in through the Vembanad Lake on the traditional kettuvallam.

It recreated an ambience of traditional Kerala with coconut palms, canals and small canoes, but most of all, the centuries-old Tharawad houses, which are built according to a unique architectural concept. Apart from the evident charm of these wooden structures, the beauty of their design lies in the fact that the built structures can be transported almost completely from one place to another, without changing the original plan. Coconut Lagoon consists of a cluster of ancient 250- to 400-year-old Tharawad houses that were dismantled from various locations and reassembled in Kumarakom.

These houses were no longer being constructed and the ancient knowledge of assembling them was dwindling. So tracking down the Aasaris, or traditional carpenters, who had the knowledge and experience of building them, was a project in itself. Four teams of Aasaris carefully took apart the old houses, bit by bit, numbering each section of wood, so that there would be no problem reconstructing it. Each piece of wood has its place in the final structure; no nails are used. The result is a feel of the old Kerala, almost untouched by modernity.

Providing heritage experiences is not about catering to the visitor alone. CGH's focus on cultural heritage tourism is conducive to the conservation of cultural resources and the accurate interpretation of resources, which in turn allows them to deliver authentic visitor experiences.

Architecturally and thematically, when it came to ancient properties, be it Kalari Kovilakom or its newest resort, Visalam, in Chettinad, Tamil Nadu, CGH followed the example of Coconut Lagoon. It has tried as much as possible to maintain the original tenor of the land and the structure.

When CGH Earth acquired Kalari Kovilakom, a late nineteenth-century women's palace built by Dhathri Thampuratti on the grounds of a disused Kalari (school for traditional martial arts), it was clear what theme should be adopted for it. The lifestyle of the Kerala royals has always been yogi-like reticence, rather than princely opulence. It was not flamboyant – they were vegetarian and their food was simple. In keeping with this austerity, the ayurvedic packages here follow a strictly governed regimen of diet and a minutely planned daily timetable, but the resort draws an international clientele. After all, the eighteen heritage suites, including Dhathri Thampuratti's room, retain the ambience of royal living.

Visalam is situated in Chettinad, the home of the Nattukottai Chettiars, a prosperous banking and business community in the early twentieth century. Vishla Vairavan, whose great-grandfather K.V.A.L.M. Ramanathan Chettiar built the house for his eldest daughter, Visalakshi, seventy-five years ago, says that Visalam is alive with stories of the past and legends about the culture of the place and its people.

The result is a unique atmosphere, an old-world charm, merged with the earthiness of the house. Restoration was done using local skills and local craftsmen. Damaged floor tiles were replaced with the brightly coloured, decorative cement tiles made on glass, which is a local industry in the nearby village of Athankudi, and is used for flooring in all Chettiar houses. The traditional plastering took a few trials before achieving perfection. The traditional shell lime plastering uses high-quality shell and quartz sand, which are ground to a fine paste and rubbed down with large quantities of egg-white, using a polishing stone. Even the furniture was copied from old samples or bought from dealers in the area.

While Kalari Kovilakom and Visalam gave CGH a basic template to work with and only required it to ensure that it kept close to the original, Brunton Boatyard, CGH's property in Fort Kochi, reflects its most audacious effort at 'restoring' heritage.

Fort Kochi is the most tourist-frequented part of the Ernakulam district of Kerala. The area celebrates the many influences that have touched its shores – Portuguese, Dutch, English, Arab, and Jewish. Brunton Boatyard is built on the site of the old English boatyard of Geo Brunton and Sons, and seems a natural extension of the Dutch buildings of the area. Everything from the airy courtyard with its old rain trees, a motif of Fort Kochi, to the punkahs, similar to the ones at the St. Francis Cathedral, has been carefully reconstructed at the resort, where every room has a view of the harbour.

With the ever-present debates about whether tourism is a positive or negative influence, CGH has tried to ensure, with its core philosophies of environmental awareness, promoting local ethos and involvement of the local community, that the scale is tilted in favour of a positive effect. Indeed, in recent years, the potential of 'culture' and its appeal to travellers to whom local traditions are not inconvenient, but quaint, have been rediscovered. At CGH Earth, the experience of promoting the local flavour, in cuisine, architecture and culture, has not only proved successful, but beneficial for the local community now involved in this growing industry.

flights from Delhi or Mumbai, the extremely high cost of air travel due to high excise/sales tax and inadequacy of fast inter-island ships and ferry services. Chennai and Kolkata are the only gateways to these islands. High-spending tourists from Europe and America take four to six days to reach the island destination. The cost of flights taken from the mainland to Port Blair is the same as those to Southeast Asian destinations such as Thailand and Malaysia, which means that travelling to the Andaman Islands is not an attractive proposition – given the fares, domestic tourists from urban centres would prefer to travel abroad.

At present, the Andamans only attract back-packers who arrive at Port Blair by ship. They avail of the subsidies available on the ship and on the inter-island ferrying. In fact, a single back-packer consumes a total subsidy of Rs 12,000 whereas he spends only Rs 9,000 during his stay in the island. In essence, the subsidy offered by the Government of India and the benefits work out at the cost of Indian tax-payers. The upscale tourist spends US$ 1500 or more during a one-week stay as compared to US$ 200 spent by a back-packer. From both the yield as well as ecological perspective, it is necessary to promote and market

193

The Maldives Model

A good example of protection and preservation of the natural environment for the future generations is the model of sustainable development of the Maldives Islands. In its environmental regulations and standards for the tourism sector it has adopted the following principles:
- Limiting the maximum built-up area to twenty percent of the total land area;
- Preserving the aesthetic integrity of the resort islands, the height of buildings is restricted to the height of vegetation. They have to be well integrated with the island, which is why the use of local materials is encouraged;
- In construction of tourist accommodation, all rooms are required to face the beach and five linear metres of the beachline have to be allocated to guest rooms, twenty percent to public use and twelve percent left as open space;
- Construction on reef flats and lagoons is discouraged. However, as waterside bungalows are very popular among tourists, their construction is permitted, provided an equal-sized open space is left on the land for each building being developed on the lagoon.

high-value tourism to provide an impetus for the growth of tourism in the islands.

Having said this, I must confess that attracting high-yield tourists is a tough proposition. The pristine surroundings of the Andamans will be a natural draw, but infrastructure inadequacies – particularly international connectivity, quality accommodation and leisure facilities – need to be addressed. A network of world-class resorts with high-quality diving and water sports would make the Andamans the most sought-after destination in the world.

A transparent private sector participation is needed to develop high-value infrastructure. The islands that are not open due to security reasons need to be made public and other islands should be opened for infrastructure development in a phased manner. The Anna University has already done studies relating to carrying capacity development, but guidelines for essentials like sewage disposal, effluent treatment, waste water management and disposal of wastes need to be in-built while inviting bids and sanctioning private sector resorts.

The Shekhar Singh report has already recommended that in forest areas, tented accommodation that can be dismantled should be encouraged. This should help to conserve nature and promote eco-tourism. There is also immense potential to develop scuba-diving holidays in these islands. To make travel easier here, a visitor who has a visa should not be asked to take a Restrictive Area Permit (RAP) on arrival and the permit for investors and employees should be issued for a period of five years. A single-window clearance should be provided for investment proposals and the Andaman and Nicobar islands need to be marketed aggressively in key source markets.

194

Tourism – An Engine of Growth for the Northeast

During my last visit to Assam, I had a fascinating experience of travelling on board the *R.S. Charidew,* a luxury boat that runs package tours on the Brahmaputra river. The boat is a refined version of the passenger boats that used to ply from Assam to what is present-day Bangladesh during British rule. The packages on board *R.S. Charidew* cost US$ 250 per person per day for a cruise lasting eight to nine days. Given the wide variety of natural flora and fauna, this is one of the most outstanding river cruises in the world. The venture has been so successful that its dynamic entrepreneur, Ashish Phookan, has launched a second boat, the *R.S. Sukapha,* to handle the big demand coming from

Assam
Nature
- Kaziranga National Park
- Manas National Park + 4 others
- Majuli (largest river island in the world)
- Chandubi Lake

Culture
- Jatinga
- Saulkuchi (renowned for silk industry)
- Madan Kamdev
- Sibasagar
- Agnigarh
- Kareighar

Religion
- Kamakhya Temple
- Umananda Temple
- Navagraha (Temple of Nine Planets)
- Batadrava
- Madan Kamdev Temple

Meghalaya
Nature
- Balpakram National Park
- Highest level of rainfall in the country
- Umiam Lake
- Wards Lake
- Nangkhnum Island

Culture
- War Cemetery
- Austra Asiatic Society (Only state in India to have one)
- Smit Village
- Lew Dun
- Jakrem Hot Springs

Religion
- Thadlaskein Lake
- Suk Mynsiem Festival
- Behdienkhlam Festival
- All Saints Cathedral (oldest church in Shillong)
- Lawkyntang /Law Lyngdoh

Sikkim
Nature
- Khangchendzonga National Park
- Bakhim – a Natural Garden
- Fambing La Wild Life Sanctuary
- Meanam Wild Life Sanctuary
- Varsey Rhodendron Sanctuary
- Kyongnosla Alpine Sanctuary

Culture
- Kabi Longstok
- Tumlong Palace Ruins
- Chungthang
- Lachung
- Yumthang
- Yuksum
- Borong

Religion
- Yoksum – Meeting of the three great Lamas
- Dhubdi Monastery
- Tashing Monastery
- Rumtek Monastery (of a total of 200 Monasteries)

Mizoram
Nature
- Dampa Tiger Reserve
- Twai Wildlife Sanctuary
- Tamdil (the largest lake in Mizoram)
- Phawangpul
- Lake Palak (home of mythical serpent wearing a ruby crown)

Culture
- Ruantiang (where age-old traditional Mizo life is still preserved)
- Kolasib
- Aizwal-Chapchar Kut Festival – Good Spring Festival
- Dances of Mizoram – Cheraw, Sartamkai, Chheih Lam, Khullarn etc.

Religion
- The famous Christian Church known for its carol singing – especially during Christmas (Christians make up 84% of the population)

Arunachal Pradesh
Nature
- Namdhapa Wildlife Sanctuary
- Mio
- Tipi, Ziro, Borndia
- Gyaker Sinyi (Ganga Lake)

Culture
- Ita Fort
- Tawang, Along
- Bhimsalmagar (important archaeological sites)

Religion
- Buddhist Monastery (largest in India)
- Tezu
- Malinithan
- Revival Church

Manipur
Nature
- Keibul Lamjao – the only floating national park in the world
- Lotak Lake (biggest fresh water lake in NE)
- Orchid Park

Culture
- War Cemeteries (maintained by the Commonwealth War Graves Commission)
- Moirang
- Khongjam

Religion
- Govindajee Temple
- Bishnu Temple – built in 1467 AD
- Kaina
- Koubru Leikha

Nagaland
Nature
- Intangki Wild Life Sanctuary
- Ghosu Bird Sanctuary
- Seithekima Waterfalls
- Dzulekie River
- Japfu Peak

Culture
- War Cemetery
- Cultural Centre of Ao Nagas
- Khasakenoa Vilklage
- Khonoma Village

Religion
- Chizarni Baptist Church
- Kali Temple
- Tripura Sundari Temple

Tripura
Nature
- Sepahijala Wildlife Sanctuary
- Jamphol Hills, Rudrasagar, Near Mahal
- Tirthamulk
- Khowra Lake

Culture
- Pilak Panther
- Lungthung
- Paus Sankranti Mela

Religion
- Benuvan Vihar
- Chaturdasha Devta Temple
- Brahmakund

196

European markets. Phookan has also started a resort overlooking the Biphi river in the Kaziranga National Park.

Sanjay Basu, another entrepreneur with a fascination for products highlighting the vibrant cultures of India, is shortly launching *M. V. Mahabahu* (a cruise-liner on the Brahmaputra river in Assam). It is already sold out for the next two years in the European and American markets.

In recent times, the northeast has witnessed the emergence of several young and dynamic tourism entrepreneurs, who have shaped the region as an exotic tourism destination. There is Manoj Jalan, who markets exotic packages in the northeast through his tour operating company 'Purvi Discovery', and Ranjit Barthakur, who operates 'Wild Grass' resort in Kaziranga and runs the exotic 'Wild Mahseer' resort in Balipara in twenty-two acres of tropical vegetation surrounded by tea gardens, with a wide variety of insects and birds. Tea tasting here is a unique ritualistic experience.

The region has several unique assets around which tourism can be developed. The northeast's competitiveness is based on three distinct pillars: nature (rich bio-diversity, national parks, wildlife sanctuaries and forest reserves); culture (diverse cultural heritage sites, numerous tribes and their multifaceted fairs and festivals); and religion (a confluence of three religions – Hinduism, Buddhism and Christianity). The wide array of tourism assets in these three distinct spheres in each of the northeastern states is elucidated below.

The focused development of these tourism assets can have an immense multiplier effect on the entire economy of the northeast. It is, however, imperative that the strategy of development is sustainable, with an emphasis on low volume and high value rather than a mass inflow of tourists. Continuing with the present policy of attracting government officials to the region under the Leave Travel Concession Scheme and subsidized fares would be disastrous, to say the least. We need to focus on the discerning traveller, the culturally enlightened eco-tourists, by carefully structuring packages, enhancing the quality of experience and positioning and branding the region as 'Paradise Unexplored'.

There is also a need to create an enabling policy environment by gradually liberalizing outdated policy regimes like the Restricted Area Permit (RAP), Protected Area Permit (PAP) and the Inner Line Permit (ILP), promoting local entrepreneurship to create environment-

Box B

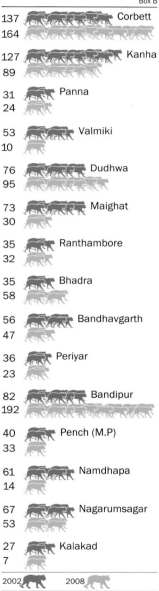

137	Corbett
164	
127	Kanha
89	
31	Panna
24	
53	Valmiki
10	
76	Dudhwa
95	
73	Maighat
30	
35	Ranthambore
32	
35	Bhadra
58	
56	Bandhavgarth
47	
36	Periyar
23	
82	Bandipur
192	
40	Pench (M.P)
33	
61	Namdhapa
14	
67	Nagarumsagar
53	
27	Kalakad
7	

2002   2008

friendly accommodation facilities and developing a supporting tourism infrastructure.

Wildlife Tourism and Tiger Conservation

A National Tiger Conservation Authority report, released in February 2008, has concluded that the number of wild tigers in India could be only around 1411.[10] In fact, if error margins are taken into account, the tiger population would range between 1165 and 1657. This confirms the worst fears of tiger lovers and conservationists – the Indian tiger is living on the edge and surviving under hazardous circumstances. (As compared to 2002, the position in 2008 in different tiger reserves is shown in Box B).

198

The objective of wildlife tourism should be to inculcate an empathy for nature and provide a communion with nature rather than to ensure sightings, a process that has to be experimental and educative. Eco-tourism must also primarily involve and benefit local communities and the benefits of tourism must flow to the local population. As stated by the National Wild Life Action Plan of 2002-06 'regulated low impact tourism has the potential to be a vital conservation tool as it helps in public support for wildlife conservation. In case of any conflict between tourism and conservation interests of a protected area, the paradigm for decision-making must be that tourism exists for the parks and not the parks for tourism, and that tourism demands must be subservient to and in consonance with the conservation interest of the protected area and all wild life.'

The Periyar Tiger Reserve, located in the Western Ghats in the Idukki district of Kerala, presents an excellent example of tourism as a tool for the preservation of the natural resources and community participation in biodiversity conservation. What makes the growth of the Periyar Tiger Reserve exceptional is that it is a successful initiative by the government to involve ex-poachers, local villagers and self-help groups of women living on the periphery of the forest with eco-development committees in the preservation and protection of the reserve. These groups are active and vociferous in promoting eco-tourism and diverse conservation programmes. Their efforts have been sustainable and dynamic.

The Periyar Tiger Reserve comprises a core zone of 350 square kilometres and a buffer zone of 427 square kilometres that encloses 50 square kilometres of the tourism zone. It is home to sixty-two species of animals, including endangered species like the tiger, the Nilgiri langur, the lion-tailed macaque, the Travancore flying squirrel, the brown palm owl and the elephant.

The park area also includes the famous religious site of Sabarimala, which is visited by millions of pilgrims. The reserve is also home to a large number of indigenous people, which include the Mannans, the Puliyars, the Ooralis, the Ulladas, the Talayarayas and the Talampandans. Apart from them, more than 2,500,000 people reside in the areas surrounding the park.

The human-wildlife conflict was fierce in Periyar. About 35,000 local people were directly dependent on linkages with the forest area. On account of religious pilgrimages, there were issues relating to fuel wood collection from forests, extensive garbage, degradation of forests and demand for land. There was also illegal ganja cultivation in the interior forests. As the cultivation of ganja takes almost six months, labourers stayed in the area for a long period, which led to poaching. The fringe area also suffered from large-scale cattle grazing.

In 1998, the eco-development project proposal was implemented. This brought in eco-development initiatives to empower the local community, improve protected area management, and impact monitoring research, environment education and awareness campaigns. The first challenge was to organize eco-development committees (EDCs), provide financial support to the tribals to repay their debts, assist them in raising pepper crops during the season and empower them to collect and market pepper. This led to freeing the tribals from the huge debt burden, an almost ten-fold increase in the tribal income from pepper, a sixty percent reduction in firewood collection for sale, and joint patrolling by the tribals and the park staff.

The second challenge was to convert poachers into park conservators. Poachers were taken into the EDCs for trust building, cases of park offences were withdrawn, and they were allowed to be eco-tourism guides. This led to regular incomes for the poachers, and the social stigma of cases against them was removed. In the process, park protection was strengthened, illegal activities were radically reduced, and the EDCs gained wide recognition. The third challenge related to the inflow of 5 million pilgrims over two months, and how this resulted in unregulated exploitation of firewood, small timber and creation of excessive solid waste. The approach adopted was to ensure that the local EDCs would provide facilities for the pilgrims and thus confine the pilgrimage to a restricted area. This led to a reduction in fuelwood collection and timber exploitation, and incomes for the EDCs was assured.

Involving the local people in bio-diversity conservation and using social capital as a management tool in the Periyar Tiger Reserve has strengthened park protection, enhanced visitors' satisfaction, reduced the local population's dependence on forests and generated revenue streams for community welfare.

Another such example has been community-based tourism in Corbett National Park, using the Appreciative Participatory Planning and Action (APPA) methodology as an integral component of sustainable development in Uttaranchal. A framework for eco-tourism was developed for the Corbett Binsar National Park (CBN) circuit, connecting two protected areas and hill resorts. In addition, Community Based Tourism (CBT) was developed in three villages on the periphery of Corbett National Park from January 2001 to November 2003.

CBT Plans were developed, involving the villagers over several rounds of meetings using the APPA Methodology – discovering what was successful, what was working, what people were proud of and would like to share with the tourists; followed by envisioning the future; designing through feasibility studies and development of action plans; and finally, delivering the plans.

The project performance was evaluated at the community and the destination level by using key indicators arrived at through a participatory process. Experience showed that communities arrived at indicators as part of the planning process and in product development. However, as the project advanced, capabilities needed to be developed to set targets, maintain records and carry out participatory evaluation so as to develop a common appreciation and identify the future course of action.

Tourism and Climate Change

It is widely recognized that in the coming decades, climate change will have a critical bearing on tourism destinations. The tourism sector is not just a major victim of climate change but also contributes to its causes. Air travel, for instance, is the fastest growing source of greenhouse gas emissions and, therefore, increases the risk of global warming. At present, aircraft account for around three percent of all emissions globally and the International Panel of Climate Change (IPCC) expects this to rise to a high figure of seven percent by 2015. The actual tonnage of carbon emitted by air traffic will increase by over seventy-five percent by 2050. The total volume of international travellers is likely to reach 1018 million by 2010 and 1.6 billion by 2020.

A technical paper, which formed the basis for a conference on 'Climate Change and Tourism' at Davos, Switzerland in October 2007, made the first attempt to calculate emissions of CO_2 from three main tourism sub-sectors – transportation, accommodation and activities – as well as the contribution to radiative forcing (inclusive of greenhouse gas) in the year 2005. International and domestic tourism emissions from three main sub-sectors were estimated to represent between four percent and six percent of global emissions in 2005 (see Box D).

Transport generated the largest proportion of CO_2 emissions (seventy-five percent) from global tourism with approximately forty percent of the total being caused by air transport alone (see Box E).

Therefore, the challenge before the tourism sector is to evolve a strategy that

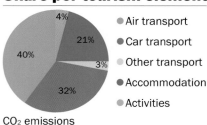

Box D

Share per tourism element

- Air transport
- Car transport
- Other transport
- Accommodation
- Activities

4%
21%
40%
3%
32%

CO₂ emissions

Source: Climate Change and Tourism : Responding to Global Challenges UNWTO

Greenhouse Gas Emissions from Global Tourism in 2005

Box E

(including same-day visitors)

Air transport	517
Other transport	468
Accommodation	274
Activities	45
Total	1307
Total world	26400
Share (%)	4.95

Source: Climate Change and Tourism : Responding to Global Challenges UNWTO

de-couples the projected, enhanced growth in tourism volumes in the coming years from increased energy usage and greenhouse gas emissions. This will enable tourism to become a positive element in society, contribute to poverty alleviation and play a significant role in achieving the 'United Nations Millennium Development Goals'.

At the Davos Conference, it was agreed that given tourism's importance in addressing climate change and poverty alleviation, the emphasis should be on sustainable tourism that reflects on the quadruple bottom line of environmental, social, economic and climate responsiveness. The conference laid down a range of specific actions to be initiated by all stakeholders in the tourism sector to establish and implement a long range carbon-neutral road map. Studies have demonstrated that there are several ways in which climate change will affect tourism destinations, their competitiveness and their sustainability.

Climate determines the sustainability of tourism destinations and is the key driver of seasonality in tourism demand. The climate change impacts will be in the form of coastal erosion, biodiversity loss and reduced landscape aesthetics, and UNESCO has identified several World Heritage Sites that are vulnerable to climate-induced environmental changes. The changes will have a severe effect on the tourism industry through increased costs in terms of infrastructure, higher operating expenses, and backup water and power systems.

Tourism policies that seek to reduce greenhouse gas emissions will also have an impact on tourist flows. Not only will they lead to an increase in travel costs but also to tourists changing their travel patterns. Long-haul destinations such as South and Southeast Asia, Australia and New Zealand, for instance, would get adversely affected. Low carbon emission transport modes like coaches and railways would greatly benefit, as would short-haul tourism destinations.

Several scholars have concluded that climate changes would pose a risk to future economic growth and the political stability of several

202

nations. The Stern report on the economics of climate change has concluded that unmitigated climate change could cause a reduction in consumption per capita of twenty percent in late twenty-first century or early twenty-second century. This reduction in wealth will also have an impact on tourism flow.

Climate change will therefore generate both positive and negative impacts in the tourism sector and these will vary, depending on the market segment and the geographic region. The figures in Box D represent the distribution of major climate change impacts affecting tourism destinations. There will, therefore, be winners and losers at the level of business destinations and nations.

The developing countries, including India, have contended that matters relating to climate change should be best left to the United Nations Framework Convention and Climate Change (UNFCCC) as the largest number of states are party to this multilateral instrument. These countries have objected to the proposals at the Davos Declaration, which called for incorporating tourism in the implementation of existing commitments under UNFCCC and the Kyoto Protocol. While stressing the need to encourage voluntary responsible tourism, India has maintained that the Davos Declaration will not only come into conflict with the Kyoto Protocol but that would also result in climate change being used as a non-tariff barrier for restricting flow of tourism to the developed countries. The contention of India is that the Kyoto Protocol does not require developing countries to cut the CO_2 emissions in the atmosphere, which means that the move of the UN World Tourism Organization to fix such cuts on all its member countries would indirectly impose emission targets on the developing world. The contention of the developing world is that, measured per person, the US, Japan and European nations make the biggest contribution to global emissions. They should, therefore, lead the way.

The issues are complex, but it is necessary for the tourism community to formulate a strategy, taking into account the concerns of the developing countries, to tackle what is the greatest challenge to the sustainability of tourism in the twenty-first century.

‘Tourism not only provides material benefits for the poor, but can also bring cultural pride, a sense of ownership and control, reduced vulnerability through diversification and development of skills and entrepreneurial capacity.’

UN World Tourism Organization (UNWTO)

205

Poverty alleviation: tourism as key catalyst

In an attempt to discover India, the British foreign secretary, David Miliband, accompanied by Rahul Gandhi, spent a night at Shivkumari Kori's house at Simara Village in Amethi district of Uttar Pradesh. The two men slept on charpoys and ate vegetarian food with their hands in true village style. Subsquently, Miliband took a guided tour of the milk collection and chilling centre and the women's self-help group training centre. For Miliband this was a glimpse of India quite unlike what he would have found in the metro cities of Delhi, Mumbai and Bangalore.

An NRI friend of mine, Mohit, a Wall Street whiz kid, and his charming wife, Neerja, came to Kerala for a holiday in 2007. On my recommendation they ended up staying two nights in the unique heritage village of Aranmula, centred around the legendary Parthasarathy temple. The village is famous for its Aranmula Vallomkali, the fabulous boat race held on the river Pamba. It is also renowned for the Aranmula Kannadi (mirrors), which are made using white lead and copper and have immense clarity of images. A French artist, Louba Schild, runs a folk art school in a hundred-year-old heritage building. The Vijnana Kala Vedi cultural centre teaches the nuances of Kathakali, Mohiniyattam and Bharatanatyam as well as percussion and Kalaripayattu (Kerala's ancient martial art form). The Vaasthu Vidya Gurukulam teaches Vaasthu Vidya, the ancient Indian science of architecture. There is also an art gallery, where you can learn the age-old techniques used to create murals on the walls of the temples. The institute and neighbouring houses in the village welcome visitors, artists and researchers from across the world.

Aranmula is one of the several villages across India implementing the Endogeneous Tourism project – a joint venture of India Tourism and the United Nations Development Programme. In 2007, it won the Pacific Asia Travel Association (PATA) Gold Award for the best cultural tourism product worldwide. For my friends Mohit and Neerja, it was a journey to a village steeped in layers of history and culture. As Mohit put it, 'everything in this heritage village had an inherent artistic and cultural tinge to it'. In 2010 they are planning a repeat holiday in Aranmula – this time for five days with four other couples based in New York.

Rural Tourism As A Unique Experience

Rural tourism is about having an experience in a rustic setting and participating in such a lifestyle. It provides impetus to creation of alternative sources of income in the non-farming sector for the rural population. The reverse cash flow from urban to rural area also leads to reinvigoration of lost folk arts and traditional handicrafts. Its significance for India, where seventy-four percent of the population resides in its seven million villages, need hardly be emphasized.

The advent of tourism in post-independent India started with the launch of a five-star deluxe hotel – the Ashoka in 1962. Since then, tourism in India has always been viewed as elitist in character, catering to the rich. This perspective would have been different if tourism in the initial years had focused on building unique experiences around the vast and varied wealth of handloom, heritage and culture that exists in Indian villages. This would have led to tourism becoming a 'transformative' agent, providing a major impetus to local economies throughout India.

This policy corrective was brought about in 2003 with the launch of endogenous tourism or, as it is better known, the rural tourism scheme. The scheme's objective was to shift the vision of tourism essentially to the local level and build links with local communities, focusing on capacity building, training, empowerment and expanding employment opportunities at the village level.

The scheme identified key villages with core competency in heritage, culture, handlooms and handicrafts, aiming to build unique experiences with infrastructure components of Rs 50 lakh per village. The more significant aspect was the community participation component of an additional Rs 20 lakh in each village to enhance the host community's tourism awareness, art and crafts skill development, training in visitor handling and gender sensitization.

The projects are being implemented through local non-governmental organizations (NGOs) whose role is critical and significant. The implementation of this scheme has provided an opportunity to position the Indian rural tourism project as a unique tourism visitor experience in a low-impact setting. The primary target has been the low volume but high yielding visitor seeking unique local community experiences.

Let me briefly dwell on the role tourism can play in reducing poverty. This focus has broadly been described as 'pro-poor' tourism and thesector is particularly conducive for pro-poor growth on account of its special features as elucidated by the World Tourism Organization study of 2002.[1](See Box A.)

Box A

World Tourism Organization Study on Pro-Poor Tourism

Pro-poor tourism is consumed at the point of production, thereby increasing opportunities for individual and micro-enterprises to sell additional products and services. Its main features are:
- The restriction of access to international markets as faced by the traditional sectors of developing countries is not applicable to tourism;
- Tourism depends not only on financial, productive and human capital, but also largely on natural and cultural capital – often assets possessed by the poor;
- Tourism is labour-intensive, providing the poor, who have large labour reserves, with many opportunities;
- Tourism thrives on diversity, drawing from a large resource base which increases scope for wider participation;
- Tourism provides important opportunities for women to find employment.

Tourism directly responds to poverty reduction objectives since it:
- Unlocks opportunities for pro-poor economic growth by providing formal and informal employment;
- Creates profit and collective income from locally owned enterprises;
- Facilitates social development by increasing access to infrastructure, by providing local people with the opportunity to access tourism infrastructure;
- Helps increase participation of the local communities in decision-making as tourism products are often assets owned by the poor;
- Reduces vulnerability by helping to diversify income opportunities;
- Promotes environmental protection as the natural and human environments are the lifelines of tourism development.

Raghurajpur – New Lease of Life to Heritage

Any strategy for pro-poor tourism should aim to enhance its positive impacts while reducing the negative ones. A tourism development strategy aimed at pro-poor objectives can lead to an increased demand for goods and services provided by the poor, increasing their asset base and supporting diversification.Raghurajpur village in Orissa is an example of how tourism can give a new lease of life to heritage, bring in infrastructural and social development, bring back the younger generation to ancient traditions, improve the quality of life of the host community and alleviate poverty. It also shows how a community can ultimately shoulder the process of tourism and administer and manage its workings.

Raghurajpur is a crafts hub comprising 123 households that conserve some of India's priceless traditional crafts – Pattachitra paintings, palm leaf manuscripts and mural paintings. It is also a centre of five major cultural art forms – Medha, a mask dance; Naga – a dance performed against the backdrop of art; Parka Akhada – a dance with fire; Gotipua dance and Rama Leela (a dance drama portraying the story of the epic hero, Rama).

209

The ministry of tourism undertook the work of creating infrastructure facilities as part of the 'hardware' component in Raghurajpur, with a grant of Rs 50 lakhs, and also conducted training programmes for the villagers as part of 'soft' component, aided by a grant of Rs 20 lakhs from UNDP under the endogenous tourism project scheme. The Indian National Trust for Art and Cultural Heritage (INTACH) was the implementing agency for the project.

The Raghurajpur project was carried out with the assistance of the local panchayat and the state government to highlight the cultural and architectural heritage of the village and thereby promote rural tourism. An important aspect of the project was to improve the quality of life in the village. Prior to the project, Raghurajpur was accessible only by the kaccha (mud) road from the highway to the village or by a local train to the nearest station at Janakeidpur. After pursuing the local authorities to take action, the village was connected to the Bhubaneshwar-Puri highway and a road was constructed, leading to the village right up to the very end near the Bhargavi river. Other agencies were contacted to undertake work in the village to improve sewage disposal, drainage, roads and telecommunications. UNICEF helped in the construction of toilets in each household, while the local authorities pitched in for the civic work in the village.

Tourism was essential for Raghurajpur; firstly, to bring in buyers to the doorstep of the villager, and secondly, to develop the infrastructure of the village such as roads, electricity, water supply, lodging facilities, and a restaurant to facilitate the tourism process.

Sustainable Tourism – Eliminating Poverty

As elucidated by WTO in its study, 'of the 100 or so poorest countries, tourism is significant in almost half of the low-income countries and virtually all of the lower-middle income countries. Tourism is a principal export (features in the top five) for eighty-three percent of the developing countries and the principal export for one-third of the developing countries. Eighty percent of the world's poor, those living on less than one US $ per day, live in twelve countries. In eleven of these countries, tourism is significant or growing, using significant to mean over two percent of GDP or five percent of exports.'[2]

Pro-poor tourism's thrust is in developing tourism strategies and plans that are aimed at eliminating and reducing poverty. This is in contrast to tourism being utilized as an agent of economic development. A United Nations Economic and Social Commission for Asia and the Pacific (UNESCAP) study on poverty alleviation through sustainable tourism development identified two models – one where there is a trickle-down of resources to the poor and the other where there is a direct thrust of all efforts towards poverty reduction (see Box B).[3]

The travel and tourism industry's focus has essentially been on sustainability with little emphasis on utilizing tourism for poverty alleviation. At its Millennium Summit in 2000, the United Nations identified poverty as one of the biggest global challenges and set forth the eradication of poverty by 2015 as one of the millennium development goals. The World Tourism Organization responded to this challenge

Box B

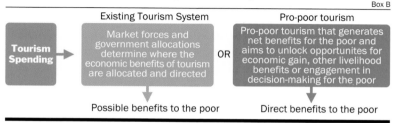

	Existing Tourism System	Pro-poor tourism
Tourism Spending →	Market forces and government allocations determine where the economic benefits of tourism are allocated and directed	**OR** Pro-poor tourism that generates net benefits for the poor and aims to unlock opportunites for economic gain, other livelihood benefits or engagement in decision-making for the poor
	↓ Possible benefits to the poor	↓ Direct benefits to the poor

Hodka – An Aesthetic Existence

A quintessentially Kachchhi village on the edge of the timeless Rann of Kachchh, Hodka village is the western gateway to the colourful diversity of India. Kachchh is a living museum in more ways than one, with geological landmarks that tell the story of the formation of prehistoric life. It also has sites of Indus Valley settlements – Dholavira, for instance, goes back to 3000 BC and is India's largest archaeological site.

There are two communities in the village. The main livelihood of the Meghmal community is art and crafts. The women are expert embroiderers, besides being adept atfashioning beautiful items out of mud and clay, and the men are traditional artisansin leather-work. The Maldhari community, on the other hand, comprises migrant cattle-breeders living off the distinctive 'banni' grasslands. (Spread across 3,846 sq km, this grassland is witness to a strange light phenomenon on any dark night. Locals call it Chhir Batti in their Kutchhi-Sindhi language, with Chhir meaning ghost and Batti meaning light.)

211

The Rann of Kachchh is a designated biosphere reserve, with trekking and camping tours. There are also overnight camel safaris and exclusive bird-watching excursions to Chaari Dhand in Rann of Kachchh.There is an amazing variety of flora and fauna featuring the wolf, hyena, black buck, wild ass and several aquatic and territorial birds, including the Great Indian Bustard. The implementation of the rural tourism project has led to the Hodka community owning and running the Shaam-e-Sarhand (Sunset on the Border) resort comprising the conical Rabari mud house or 'boonga', cappedwith a thatched roof, and ornate interiors. Visits to the Hodka village are organized regularly, with local Bhomyas (interpreters/guides) acquainting tourists with the local traditions, crafts and architecture. The Kutch Mahila Vikas Sangathan is the NGO partner implementing the project. The shopping experience comprises leather craft, traditional textiles and lacquer work.

and opportunity by launching the Sustainable Tourism Eliminating Poverty (ST–EP) initiative at the World Summit on Sustainable Development in Johannesburg in 2002.

The ST–EP initiative focuses on activities that specifically alleviate poverty, providing development and jobs to people living on less than a dollar a day. The initial financial contributioncame from the governmentof the Republic of Korea, leading to the establishment of the ST–EP Foundation in Seoul.Contributions from the government of Italy and the Netherlands Development Organization, SNV also made possible a series of pilot projects to identify and test various interventions to make the tourism sector work.

One of the main objectives of the ST–EP initiative is to work with governments, NGOs, bilateral and multilateral organizations, and business and local communities to identify and support a wide range of tourism projects for poverty alleviation. More than 150 ST–EP projects have been identified for future implementation around the world.ST–EP projects are primarily implemented in the least developed countries (LDCs) as well as in poor regions of other developing countries.[4]

212

In India, the realization that tourism can be a major employment generator emerged from the 2001 report of the Task Force on Employment Opportunities constituted by the Planning Commission. It targeted ten million employment opportunities per year over the next ten year period. It stated that tourism once re-oriented would be labour-intensive, a provider oflarge-scale employment and would be able to provide extensive forward and backward economic linkages that could build income and employment, especially for women, youthand other disadvantaged groups. It felt that in the absence of sufficient openings in the organized and agricultural sector, the rural non-farm sector was a critical area for generating productive employment, thus alleviating poverty and improving the living conditions and quality of life of the rural poor. It stated, 'the government's thrust on areas such as tourism would lead to a greater articulation of grassroots enterprises, skills, institutions and indigenous knowledge and would employ a sizeable proportion of the local populace.'[5] Since then several initiatives have been taken to exploit the multiplier impact of tourism for employment generation.

A study was conducted to assess the impact of tourism on folk artists and artisans in Kerala and Rajasthan.[6] Artists and artisans who

Endogenous Tourism

Endogenous or 'transformative' tourism has been used in the context of travel, not merely for pleasure but also for broadening the traveller's outlook. It seeks to transform attitudes and mindsets, effect a change in people's consciousness and instil in them a sense of appreciation and pride in the culture, heritage and environment of the region. It encompasses cultural tourism, craft tourism as also eco-tourism and all sustainable forms that value and celebrate the diversity and resources of the country. This concept of tourism aims to target the host community so that they take pride in their own identity and their environment and attract visitors who are interested and fascinated by their culture, artistic skills and lives.

The endogenous tourism project of the tourism ministry undertaken in collaboration with the UNDP (United Nations Development Programme) became an investment for alleviating poverty, achieving economic growth and enhancing the quality of life in rural areas. Its objectives are building capacity at the grassroots level by creating new entrepreneurs and tourism volunteers; experimenting with location-specific models of community-based tourism; and building strong people-public-private partnership.

There were several key challenges to be confronted in the implementation of this novel project. It was a unique learning experience with constant innovation as we went along. Some of the challenges that were faced during the implementation process are elucidated:

(i)   The primary task was to identify, in partnership with the state government, villages that could showcase rural life, art, culture and heritage that were in close geographical proximity to existing circuits and destinations and could provide an enriching tourism experience;

(ii) The project was to be coordinated through a convergence committee headed by the district collector so that resources from various government schemes could be brought together. The software component of advocacy, training, capacity-building, skill development, promotion and marketing was undertaken at the field level through an NGO with a proven track record;

(iii) The hardware infrastructure requirement of the tourism village emerged from software elements based on interaction and requirements of the local community;

(iv) The basic task was to create unique rural experiences for the visitor through community participation, together with locally styled accommodation. This was to become the process for strengthening rural livelihood and employment via tourism. The visitors were to be given the experience of rural life with clean living room, toilets, local culture and cuisine;

(v) To ensure that hardware components (construction work) were not hijacked by PWD agencies, the district-level implementation committee chaired by the district collector was given the freedom to adopt the rates of local District Rural Developement Agency (DRDA), rural engineering, panchayats and zila parishads based on certification of reasonableness;

(vi) To ensure flexibility and innovation while implementing the projects, the district-level committees were given the freedom to change items based on new perceptions emerging during community consultation, within the overall work plan already sanctioned for hardware and software components;

(vii) To facilitate and ensure adherence to local building styles, local materials and local skill, a regional panel of architects was created. District committees were asked to seek assistance of these architects so that construction was based on local architectural idioms and materials;

(viii) All selected villages were asked to build into their hardware plans internet capability, clean governance, sanitation, toilet, solid waste management, local home stays or community-operated lodges and local craft outlets;

(ix) A system of operation and maintenance based on a user's fee was to be inbuilt in the project;

(x) Villages were asked to target domestic and international tourists with an appropriate pricing strategy to attract sensitive visitors. The linkage with the travel trade was established to promote and market the rural experience being created. An experiential content-rich website, www.exploreruralindia.org, was created;

(xi) The concept of gurukul was revived to encourage students to come and stay with rural host communities to learn the resources of Indian culture, art and craft.

An evaluation study[7] of the rural tourism project has concluded that it has led to:

• Gainful employment of local youths as tour guides;
• Revival of the folk arts and providing livelihood to the practitioners of the arts;
• Enhanced income and stopping of migration of artisans like pot-makers, weavers, wood-carvers.

Solid waste management (SWM) training has improved the environment and facilitated the arrival of tourists. After training, the villagers have initiated waste management and started collection, segregation and dumping of the waste in designated areas.

The quality of the living conditions of the local community and their sanitation and hygiene practices have also improved. The project has led to the creation of toilet facilities for the local community and enhancement in awareness on the utilization of the created infrastructure.[7]

made their livelihood from small businesses in and around selected heritage sites – fifteen in Kerala and twenty in Rajasthan – were selected for the study. It was found that ninety-six percent of the total income of artisan households in Kerala and ninety percent in Rajasthan came from tourism-related income. These people now have better housing, and access to safe and clean drinking water, electricity and toilet facilities, within their home premises. They are also able to afford household assets like consumer durables, which otherwise would have been a faraway dream for them.

The per capita income of folk artists during peak tourism season is easily about four times that of the lean season – even though there is a high level of variation between both the states in terms of average employment and productivity during peak seasons.

Education too has become an important prerogative among artisans and folk artists in both states, with the incidence of hundred percent formal education for both male and female children. Artisans in Kerala do not encourage child labour, but in Rajasthan, children still work alongside their parents in the lower income groups. Given the fact that these children do get some formal education, their contribution to the family business can be considered as learning the trade.

In February 2009, Hugh and Colleen Gantzer travelled to several rural villages where the endogenous tourism project is being implemented. On their return, I interacted with them to learn from their experience. They felt that it was necessary to differentiate between rural tourism and rural homestays. In rural homestays tourists share the lifestyle of the families they stay with. In contrast, in rural tourism the standards of accommodation must be able to cater to tourists in terms of hygiene, security, safety and basic levels of comforts. According to them, 'the choice of site of rural tourism projects are of prime importance. They should not be more than two hours of driving distance from an airport-or-railhead town unless they are on a tourist circuit....While conforming to these criteria, the ambience of the rural tourism resort must assert the indigenous architectural idioms of the area in which it stands, or in the absence of such identifiable features, use vernacular, recyclable materials such as wood in preference to non-reusable ones such as cement or concrete.'

Mahatma Gandhi once said that India lives in her villages. The Indian rural tourism community is steeped in folklore, indigenous art, craft and natural heritage. The geographical spread and cultural

Khonoma – Green Village Communitization in Nagaland

Khonoma is a small village 20 kilometres southwest of Kohima, the capital of Nagaland. It is home to the Angami tribesmen who toil in their fields, cultivating paddy. The village gets its name from the plant Khnumo (*Glouthera fragrantisma*), which grows here, but its fame is largely due to its reputation as a village of warriors.

In Khonoma, the government has worked in partnership with the community to create a valuable rural experience. The government facilitated investment in infrastructure while the community took the responsibility for its maintenance, upkeep and management. The project was sanctioned in March 2004 by the ministry of tourism with an outlay of Rs 300 lakhs. This has led to an improvement of walkways in the village and construction of accommodation facilities.

216

The capacity-building of the community was the key factor as it encouraged the growth of local entrepreneurship, ownership by the community and provision of standard services. As a community initiative, the village banned hunting and fishing and took responsibility for protecting natural resources and forests.

The infrastructure component of the project has included public sanitation, solar lighting, a base camp for eco-tourism, and trekking and tent equipment. The entire project is managed by the village tourism management board, which has taken the management responsibility for tourist accommodation, catering and hospitality, cultural entertainment and souvenir outlets – together with Equitable Tourism Option, an NGO that acted as the catalyst. Local village members have been trained as tourist guides. A similar project has been implemented in the Touphema tourist village of Nagaland. In fact, the success of these projects has led to Nagaland Tourism focusing on community-participation as the key strategy for tourism development in the state.

diversity of India provide multiple areas of interest for the all-season visitor. Local communities have the potential to participate in sustainable strategies encompassing the country's bio-geographic zones. This paradigm shift heralds a fresh approach, based on India's rural assets.

A recent *Washington Post* article entitled 'In Rural India, it (Finally) Took a Village'[8] states, 'I'd come to Rajasthan for a two-week journey through rural India – a world that Gandhi called the heart and soul of the country, and where most of India still lives.... A woman boiled milk for chai, another placed sugar wafers on the cot, then rice and puri, a wheat flatbread. A grey-bearded man, a Rajput farmer with ruby-studded earrings, a vermilion smudge between his brow and the turban of red, green and purple, stood looking down. He handed me his children's wedding invitations.... Here in India's heartland, they really do treat guests like gods.'

People from across the world were held in thrall recently by the film *Slumdog Millionaire,* set in Mumbai's slums. Its message of hope and joyous spirit emerges from the portrayal of what *New York Times* terms as a land of self-makers where a scruffy son of the slums can, solely of his own effort, foist himself up, flout his origin, break with fate. It calls the film a tribute to the irrepressible self.

Public policy prescription battling economic downturn through stimulus packages can derive motivation from the essence of the film. Given the opportunity, people have an immense capacity to remake their lives. Rural tourism in India has the potential to stimulate both the economy and employment.

'The convergence of trends within the domains of demography, economy and culture...in other words, people, place and desires ...is creating the biggest boom in travel, tourism, and lifestyle trends in over a hundred years.'

Ho Kwon Ping, Executive Chairman, Banyan Tree Group

219

Through the looking glass: future of tourism

In the early 1980s, a schoolmate of mine from a fairly privileged background wanted to give his wife a memorable holiday on her birthday. The best he could plan was a trip to Ootacamond (Ooty), a celebrated hill station in south India. Since then, my friend has gone on to become a leading lawyer in the Delhi high court. He now takes multiple short breaks – up to four holidays a year. His selection of the destination, and the nature and duration of these holidays is influenced by his pursuit of authenticity and exotic experiences.

He represents one of the 9.5 million Indians undertaking close to 20 million outbound trips a year from India. In recent times, outbound tourism has thrived and flourished. This trend has grown on account of several factors that are affecting the very nature of global tourism.

Rise of BRICs as an Economic Power

The rise in status of BRIC (Brazil, Russia, India and China) countries as economic powers will have a radical impact on tourism.

Towards the end of 2001, Goldman Sachs economist Jim O' Neill, in his research paper entitled 'Building Better Global Economic Brics', argued that the four economies of Brazil, Russia, India and China, which he termed BRICs, would contribute almost ten percent of the world's gross domestic product by the end of the decade. These countries encompass over twenty-five percent of the world's land coverage, forty percent of the world's population and hold a combined GDP of 15.435 trillion dollars. On every scale, they would be the largest entity on the world's stage. In an updated 2007 report, Goldman Sachs asserted that 'India's influence on the world economy will be bigger and quicker.... India has ten of the thirty fastest growing urban areas in the world and a massive 700 million people will move to cities by 2050. This will have significant implications on demand for urban infrastructure, real estate and services.'

In the revised 2007 figure, Goldman Sachs has predicted that 'from 2007 to 2020, India's GDP per capita in US$ terms will quadruple', and that the Indian economy will surpass the US in US$ by 2043. It states that the four BRIC nations as a group will overtake the G7 in 2032.

The International Monetary Fund has recently calculated that the BRICs and the emerging markets they are driving account for almost thirty percent of the global economy and forty-seven percent of the entire global growth. India and the emerging markets are catering to nearly twenty-six percent of the global information technology services market and their market share is actually growing at a much faster annual rate than information technology services in developed markets. A Professional Wealth Management Study has highlighted that BRIC countries have pushed the share of global exports from emerging markets from a mere twenty percent in 1970 to almost forty-two percent in 2006 and fifty percent of consumers spending in purchasing power parity terms will come from emerging economies by 2010. Almost seventy-five percent of the world's growth will come from Asia, with almost forty-five percent from China and India. In the next ten years almost 1 billion new consumers will enter the market. Most economists have argued that the BRIC countries will be instrumental in driving the global economy and remain a key factor in future global economic growth.

What will be the impact of sustained economic growth in BRIC countries on travel and tourism? Though the BRIC countries account for half of the world's population, only five percent of their population has travelled abroad as compared to almost fifty percent in developed countries. China and India together have a population double the size of the US, Japan and Western Europe. With their basic needs getting fulfilled, people in these countries have started travelling – not merely to domestic locations but abroad – discovering new destinations, exploring new tourism products, indulging in shopping and trying out unexplored cuisines. This trend was witnessed in America in the 1950s, Japan in the 1970s and Korea in the 1990s – and is becoming highly visible in China and India in the present millennium. No wonder the World Travel and Tourism Council has estimated that India, with an annualized real growth of 9.4 percent, along with China at 8.9 percent, are countries expected to increase their travel and tourism demand most rapidly between 2008 and 2018.[1] Indians are already being considered the highest spenders in several destinations in the Asia-Pacific Region. The Singapore Tourism Board reported that spending by Indians stood at around SG$ 1,500 (US$ 900) per person, per trip in 2005, while in Hong Kong, the figure was HK$ 4,967 (US$ 640)

On a Relative Scale

Countries expected to increase their Travel & Tourism demand most rapidly between 2008 – 2018

T&T demand, 2008-18   (% annualized real growth)

#	Country	%
1	India	9.4
2	China	8.9
3	Libya	8.1
4	Vietnam	8.1
5	Montenegro	7.4
6	Romania	7.1
7	Macau	7.1
8	Namibia	6.9
9	Croatia	6.9
10	Czech Republic	6.8

Source: World Travel & Tourism Council (WTTC) Progress & Priorities 2008/09

in the same year.[2] A recent report by Visit Britain highlights the fact that Indian tourists outspend Americans in Britain.[3] Whereas the average American tourist spent £710 in 2007, the Indian traveller spent £793. In contrast to Indians, there had been a 7.9 percent reduction in the number of American tourists between 2006 and 2007. These figures show that China and India will be the future tourism tigers and Asian-led growth will be the key feature of the travel and tourism industry in the coming years.

The implosion of the global economic and financial systems also has severe implications. The recession in America has been a consequence of Americans consuming more than they produce and making up the difference by borrowing through little understood financial instruments. The current global financial crisis signals a historic shift in world politics and economics – a moment that both marks and accelerates the decline of American and European power.

Impact of Demographic Changes

The second key trend is the rapidly changing demographics of the world. The ageing of the population in European countries is the most salient social, economic and demographic phenomenon. By 2050, the number of people over sixty years of age in Europe will reach forty percent of the total population or sixty percent of the working age population. This ageing of population will lead to reduced incomes, consumption and wealth. Several studies have predicted that European countries would be characterized by a dwindling population in the cities, the solution for which would lie in migrant workers. This in turn will lead to a substantial increase in the VFR (visiting friends and relatives) segment of tourism. The demographics are altering as those born between 1946 and 1964 (baby boomers), who form the largest population bulge in history, have just begun retiring. Post World War II, the US experienced an explosion of births (hence the term 'baby boom') that continued for the next eighteen years, after which the birth rate began to drop. In 1964, 'baby boomers' representing forty percent, or more than one-third, of the American population, were under nineteen years of age. Since they comprised a sizeable portion of the consuming public, their spending habits and lifestyles have always had a powerful influence on the economy. Their economic impact can be assessed from the fact that in 2004 in UK 'baby boomers' held eighty percent of UK's wealth and bought eighty percent of all top-of-the-range cars and fifty percent of skincare products.[4]

In USA alone, 77 million baby boomers have begun to retire from 2006 onwards – 8000 Americans are retiring at the age of sixty every day while 8500 Japanese are reaching this age every day. These people will represent 'a dynamic market of active, adventurous, affluent consumers, for whom travel will be an integral part of a fulfilling retirement'[5] and the retiring people in the US and Europe will set the next new trend in travel and tourism.

In contrast, India will pass through 'the demographic window' during the next fifty years. This will be a period when the proportion of children and youth under fifteen years will fall below thirty percent of the population and the proportion of people over sixty-five will be below fifteen percent. For the next thirty to forty years, the proportion of working age people in society will be dominant and the population will have light dependency burdens. If effectively managed, India will have the potential for rapid economic growth since the country is expected to have the largest pool of manpower in 2020. A study entitled 'India's New Opportunity – 2020' has concluded that developed countries will face a net workforce shortfall of 32-39 million by 2020.[6] India can target this shortage by providing remote services to these countries and also by importing customers and servicing their needs in India. By enhancing its capabilities in several areas, India would be in a strong position to capitalize on these opportunities.

The Rise of the Urban Middle Classes

The third key trend will be the rise of urban middle classes in India and China. It is estimated that by 2050, over fifty-five percent of the Indian population would be living in urban cities. In China, only thirty percent of the population is expected to be living in the countryside as against sixty percent at present. This will fuel consumerism. A recent report has alluded to India overtaking the US to become the world's second largest mobile phone market in terms of subscribers after China. By the end of October 2008, the number of mobile phone subscribers in India stood at 325 million as compared to 280 million in the US.[7] China leads the pack with 540 million connections. Another aspect is credit card usage, which in India is growing at the phenomenal pace of thirty-seven percent annually, while personal consumption in India accounts for sixty-seven percent of GDP as compared to forty-two percent for China. All these are signs of a growing, expanding middle class. Similar trends are being witnessed in the other BRIC countries where GDP figures are likely to rise significantly by 2020. Though GDP per capita is not an adequate measure of the capacity to consume, it is forecast that GDP per capita will rise to US$ 12,527 in Russia, US$ 6,302 in Brazil, US$ 4,965 in China and US$ 1,622 in India. While their GDP per capita will be much lower than in the US and UK, the purchasing power will rise significantly. There will be considerable disposable incomes in the hands of the middle classes and their desire to travel and discover new destinations will start getting fulfilled. It has been argued that the size of the 'bottom of the pyramid' market in India is 650 million people, who collectively account for about thirty percent of the national income, a little over thirty-three percent consumption expenditure and some twenty percent of India's savings. The total income of the bottom of the pyramid consumer in India is 1.4 times that of Malaysia, 1.6 times that of Singapore, equal to that of South Africa and ninety percent that of Hongkong.[8] In most BRIC countries, the increase in consumer income is being accompanied by a change in business models, with a substantial drop in price thresholds. This is leading to an explosive growth in products and services, a classic example of which is the sale of televisions and cell phones to all segments of society.

The immense growth in outbound tourism from India – 10.02 million in 2008 – has been a consequence of innovative and aggressive products launched by outbound tour operators such as Kuoni, Thomas Cook, Cox & Kings and Le Passage. They have vigorously promoted and marketed their packages in partnership with tourism boards, airlines and even financial services agencies, enabling consumers to experience a wide range of products. As Arjun Sharma, chief executive of Le Passage, says, 'The potential of the Indian outbound travel market is vast. The capacity to travel has spread to smaller towns and rural areas. This has prompted UNWTO to brand India as an emerging tourism destination of the future.'

The vast numbers of travellers from China and India are the key features of today's travel and tourism world. To meet their growing demands and aspirations, particularly in aspects relating to cuisine and hospitality, trained workers and managers from these countries are in huge demand in Europe. India therefore needs to tap this opportunity and establish hospitality and catering institutes which function as centres of excellence. These in due course would eclipse the hospitality institutes of Switzerland, whose curriculum was and remains primarily designed to produce managers catering to European, not Asian, travellers.

The Shift Towards Experiential Tourism

Fourthly, there will be a huge shift towards experiential and cultural tourism.

When the hotel chain CGH Earth Experience started Kalari Kovilakam, its new resort in Palghat district of Kerala, they called it the 'Palace for Ayurveda'. Their fortnightly, twenty-one day and month-long ayurvedic packages follow a strictly governed vegetarian diet regimen and a minutely planned daily timetable. No meat, alcohol or even leather footwear are allowed at Kalari. Can one define Kalari as a spa? A palace hotel? An ayurvedic hospital? An ashram? Kalari's experience is a little of all of these. The intent and purpose of Kalari Kovilakam is to give one a chance to start one's life all over again. Its contention is that ayurveda, correctly followed, promises not only a new body and mind, but a deep connection with the spirit. To ancient Indians, this was a cosmic connection, a chance to be reborn in life itself. This authentic experience attracts an international clientele and operates to an almost hundred percent occupancy with a high waiting list.

The rapid rise of post-material consumerism, motivated by the pursuit of individualism, is responsible for a significant trend in the travel and tourism industry – the desire for authentic experiences. This desire has been a response to globalization and the spread of a corporate mono-culture driven by ubiquitous global brands cutting across geographical boundaries. The search for real and authentic experiences through travel has been a way of escaping from the stress and sometimes harsh reality of modern life. The popularity of multiple short breaks is rising, with tourists wanting to get away from their routine existence for cultural and natural holidays.

Zubin Karkaria, the young chief executive officer and managing director of Kuoni India, has a spiritual side; he is a Parsi priest. Knowing the importance of God in life has enabled him to face challenging times with calmness. He has always focused on new areas of growth and opportunity.

Karkaria not only tapped the market for Indians wanting to travel abroad, but also aimed at the vast numbers of Indians staying abroad who wanted to travel to India. His constant thirst for innovation led him to create 'Holiday Now, Pay Later' scheme with a loan for travellers through a financial institution. He has always been on the lookout for consumer trends and new patterns of behaviour. As he says, 'Today people prefer shorter holidays as opposed to longer ones. The accent is on having fun and spending quality time with the family as opposed to shopping. People simply do not have the time so they would rather spend whatever time they have with their close ones.'

In India, a number of young entrepreneurs have successfully tapped this market. Samit Sawhney, a graduate of Indian Institute of Management, Ahmedabad, quit his job with Ernst & Young to establish and operate Barefort Resort in Havelock Island of the Andamans. The name itself was chosen to signify an environment-friendly approach in a beach rated by *Time* magazine as the finest in the world. Aman Nath and Francis Wacziarg operate the Neemrana 'Non-hotels' and provide a cultural experience thorugh the heritage properties they have restored. Apart from the Neemrana Fort Resort, they have the Bungalow on the Beach in Tranquebar in Tamil Nadu, Glasshouse on the Ganges in Rishikesh and the Rambagh Bungalows in Uttranchal. Sanjay Basu of Far Horizon Tours launched his career by organizing luxury tented accommodation during festivals in Rajasthan and Kerala. He then went on to establish *Vaikuntham*, the largest houseboat in the backwaters of Kerala, especially catering to the Spanish inbound tourists. Sanjay's next initiative in the sphere of experiential tourism was the Dera Sand Dune Resort in Rajasthan. This is the only resort built atop a sand dune with private pool villas. His next venture is the launch of *Mt. Mahababu*, an eco-friendly cruise liner operating on the Brahmaputra river in

Assam. Ibex Expeditions, led by mountaineer and explorer Mandip Singh Soin and his enterprising wife, Anita, has the care of environment at the very heart of its business philosophy. It promotes nature-based tourism and allows an open audit system of its environmental safeguards by its clients. Ibex supports NGOs through efforts of tree plantation, books and medicines to hill village schools and purchase of artifacts produced by tribal communities. The National Geographic Adventure magazine recently selected it as one of the best adventure travel companies on earth.

Ranjit Barathakur is an entrepreneur focusing on creating unique experiences in the northeast. He feels that naturenomics will become the dominant economic paradigm in the coming years. He is convinced that tourism is the vehicle on which the northeast will evolve and develop in a sustained way. He feels that by unlocking the three tourism pillars of the northeast, namely, nature, culture and religion, he can give the region a sustainable competitiveness. In my long and fascinating conversation with him, he stated that the discerning travellers are looking to break out of traditional holiday-making. Through a differentiated strategy based on the northeast's rich bio-diversity, its

spectacularly diverse cultural heritage and the confluence of the three religions (Hinduism, Buddhism and Christianity), tourism can be its engine of growth. Ranjit, with his dedicated team, is implementing a range of projects to fulfill his worldview. He already runs and operates the Wild Grass in Kaziranga and the Wild Mahseer in the Balipara region of Assam.

I have mentioned the trend of young entrepreneurs driven by dynamism breaking away from the five-star deluxe world of tourism. They are influenced by new market opportunities, sensitivity, and innovativeness, which differentiates them from tourism professionals in the past. Jose Dominic of CGH Earth Experience never tires of quoting the statistical research carried out by an eminent tourism researcher, Peter Aderhold. Based on holiday traveller characteristics, he grouped his sample surveyed in 1996 into two 'baskets', one called the 'Sun–Sand–Surf' (SSS) basket and the other the 'Alert Independent Traveller' (AIT) basket. While the SSS was the mass market, the AIT was the newly emerging niche. His research provided clear evidence that the up-market clientele was increasingly moving towards becoming 'Alert Independent Travellers' wanting to learn about the destination, contribute towards it and give more to the destination than they received from it during their holiday. In this context, the retiring 'baby boomers' in the US and Europe will comprise the affluent older consumers in this category. They will set a new trend of short breaks – multiple short holidays in a year – seeking authenticity of experience. This will fuel an immense demand for cultural tourism as their desire will be to experience different cultures, meet different communities and explore historical sites. This trend will provide an impetus for countries like India with a rich component of history and culture. Young entrepreneurs providing this experience will be the beneficiaries as holiday experiences get reshaped.

Raymond Bickson, the committed and passionate chief executive of Taj hotels, and I participated in the Kellog Business School India Summit in 2008.Speaking on the global trends, Bickson said, 'Thinking local and acting global is not just about environment today – it is a way of life and a mode of being.' Breaking new ground, Taj, in collaboration with Conservation Corporation Africa (CC, Africa), provides interpretive wildlife experiences. Its first lodges, Mahua Kothi in Bandhavgarh and Baghavan in Pench, offer an alternative to Africa in wildness experience. The safari comprises game viewing, jungle walks and meditative solitude. The lodges with six to twelve suites are designed with a light footprint.

The Impact of Climate Change

Fifthly, climate changes will play a major role in tourism demand, and its development and management. Tourists normally take their travel decisions based on the climate, the natural environment and their personal safety. All these factors will be reshaped on account of global climatic changes. The Intergovernmental Panel on Climate Change (IPCC) forecast for climate change from 1999 to 2100 states that:

- Average global temperatures will rise by between 1.4 and 5.8° C, a rate unprecedented in the past 10,000 years.
- Sea levels will rise by between 9 and 88 centimetres by 2100, with a central forecast of 48 centimetres, implying a rate of increase that will be between two and four times greater than that during the twentieth century.
- There will be substantial regional variations around these temperatures.[9]

There is a likelihood of geographic and seasonal redistribution of tourist demand based on the altered climatic conditions. Anticipated impacts envisage a slow but definite shift in preferred destinations to higher altitudes and to higher elevations in mountainous areas. Tourists from temperate nations, such as northern Europe, are likely to holiday in their home country, taking advantage of the new climatic conditions. Tourism seasons will be altered, with a majority of tourists travelling during shoulder or winter seasons, as the climate will be far more pleasant. The shift in travel patterns will have major implications, with increased tourism spending in temperate nations and proportionately less spending in warmer nations now frequented by tourists from temperate nations. Several scenarios have been forecasted – the low-lying countries like the Maldives and Caribbean Islands could be overrun by rising sea levels, key sunny destinations like Greece and Turkey may become unbearably hot, while ski destinations may suffer from lack of snow. Almost one-sixth of all tourists trips worldwide are by holiday-makers from northern Europe to the Mediterranean to enjoy the sun, sand and sea. This could witness a huge decline if summer temperatures become too hot or coastlines are eroded by the rising sea. In fact, the present trend could be reversed, with southern Europeans travelling to north European destinations to escape the heat.

What is the likely impact of climate change on India? An analysis by the Indian Space Research Organization (ISRO) has shown that Indian seas are rising at the rate of 2.5 millimetres per year as against an earlier trend of 1 mm. If this trend continues, the sea level would rise between 15 to 38 centimetres by the middle of the century and 46 to 59 centimetres by the end of this century.[10] The research by the Indian Institute of Technology (IIT, Delhi) on ISRO data confirms the findings of the Intergovernmental Panel on Climate Change, which has stated that half of Mumbai and several coastal cities of India might be submerged when the sea level rises by 50 centimetres. The intensity of cyclones hitting India, especially the east coast, will increase substantially, with Andhra Pradesh, Orissa and West Bengal becoming more vulnerable than the west coast. Various studies have shown that the surface air temperatures in India are going up at the rate of 0.4°C every hundred years, particularly in the post-monsoon and winter seasons. It has been forecast that mean winter temperatures will increase by as much as 3.2°C in the 2050s and 4.5°C by the 2080s due to greenhouse gases. Summer temperatures will increase by 2.2°C in the 2050s and 3.2°C in the 2080s.

Recent research conducted by scientists at Pune's India Institute of Tropical Meteorology, a key government institution studying climate change in India, has concluded that after 2050, temperatures would rise by three to four degrees over current levels and rainfall would become both heavier and less regular.[11]

Developing countries, including India, China and Brazil, have strongly argued that the developed world, including the US, should reduce its greenhouse gas emissions by thirty percent from their 1990 levels before 2020 and by eighty percent before 2050. They point out that the developed world is largely responsible for greenhouse gas emissions across the earth's atmosphere. The carbon footprints left by the US are almost four times that of China and fifteen times that of India. The polluter must pay and the US should take the responsibility of cleaning the earth's atmosphere. The counter agreement from the US is that greenhouse gas emissions of emerging economies are spiralling and China is likely to overtake the US as the world's largest greenhouse gas emitter, with India being the fourth largest gas emitter. Their contention is that the developing world, notably China and India, should also cut their greenhouse gas emissions by twenty percent from the 1990 levels.

The trend of global warming for the last fifty years is twice that of the last hundred years. Eleven of the twelve warmest years since 1850 have occurred between 1995 and 2006, which means that irrespective of arguments on either side, there is a need to adopt sensible energy conservation measures.

On account of these factors, our lifestyle, health and social well-being will all be affected by climate change – and tourism will be no exception. Climate change will be an increasingly pivotal issue impacting tourism development and management.

Technological Changes as the Key Influence on Tourism

The sixth driver of change in travel and tourism will be technology. The internet has already had a phenomenal impact on the industry. In fact, the usage of the internet for researching and booking holidays has increased by over 900 percent since 1997. Hand-held devices and the use of digital technology will enable travellers to book and travel without intermediaries. The surge of information will truly empower the future traveller. The use of technology has already brought down costs and led to the successful emergence of low-cost carriers.

The contribution of tourism to human-induced climate change will come under severe challenge. Tourism at present represents around five percent of the global emissions. Transport generates the largest proportion of CO_2 emissions (seventy-five percent) from global tourism with almost forty percent of this being caused by air transport. Analysis has revealed that a small share of tourism trips are found to cause the main share of emissions. Thus, seventeen percent of the aviation-based trips cause forty percent of all emissions. Long-haul air travel, representing only 2.7 percent of all tourist trips, contributes to seventeen percent of global tourism-related CO_2 emissions.[12] The travel industry will, in the coming years, be investing heavily in carbon-free technology to ensure that it does not pollute the atmosphere. Its target will be to achieve carbon neutral growth, a challenging but feasible task.

Technology will be the driving force for the emergence of newer and cheaper aircraft. Airbus has already launched its Airbus AB 380, a super plane known as the 'flying fortress', with a capacity for 555 passengers. Airbus's assumption is that air travel in the twenty-first century will be between urban hubs – New York, Paris, London, Shanghai, Tokyo. With further technological innovation, it will be possible to develop larger aircraft with a capacity for 800 seats. In contrast, Boeing has a different worldview. It is developing the 7E7 Dreamliner, a medium-sized jet with high-speed travel for middle-range holiday-makers to specialized locations. Though badly delayed, the Dreamliner is an ambitious project with better fuel efficiency, bigger windows and larger overhead cabins. Then there is Virgin Galactic, which has utilized technology to conduct the first civilian flights to space. The Virgin Space Project has progressed at a dramatic speed and over 200 people have paid for the sub-space experience in response to Virgin's aggressive promotion of the experience by selling marriages as well as honeymoons in space. One view is that this technology of sending people beyond the upper atmosphere would, in the coming years, be used to conduct speedier long-distance travel between cities on different sides of the earth. The use of newer technology will make travel faster and lower passenger fuel costs.

Tourism is in the midst of unprecedented change and growth. In the coming decades, there will be developments that are difficult to even imagine today. There will be immense challenges posed on the travel world, on its organization and on its creativity in anticipating and meeting tourist expectations – challenges that we need to overcome with vision, flexibility and creativity.

As far as putting India into the consciousness of the world is concerned, I think 'Incredible India' has arrived. I will give you a very small example. Danish prime minister Anders Fogh Rasmussen on his recent visit to India was hosted by our prime minister at a banquet and I happened to be there. When he began his speech, he addressed Manmohan Singhji, saying 'Excellency, till now I had only heard about "Incredible India". But after coming, here I have seen how India is really incredible.' Wherever you go people say 'Ah! Incredible India.'

Ambika Soni, minister of tourism and culture, quoted in *India Today*, May, 2008

Appendix

Brand India – where next?

Excerpts from a panel discussion held during Incredible India @ 60 at the Harvard Club, New York City, on 26 September 2007, sponsored by the Confederation of Indian Industry, The NewsMarket and Mirabilis Advisory.

Andrew Heyward: Good morning, and on behalf of the Confederation of Indian Industry and its partners in this event, The NewsMarket and Mirabilis Advisory, I want to welcome you all to this discussion. Our subject is the economic transformation and future of India, and the building of what we are calling 'Brand India'. It's a great pleasure to be here in this beautiful room at the Harvard Club on this wonderful occasion celebrating India's sixtieth year of independence.

I'm Andrew Heyward, a board member of The NewsMarket as well as a former President of CBS News, and I'm going to serve as moderator. We have a terrific panel of speakers. And after I introduce each of them, we will talk about the ground rules and get the discussion going.

At the far left end of the table from me is Vir Sanghvi, who is one of India's most prominent journalists. Mr Sanghvi is the Advisory Editorial Director of HT Media Ltd, a company he joined as an editor of the Hindustan Times in 1999. He is also a well-known and award-winning television anchor – and, having run CBS News for ten years, I've seen a few of those in my day.

Next to Vir is Arun Sarin, who is the Chief Executive Officer of Vodafone, which calls itself 'the world's leading mobile telecommunications company' – and which, at least as measured by sales, is the world's largest. With 250 million customers, a total revenue of over $ 60 billion, and a market cap of some $173 billion, the company is a major presence in Europe, the US, the Middle East, Africa, and Asia Pacific. In recent years, Vodafone has made big investments in China and India, the largest and latest of which is its $11 billion acquisition of the Indian mobile operator Hutch Essar in May 2007. That is far and away the largest direct foreign investment in India to date – and I imagine Arun will be telling us a bit about this. He has served on the boards of such companies as Gap, Charles Schwab, and Cisco.

Next to Arun is Amitabh Kant, who is Joint Secretary of the Indian Ministry of Tourism, where he oversees policy planning and international marketing and promotion. In this role, Amitabh is responsible for marketing India to people his promotional literature refers to as 'discerning' travellers. Amitabh is the main architect of the campaign called 'Incredible India@60', which is why we're all here today. And he's also the creator of the modestly titled 'God's Own Country' campaign for his home state of Kerala in southern India – a campaign that has helped turn Kerala into the fastest-growing tourist destination in the country.

Next to Amitabh is Nandan Nilekani, who is the Co-chairman of Infosys Technologies, one of the great success stories of Indian business. One of the co-founders of Infosys in 1981, Nandan has since served as its President and Chief Operating Officer and, from 2002 until this past June, as its CEO. He has also played important roles in several government initiatives, having served as Chairman of India's IT Task Force for power and as a member of the Reserve Bank of India's Advisory Group on corporate governance. Nandan has received many awards from civic and corporate organizations, including recognition this past year by *Forbes* magazine as its 'Businessman of the Year'.

Last, and seated next to me, is Sir Martin Sorrell, who is CEO of the WPP Group, one of the world's leading communications services and advertising companies. Producing annual revenues of $12 billion, WPP has over 100 operating companies that employ 102,000 people in 106 countries. After joining WPP in 1985 as a director and becoming the chief executive in 1986, Sir Martin spent the next three years acquiring eighteen advertising-related companies, including J. Walter Thompson in 1987 and Ogilvy & Mather in 1989. He may well be the best-known advertising executive in the world – at least, that's what he has instructed me to tell you.

Now that you have our cast of characters, a word on the ground rules. We're going to model this discussion on the new faster form of cricket that India's recently had some success with – and my congratulations, by the way, on India's victory in the Twenty20. I'm going to ask each of the panelists to start with just three minutes of opening remarks. And after we've made the rounds, I'm hoping that a spontaneous discussion of the opportunities and challenges facing India after sixty years of independence will emerge from the observations of these five really interesting people.

And I thought we would start with Mr Kant in his role as creator of the 'Incredible India@60' campaign. What does Brand India mean to you?

The Challenge of Branding India

Amitabh Kant: Thanks, Andrew. Well, let me start off by saying that this thing that we are calling 'Brand India' – the global set of perceptions and associations that now surround the country – is multi-layered in many ways. It's very difficult to make generalizations about India because it's such a vast and diverse country. There are twenty-seven states where the people look different, the religions are different, and the languages are different. It's also a constantly evolving brand. Many years ago when I was in school, our brand had to do primarily with food exports. Then it became software. And now we have a growing reputation in mobile telecom.

So I think it's misleading to say there's a single Brand India. It's in many ways an aggregate, a composite, of several brands. There's Brand Bangalore, there's Brand Chennai, there's God's Own Country of Kerala, and so on. And I think the first glimpse of India should be one that gives you a sense of its diversity and, above all, its vibrancy.

The process of branding is essentially one of differentiation, of distinguishing your products or services from those of the rest of the world. Many years back, when I was working in Kerala, our only attraction for tourists was our beaches. And we used to get charter flights from London, bringing mainly people who were paying about £15 a night for a room. But we stopped marketing just our beaches and concentrated on the other features that really set Kerala apart – and that was the backwaters and hillside plantations as well as our forts and temples and wildlife. It was these other attractions, all located within a few hours of our beaches, that really took Kerala forward.

Our branding strategy came out of the realization that it was not mass tourism that was going to drive Kerala's economy, but rather the search for more discriminating tourists willing to pay more for a different kind of experience. We decided to move up the value chain. And as Andrew was kind enough to tell you, that campaign has been a great success.

But now I'm at the Indian Ministry of Tourism. And India, as suggested, is a far more complex game. It's a multi-product destination, if you will. It's much easier to brand a single-product destination like the Maldives, or a wildlife destination like South Africa. But how do you brand a country like India, with its twenty-seven different states, and its amazing variety of people and languages and customs and architecture.

To come up with a plan, you have to start by doing research on market segmentation and positioning to answer questions like: Which markets do you want to defend? Which markets do you want to invest in? Which media should you use to accomplish these goals? Research designed to answer these questions is critical to developing a strategy of differentiation.

It's also important to realize that any branding with reference to India as an entire country can serve only as a kind of model branding campaign. It's a broad template, if you will. And each of our twenty-seven states can then use this template when designing their own 'sub-brand' campaigns. The potential for such campaigns was first realized with Kerala many years ago. But much the same has been done in states such as Rajasthan. Each of these cases has shown the benefits of aggressive international marketing and establishing a distinctive brand.

Now, on the subject of our countrywide campaign called 'Incredible India', I think there are a few important lessons. One is the importance of working with the brightest people in the creative field, which we think we are doing. A second lesson is the need for continuous innovation. Keep the brand campaign alive; keep it fresh all the time. We've spun out a new campaign every year. Perhaps even more important, we've tried to do a so-called '360-degree' campaign that has elements of both print and the internet. In the future, the internet is going to be driving the brand campaigns in many ways.

But when we're talking about the global branding of India, it's very important to keep looking back to see that the brand that we're building matches the reality back home. And that's why we have launched a complementary branding campaign in our domestic market. The purpose of this campaign is to ensure that all the stakeholders in the Indian economy – the taxi drivers, for example, and the customs and immigration officers – share our vision of a thriving tourist industry. They all must recognize that tourism is going to be a key driver of India's economic growth, and a major source of new jobs. So we're talking here about equitable, or inclusive, growth – about the importance of getting all the stakeholders to understand the role they can play and the benefits to them from so doing. We're making an effort to bring people on board and include everyone.

But, as we move forward with our branding campaign, I think there are four challenges that will be critical to realizing this vision.

The first is the need to upgrade our infrastructure – for example, by continuing to invest in roads, highways, and airports. If we keep expanding travellers' access to new locations and markets, we will get continued growth in tourism and in our general economy.

Second is greater attention to civic governance, finding ways to encourage the growth and capacity of all kinds of service-providers.

Third is constant communication, along with continuous evolution of the communication strategy. For example, until we began using the internet, we did not fully grasp the huge overseas interest in yoga – 40,000 hits a week! Since that discovery, our communications never miss an opportunity to mention yoga programmes and facilities. The internet really shows us what people are looking for – and it has reinforced our conviction that the experience they want is different from what they find in America, and different from what they get in Europe.

Fourth and finally, our branding campaign needs to be coordinated with the promotional efforts of other sectors of the Indian economy, as we've tried to do in New York with this event. We need to link tourism with business. If that happens, Brand India will keep moving forward. Thank you.

A Westerner's Thoughts on India and China

Heyward: Thanks, Amitabh. Now, let's hear from Sir Martin Sorrell, the CEO of WPP, which has long been the largest marketing communications company in India. Sir Martin has also been a leader in thinking about China and its role in the future. What you think when you hear the words 'Brand India'?

Martin Sorrell: Thanks for the kind words, Andrew.

What does India mean to me? Well, the first thing that comes to mind – at this very moment – is a fantastically outstanding performance on the cricket field. It was in a somewhat strange part of the game. But it's a part of the game that will now, thanks to that performance, live in the memory of all fans of the sport.

Interestingly, that particular game was won by a young team, a team without any of the old stars. And, in that sense, it's emblematic of the opportunities in India today. Because my second thought about India is the size – 1.1 billion people – and, even more important, the youthfulness of its population. Although China now has more people – probably closer to 1.5 billion than the 1.3 billion commonly reported – in the next fifty years India is likely to overtake China as the world's most populous country because of its much higher growth rate.

India also, at least for now, means service companies. But our own view is that India will increasingly become more of a manufacturing-based economy. And where people think of China as mainly a manufacturing economy, we think China is about to make a major shift toward services. So, at the same time as the Mayor of Shanghai is saying that he expects Shanghai to become the services centre of the world, we expect to see India becoming more of a manufacturing heartland. Given what some of India's major entrepreneurs and industrialists are now doing in sectors like retailing or auto-manufacturing or technology, I think we can expect to see an economy that will become known not just for services but manufacturing as well. And, as a result of these shifts, both China and India will end up with economies that are much more balanced between manufacturing and services.

Perhaps most important, what India and China both say to me is captured by the old movie title *Back to the Future*. Both India and China have been on the wrong side of history for the last 200 years – and our prediction is that they will be on the right side for the next 200 years. To put things in perspective, it's helpful to recall that, in the early nineteenth century, India and China accounted for some 40% of worldwide GNP – and we could see numbers like that again.

On the negative side, India means to me lack of infrastructure, particularly in comparison to China as it gets ready for Beijing 2008. I wonder about the eventual consequences of that lack of infrastructure in India. Obviously, there's an element of chaos that comes with that. 'Chaos' may be a harsh word to use, but since it's part of what makes some people nervous about doing business in India, it's something we should be aware of and address. This is an area where perceptions are likely to fail to keep up with reality. But that's, of course, where brand campaigns like this one can help.

Historically, India has meant slow growth to me. But perhaps because of neighbourhood envy and the growth of China, India has now fully awakened; it is clearly on a path of much more rapid growth. India also has meant a bit of bureaucracy. But I have to say that WPP has never encountered any significant problems in that area.

India stands for the potential of education. In fact, education is revered in India. There are some very high-quality schools. But, obviously, there's an awful lot more to be done in this area.

India also means, as we've already heard, different states. It doesn't mean one country. And it means, from WPP's point of view, not just being in New Delhi or Mumbai, but penetrating as we have done with companies such as Pramers or Genesis, the whole of the Indian opportunity. And the same is true in China, with its thirty-two provinces. In India and China alike, seizing the entire opportunity means thinking about it not as a single country, but as lots of different opportunities with different requirements.

Finally, on a negative note, India also means to me the possibility of protectionism by Western governments. India's competitive advantage, particularly in services, has been so powerful that it has started to trouble the developed economies. Both India and China represent newer forces that threaten the operations of developed economies, at least in certain sectors. One of the toughest things for Westerners – for the British and the Americans and the French and the Germans and the Italians – to get their minds around is the possibility that they will no longer be the dominant forces in the world economy. And that's why the biggest risk to me is that the politicians in these developed nations will win votes by taking populist, protectionist stances. If these politicians get elected, they may well succeed in passing measures that reduce not just Indian growth, but world growth as well. And we will all be the worse for that. Thank you.

Brand India as a Public–Private Partnership

Heyward: Terrific, Martin. Now, let's hear from Nandan Nilekani, co-founder, and now the Co-chairman, of Infosys, which, as I said before, is one of India's great success stories.

Nandan Nilekani: Thank you, Andrew. I thought I'd start by talking about business involvement in Brand India and how it's converging with some government initiatives toward one goal.

About three years ago, business leaders in the Confederation of Indian Industry felt there was a need for a much more strategic projection of India's brand. We chose Davos 2006 as the occasion to launch the campaign. And we came up with a comprehensive, high-impact campaign that we called 'India Everywhere at Davos'. The basic idea was that, for anybody who came to Davos for that one week, whatever they ate, whatever they drank, whatever conference they went to, and whatever they saw on the buses would reflect some aspect of Indian commerce or culture.

What was unusual, if not unique, about this effort was that it was initially financed by the private sector. The CII was able to convince many of its members to give money and make a contribution to making this event happen. And when people from our public sector saw private companies contributing to this effort, the Ministry of Commerce and Industry then provided leadership and support through its India Brand Equity funds. So it became a public-private partnership, and a very successful one.

When planning our campaign, we started by asking ourselves the same question Amitabh posed earlier: how do we differentiate the brand? The first thing we thought of was economic growth; at that time, India was growing at a rate of 7% or 8% a year. We also felt that, given the major push by Indian policy-makers toward a free-market environment that started in 1991, economic liberalization and free markets should be an important part of our message. Finally, it also became very clear to us that if we wanted to create a clearly differentiated brand that could not be easily appropriated by other nations, we would have to emphasize the democratic nature of India's values.

So that's how we came up with the slogan for our campaign in which India was identified as 'the world's fastest-growing, free-market democracy'. We concluded that each of these three attributes – fast-growing, free-market, and democratic – had an important role to play, and that a combination of the three was a unique selling proposition. The great appeal of the slogan in this situation was that it was not only a plausible description of our country, but it was a claim that no other economy, developing or otherwise, could comfortably make.

And I think this campaign has been very successful. For the last three years, we have been taking it around the world. We have done it in Japan, and in China – and we took it to the Cannes Film Festival this year. It has had a considerable impact, especially given our relatively modest investment of resources. And so we've had a wonderful experiment in cost-effective marketing, in learning how to create high impact with limited resources, to get the biggest bang for our buck.

We have also concluded that creating these high-impact events is really quite effective in extending what might be called the 'face' of the brand. What is unusual about what we're doing in New York with our Brand India celebrations is that they effectively unite and combine the strengths of two different but parallel brand campaigns. While Amitabh and his colleagues at the Ministry of Tourism have been doing these extraordinarily successful Incredible India brand promotions, with the main aim of driving tourism, we at the CII have been promoting India's free markets and big consumer as great investments. And what has really provided momentum for our current branding program is the decision of these two groups to join forces and work together. For example, today's Brand India campaign – with events going on all over the city, at the Asia Society, and at Columbia and Yale – is a truly joint undertaking between the Ministry of Tourism, which is promoting Indian culture and diversity, and our CII-led activity, which is really about business.

So bringing these two campaigns together has been a major key to our success. It has also reinforced our understanding that, to be successful, we must continue to focus on our strengths, on the benefits that come from being the world's fastest-growing, free-market democracy. A big part of our strength is our demographics. It's about young people, about the future generations that are going to support the world. And our strength also comes from our diversity, and from the development of our people and resources and commerce that is happening all over India.

Finally, our strength lies in the breadth and depth of our entrepreneurial talent. We recognize that one of the best ways to showcase India globally is to take a number of its top business leaders and showcase them. Which is why there were lots of prominent Indian executives at Davos in 2006. Our idea is that if all our top business leaders become part of India's brand projection, we will have something that is very distinctive, something no other developing economy can match.

Let me also point out that this process of global branding can have internal as well as external benefits. That is, while we are using branding to persuade outsiders that India has become a better place to travel and do business, we are also using the same story to put pressure on our own system to bring about change. Although Brand India may be somewhat of an exaggeration, it's not much of an exaggeration – and it's becoming more of a reality with each passing year. And my point here is that branding helps change the reality: once you position India as a great consumer brand, or as a great investor brand, it automatically forces the system to respond, whether by building out the infrastructure or improving investor protection and corporate governance rules.

So I think there's been a lot of progress. And much of this progress can be attributed to a unique kind of public-private partnership. Along with some support from the Indian government, thirty-three Indian companies have contributed to making this event happen. This model of public-private partnership – one that is promoting both the cultural, or 'soft', side of India as well as its business side – may well be the only one of its kind. I don't know of any country that has taken this approach.

And let me close by making one last point about Brand India. We have been very conscious and deliberate in presenting it as a softer brand. It's really not a hard or a dominant brand to begin with. The quest for efficiency through knowledge and knowledge-sharing is an important part of Brand India. But it is not only about efficiency. It is also about democracy and reverence for learning and the past, about art and architecture, and Bollywood and yoga, all of which have a cultural and even a spiritual dimension.

With this in mind, we have been positioning our engagement with the world not so much as a competition for scarce goods, but as a win-win proposition. I believe it was Adam Smith who said that economic success is not about creating a mercantilist economy; it's not just about exporting goods and building up a nation's reserves of gold or, in these days, hard currencies. Success is better measured in terms of the gains from trade by all parties, by the consumers and companies of importing as well as exporting nations. And so one of the basic messages of Brand India is that, to the extent that India succeeds, the world is going to be the richer for it. Thank you.

Vodafone and the Case for Investing in India

Heyward: That was great, Nandan, thanks. Let's now turn to Arun Sarin, CEO of Vodafone, a UK company that has come storming into India, invested $11 billion in Hutch Essar, and rebranded the company as a Vodafone subsidiary. Arun, would you start by giving us your thoughts about Brand India?

Sarin: Thank you, and good morning to everybody. First of all, let me thank the arrangers of this conference for allowing me to meet with Martin

Sorrell in person. Although my company is one of his larger clients, it's actually very hard to schedule a meeting with Martin in London, and so I feel somewhat privileged to see him here in New York.

Let me also say at the outset that I think my fellow panellists have done a great job of talking about the marketing or branding of India. Brand India, in my mind, is about raising the awareness of where India is today as a nation and as a place to do business. In my view, the emergence of India is a phenomenon that has really taken off in the last three to five years. The kind of confidence and self-assurance that you now find amongst young people when you go to India is very recent. And I think what we're talking about is that awakening. There are now a number of Indian companies that either have become, or are on the verge of becoming, truly world-class multinational corporations – companies like Infosys, and like Tata and the two Reliances. It is important for the world, and for Indians as well, to understand that India now occupies a certain place in the geo-political world that it did not occupy five or ten years ago – and definitely not twenty years ago.

But having said that, I am going to make most of my comments from the standpoint of my company and global investors. As Andrew told you, we've recently spent $11 billion buying a controlling ownership position in a company in India. Our primary motive for spending this money has been to produce profitable growth and terrific returns for our shareholders. But I want to say a couple of things about brands and their importance in business.

Vodafone is one of the biggest brands in the world. As Andrew also mentioned earlier, we have 250 million customers around the world and our market cap is about $173 billion. And the one thing about brands that I never get tired of telling my people is that 'a brand is what a brand does'. Building a brand is not just about advertising, or saying how great things are. Brand-building is about delivering what you're telling people you can and will deliver. And in that sense, our decision to make a major investment in India says a lot about the success of the Brand India campaign. If we didn't think India was a terrific place to invest, we would not have put down our $11 billion. But we have – and, as a result, we are now the largest single foreign investor in India by a factor of four.

Vodafone is a relative newcomer to India. We started with a very small investment back in 1995, when India's telecom industry was just opening up. Then three or four years ago, we got bolder and made a $1.5 billion investment in a company called Bharti Airtel. And then we got bolder yet, buying majority control in Hutch. It's taken us only about four months to re-brand the company, and it's been a fantastic experience for us. For those of you who haven't seen our new advertising, I urge you to do so. I think you will get a chuckle out of it, while also seeing a nice example of taking something old and established and turning it into something new.

But now let me talk a bit about the Indian consumer. Indian consumers are very discerning, and very demanding, customers. For that reason, simply exporting ideas from America or from Europe to India will often not work. Because India's a very competitive market place, you need to find some way to combine the low-cost aspects of Indian distribution and low-cost Indian handsets with differentiation and customer service. It's not an easy thing to do.

But one thing I have learned during the past four or five months is not to underestimate the quality of people in these companies. I was visiting our new company in India this past weekend, and we spent a lot of time talking with our Delhi and northern Indian management team. And I continue to be amazed by the quality of people in India. If you're getting a marketing person there, that marketing person is as good as anybody on the planet. If you're getting a technical person, the technical people are simply outstanding. If you're getting a general manager, the manager understands management. All of these folks have been well educated and well trained.

What's also surprising to me is how deep the Indian labour market really is. For those of you who are thinking about investing in India or having operations in India, I think you're going to be very pleasantly surprised. And the farther away from India you are, the less you're likely to know about it. I find it interesting that Europeans – Brits in particular – know a lot more about India than, for example, Americans. That has a lot to do with history, of course, and also with the fact that India is literally the other side of the world from America.

The second thing I would highlight, which has also been a real positive surprise for us, is what I like to call 'reverse synergies'. When we were buying this company in India, we said to ourselves, 'Okay, we will bring low-cost handsets and we'll bring our brand. And we'll bring this and that.' And most of those synergies have been realized, they are happening. But in just four short months, we have now begun exporting great ideas from India. This is what I mean by 'reverse synergies'. There is so much we are learning about how to build new operations, how to create a global company. Whether it's in the area of mobile payments, or in the area of distribution or cost management, there have been many great ideas that we've brought out of India and back to Europe.

So, again, as you think about investing in India, think about what you might be able to bring. But also be prepared to have your company changed by operating in India.

The final point I'd make is that if you're not in India today – and by the way, when I travel around and meet Fortune 500 chief executives, I haven't come across a single CEO who doesn't have an operation in India – you might want to revisit that possibility. Because if you're staying away, you could be missing some major growth opportunities – opportunities not just for profitable operations in India, but perhaps for improving your own business model. Thank you.

A Journalist's Perspective

Heyward: Thanks very much, Arun. Now let's hear from Vir Sanghvi. Vir, can you shed some journalistic light on the subject? We're hearing a lot of passion, enthusiasm, and perhaps a bit of marketing on the panel here. What do you have to say?

Vir Sanghvi: Thanks, Andrew. I'll try my best. Since I am neither a marketer nor a captain of industry like the other people on this panel, I will talk about things from a journalistic perspective. While I think it's important to talk about where Brand India is today, it's also important to have some historical perspective on how we got here, and I will try to provide just a bit.

If you asked people in the West, especially educated people, what India represents to them, here are some of the things you would be told:

You would hear about the huge market for goods and services. Arun just mentioned that every Fortune 500 company wants to come to India. You would hear about the economy and how fast it is growing – second only to China. You would hear Martin Sorrell's point about how India and China are economies of the future. You would hear about information technology. You would hear the success stories of Infosys, Tata, and other technology superpowers.

You would also hear about our vibrant popular culture. I think Bollywood is a very big part of Brand India – and by most estimates it is bigger than Hollywood. And Bollywood is very, very important for us.

You would also hear about nuclear power. You would hear about India as an emerging superpower in Asia. And you'd hear about the quality of the people that Arun just told us about. The Westerners I talk to always seem to be amazed by the quality of people in India. As Martin said, it's a country where people are highly educated, where people are bright and competent. And though many of them could find jobs anywhere, they're quite happy to be in India.

So that, I think, is the essence of Brand India today. But this is a new development. If you came into a room like this twenty-five or thirty years ago, and you asked people what images India evoked, you would have gotten a very different response. The old images of India were pictures of starving peasants and farmers, earthquakes and floods rendering thousands homeless, and urban chaos. Martin spoke about the chaos – and of course it's true: India is chaotic. Even people who are affectionate toward India speak about the chaos. John Kenneth Galbraith described India in the 1960s as 'the world's only functioning anarchy'. And I think he's right.

But chaos and mismanagement were then a much larger part of both our image and the reality behind it than they are now. Today the 'Made in India' brand has lots of positive associations. But twenty-five or thirty years ago, you would think of shoddy products. There was a time when if you saw something that was made in India, you wouldn't buy it.

So how did all this change? How have we gotten to this point where celebrations of Indian progress are taking place all over New York City, where we're sitting in the Harvard Club talking about Brand India? What's made the difference?

I will give you my personal perspective on this. And let me warn you that it's one that reflects many generalizations. And as we've been told several times this morning, all generalizations about India – with the possible exception of this one – are wrong. We know that for almost everything you might say about India, the opposite is also likely to be true.

So when did this change come about? When did India change from the old brand to the new one? My view is that India began to transform itself in 1991. Although this date may be a little arbitrary, those of you who are familiar with India will know why I picked 1991. That was the year in which the first of a series of major economic reforms were instituted. That was the year India really began the process of opening itself up to the working of markets, to outside goods and to capital.

These economic reforms have been far more important to India than many people abroad realize. Nandan once told me in an interview that if the economy had not been liberalized in 1991, Infosys would have gone bust. They were considering closing down the company. And that was what, just fifteen years ago?

The reforms changed India much more dramatically than most people in the West realized. But there were other things going on in 1991 as well. That was the year that educated Indians, including Indian politicians – with the exception of the communists – largely came to terms with the fact that the Soviet Bloc was dead, that communism had been defeated, and that India could no longer play its old balancing act between two superpowers. We knew that the old ways of state power were dead, and that we had to make new choices.

This was also the time that satellite television arrived in India, along with the flood of global products that accompanied the 1991 liberalization. It was a time when we finally began to see the world in real time. We finally felt part of the world, we felt connected. And I don't think the significance of this has ever been fully appreciated. It was hugely important for the Indian middle-class. We felt, finally, like citizens of the world.

And there were other factors. One of the most important, and I think everyone's talked about it, has to do with Indian demographics. By 1991, the generations that had run India from around the time of independence were gone. We had lots of young people then. And today with something like 65% of the population of India under thirty, that's even more true. India is one of the world's youngest countries. And this means that the people who are now transforming the way in which the government works in India are people who don't remember an earlier time. They don't remember the colonial era; they are products of an independent India. And the people you get when you reach a call centre in India today are people who remember only the last ten or fifteen years. They don't even remember what India was like before economic liberalization. And, as I suggested, these demographics have been very important in changing the way middle-class India behaves.

Demographics have also been important in terms of the Indian diaspora, in terms of all those Indian emigrants and their children who have had successful careers in their new countries. Not much is said about the diaspora. But the success of people like Arun, which perhaps wouldn't have happened thirty years ago, has had a major effect on how India is perceived. And the fact that there are so many Indians, perhaps not as successful as Arun, but certainly in top corporate jobs all over the West, has changed the way India is perceived. The diaspora has also become a huge market for Indian popular culture. They've become cheerleaders and lobbyists for India. And, as we have seen in the United States, they have done a lot to change the image of India.

So, to sum up my argument, in 1991 something happened in India that led to the withering away of Old India – and a new India was born. But, as I've also suggested, it is a generalization that is bound to be misleading, especially when applied to a complex place like India. Brand India is essentially a middle-class phenomenon. But, as several people have said, there are many Indias. And, of course, there is much of India that does not shine. Much of India is still in darkness. There's a lot of poverty, a lot of chaos. There are many, many deliverables that haven't reached the poorest in India. But with a bit of luck, we'll get there. And it's 1991 that got things started.

Balancing Global and Local Management

Heyward: Thanks very much, Vir. That ends our opening round of comments by each speaker. Now let me pose a few questions to the entire group.

Several of you have suggested the potential for conflict or tension between Western and Indian consumers and management methods. To what degree are Western companies adapting to an increasingly empowered Indian business culture, as opposed to trying to make India adapt to Western ways? Arun, perhaps you could start this by telling us about your recent experience in rebranding Hutch.

Sarin: We bought our position in this company just six months ago. And what we've since found is that Hutch was actually a very well-run company, even better than we thought when we made our investment. And this was not a company, by the way, where we planned to add value by overhauling its management or systems. We found both to be in very good shape. And we're still very early in the process of integrating the company with the rest of Vodafone.

We now have operations in thirty countries, and we've grown principally through acquisitions. So we're quite used to acquiring companies and then instilling in them our Vodafone values. But, at the same time, it's also important for the companies that we acquire to retain their local character and customs. As I like to say to all our employees, 'When we're in Germany, Vodafone is a German company. When we're in the UK, it's a British company. And when we're in India, it's an Indian company.'

But while we want our overseas businesses to keep their regional or local character, we also want them to understand and become part of our corporate culture at Vodafone – to understand who we are and what we expect of them. There are three words, or traits, that we use to describe Vodafone to our own people and to our customers. Those words are 'red', 'rock solid' and 'restless'. 'Red' is for passion, passion for serving the customer and for everything you do. 'Rock solid' means dependability; it tells people they can rely on us. And 'restless' is meant to suggest our pursuit of innovation in whatever we do; we want to do better the next time.

 This three-point slogan is also meant to remind people of our firm-wide commitment to principles of business ethics and corporate social responsibility. As you can imagine, when you have a global brand, if you have trouble anywhere around the world, that trouble travels at internet speed these days. So I personally try to make sure that the leaders of our businesses around the world are all people we would be proud of calling 'Vodafoners'. And if I'm not comfortable, then we change the people. That's a big part of the process of integrating companies into Vodafone – and it helps me sleep at night.

Heyward: Martin, what about your own experience in integrating companies?

Sorrell: I obviously have to agree with everything that Arun says since he's my client – and in fact I do. But WPP is in a somewhat different situation than Vodafone in the sense that WPP's experience in India goes back a long way. Our investment and operation in India started in 1987 with the acquisition of J. Walter Thompson in India, a firm that at the time had been around for, I think, about fifty years. So our roots in India – through the acquisitions and the development of WPP, and through our purchases of Ogilvy, Young & Rubicam, and Hill & Knowlton, among others – go back many, many years.

Now, to answer Andrew's question, I think it's a matter of achieving a delicate balance – a balance between keeping some degree of control and direction by headquarters while also encouraging local or regional decision-making, and bringing in local management at the highest levels. If you're running a portfolio of global companies, you want a group of companies that are not only the best at what they do, but that are also operating in the strongest countries. Our operation in India is a good example. By the end of this August, it was growing its top line by well over 20%, as compared to GNP growth in India of about 10%. There's an iron law that in these faster-growing markets advertising and marketing sales typically grow at about twice the level of GNP growth – and our India business is living up to that expectation.

When foreign multinationals come into a new country, they often feel more comfortable having expatriate managers oversee and develop the business. But my own view is that expatriates are not the answer; they are not part of a viable long-term strategy. At the risk of sounding a bit callous, the Asian recession in 1997 gave us an opportunity to take out a number of expatriate posts not just in India, but in Asia as a whole. And while that was clearly good from a cost point of view, it had the more important benefit of sending a clear signal to the locals and nationals that the opportunities inside the company were totally open.

Ultimately, the growth and success of our businesses in those countries – in the BRIC and in countries like Indonesia, Vietnam and Pakistan – have depended on our having national staff to run and develop them. The growing complexity of businesses at a local level means that important local and national functions must be fulfilled by national management. And besides staffing with nationals, the success of multinationals also depends on their ability to provide their most talented local managers with opportunities to manage outside their own countries.

But if business has become more local in this sense, we have also seen a significant trend in our multinational clients toward an emphasis on global branding, toward the creation of so-called 'billion dollar' brands. And this means that country managers must focus not only on building the local business, but on matters that could affect the global reputation of the entire firm. Corporate social responsibility initiatives are a good example. Government relations, relations with educational institutions, and development of R&D programs are other examples where global and local concerns will come into play and have to be balanced. Like all things in life, it's not a matter of black and white, but discriminating amongst shades of grey. If you go too far to either the global extreme or the local extreme, you can be penalized.

So, again, multinationals are increasingly finding themselves faced with balancing global and local imperatives. And, frankly, market conditions will demand that you pull a little bit more one way at some times and a little bit more the opposite way in others. And I would predict that some of the functions now exercised by regional managers will be transferred to headquarters, thereby reducing overhead. My prediction is based in part on the fact that the technology represented by Nandan's and Arun's companies is giving us the opportunity to enlarge our span of control, to run at least parts of our business in a more centralized way.

Heyward: Nandan, can you give us some perspective on this? Is Infosys increasingly working in other countries and really spreading its footprint around the world?

Nilekani: As you said, Andrew, the rise of IT companies like Infosys and TCS is one of the big success stories in India. This was an industry that had only about $ 50 million in revenue during that make-or-break year of 1991. But it's now a $ 30 billion industry, accounting for 3% of India's GDP and employing 1.6 million people. And given the current growth rates, we see no reason why the industry won't double to $60 billion in the next four to five years.

The success of these companies has played a huge role in building the India brand and demonstrating the quality of India's human capital. So I think our challenge today is to build on this brand – or to build within this broad umbrella brand of technology savvy companies. A big part of this challenge, however, is to transform our current brand, which is based mainly on our successes in outsourcing, into one that stands for the capability of doing what we call business 'transformations'. That's the goal we are all working toward now.

And in working towards that goal, we face the task of demonstrating to the global business community that we are not just an Indian company, but a company that is truly global in our operations and in our work force. We have recently started hiring American college graduates and training them in India, and then sending them back to work for us in the US. And our friends at TCS now have employees in a variety of countries all over the world. This is the wave of the future for the most successful Indian companies. As Arun said earlier, we will become truly multinational corporations, with local operations and employees all over the world, and a multicultural work force.

Challenges to Brand India

Heyward: Okay, we've now heard a lot about the promise of Brand India. Let's talk about the challenges that stand in the way of realizing this promise. We have heard several references to infrastructure problems, and to the 'bit of chaos' mentioned by Martin Sorrell. These are still issues that have to be confronted. And then there's obviously the challenge of addressing the poverty, the whole notion of 'two Indias' that has become something of a cliché. How do we deal with that?

Let's start again with Amitabh. As somebody who has had such success in your home state of Kerala, and also nationally, with 'upscale' marketing, what do you see as the main challenges? What do you see as the contradictions that have to be resolved?

Kant: Well, in the long run, no brand will succeed if the message and the perception do not match the reality. The 'God's Own Country' campaign ultimately worked in Kerala because the state was able to deliver its promises to tourists. Our social indices were very high. We had 100% literacy, and the health standards were also very high. It was the most advanced state in India. Even if you were touring in the backwater, the person driving the boat was probably reading three newspapers as well as Arun's book. So, most international tourists who came into Kerala had an amazing experience.

But now let's take the question of infrastructure. In India today, there is increased focus on infrastructure. And much of the work is being carried out and funded by partnerships between the states and the private sector. Airports, for example, have been privatized in Mumbai and Delhi. And there are now thirty-five provincial airports that are being developed or expanded. There is also a lot of investment in improving roads and highways. So there's a huge amount of work going on.

But let me point to one impediment to progress in this area. As India has changed from being a more centralized democracy to a highly decentralized form of governance by the states, much of the real decision-making authority has moved to the states. And for the branding of India to move forward, the states themselves must play a more active role. The political and civic leaders of each state – and even, in some cases, the panchayats – must take ownership of their brand and drive it forward. And when that happens, when there are good roads and effective civic governance in each state, then we will have realized the promise of Brand India. For Brand India, as I said earlier, is just the aggregation of the brands of its individual states.

Heyward: Nandan, do you have a perspective on this?

Nilekani: I think there is an important difference between building a corporate brand and a country brand. In the corporate case, if you're launching a product, you can design it, price it, and distribute it. You have complete control over that brand launch. But when you are dealing with a country brand, you have absolutely no means of ensuring that the brand delivers on its promises. If you're creating a brand for India, you can't guarantee that the taxi driver will be nice to the guy who lands at Delhi Airport. And because there are so many uncontrollables, we have to be very careful that the promise does not get ahead of the reality. Because if that happens, you have a backlash – and then you're farther behind than where you started.

But having said that, we still need to go forward with our brand-building. We need brand-building to bring in foreign investors and companies, which in turn creates jobs and tax revenues and other benefits. So, I think for the people running the Brand India campaign, managing this potential gap between reality and perception is a delicate, and very important, task. But at the same time, you have to keep pushing the brand; it's an essential, a strategic, requirement.

Sorrell: I agree with that completely. But let me raise this question of infrastructure because I think it's the main advantage that China has over India at the moment. China is investing $ 45 billion in one way or another in the Beijing Olympics. And when I say 'in one way or another', I'm talking, among other things, about its airports. Anyone who's landed at Beijing Airport and seen Terminal 5, the Dragon or Foster design terminal, will have seen what I'm talking about.

Now, I'm far from suggesting that India's lack of infrastructure will prevent it from attracting foreign investment. Anyone running a multinational will not choose between China and India. You will do both. You will choose to invest in the faster-growing economies rather than the slow-growth economies of, say, Western Europe – economies like the UK, France, Germany, and Italy – though Spain and Ireland may be exceptions here.

So, again, it's not a question of either China or India. But, on the margin, I think infrastructure can be a critical issue for, say, investment decisions by overseas companies. For example, India is seeing significant development of its airports. But our own experience in working with the development of those airports suggests that things are, if not chaotic – and that's much too strong a word – then a bit disorganized. And I do think there is considerable room, and good reason, to improve this situation.

In this respect, Amitabh's emphasis on the role of the twenty-seven states is helpful in one sense, but unhelpful in another. If you want to have a national network of highways and airports, you have to have a national plan. And that kind of central planning is, of course, the strength of the Chinese system. It's state-controlled capitalism. They're trying to harness the best of both systems, central planning and decentralized markets.

But I also think that Nandan's theme for Davos – the promotion of India as the world's fastest growing democracy – is a good one. It's the right strategic line for India. But let me also suggest that a bit more central coordination of some infrastructure initiatives might help India attract even more foreign investment. WPP now has some 5,500 employees in India. And there are all kinds of businesses, from manufacturing to the different types of services business, that rely on infrastructure in various ways and to varying degrees. And I think the dependability of that infrastructure – in the sense that Arun identified as one of the three main contributors to Vodafone's brand – is pretty important. It's important for India to have a reliable infrastructure.

Sarin: I just want to underscore Martin's point that investing in India and China is not an either/or proposition. In addition to our $11 billion investment in India, we have a minority position – a 3.27% stake – in a very large company in China that has 350 million customers. In India, by comparison, our company has 35 million customers, though that number is growing at 1.7 million customers a month.

So the point here, as Martin said, is to invest in growth, in profitable growth. You take the opportunities wherever you can find them.

The Problem of Two Indias

Sanghvi: I want to respond to Andrew's comment about 'two Indias', which, I agree with him, is a cliché. Nevertheless, it is a cliché that seems to have a lot of credibility. There is very little evidence to suggest that the economic reforms I cited as initiating India's progress have much popular or political support. The last government went to the elections with the slogan 'India shining', and describing India's economy as the envy of the world. But that government went down to a sharp defeat.

Since then, all Indian politicians have been very careful about emphasizing economic growth. There is a greater, vaster India – the one that elects the politicians – that doesn't necessarily buy into Brand India. And unless we find a way to get that buy-in, this growth may not be sustainable.

One approach might be to emphasize the benefits that can be traced to the economic reforms – for example, the ability of the Indian economy to keep growing in spite of agricultural disasters and the huge oil price increases. We could also point to India's Five Year Plan to invest a record $25 billion in education, all made possible by robust economic growth and tax revenues. But I don't hear these arguments being made. There are some fairly direct links between higher economic growth and the potential for social change, social progress. But these links have not been well articulated – in part perhaps because of our past tendency to be reticent in promoting our successes.

Sorrell: One way to make the case for growth is to focus on the alternative – that is, what happens to countries that fail to grow. Why is it that Latin American countries like Brazil and Mexico have always promised, but never really delivered? It's because the populist argument has always prevailed in their politics. The leaders of Brazil and Mexico have been unwilling to discipline their unions and cut their government programs and bureaucracy because it is not a popular thing to do.

So the clear alternative to Brand India is a slow-growth India. That's what you get if the populist and protectionist politicians win. But as I said earlier, I think the biggest spur to Indian growth has been the development of China. The liberalization of the economy in 1991 might have been a necessary condition for this, but I think the biggest stimulus to growth in India has been neighbourhood envy. The Indians looked at what was happening in China, and they recognized they could do it, too. And as long as China continues to grow, I think that will be a big political, social, and economic stimulus.

Kant: I agree that the underlying premise of Brand India is that the only way to eradicate poverty is through free markets and economic growth. But there is definitely a failure of communication at work here. The polls will tell you, for instance, that despite all our efforts to promote the benefits of privatization, even the vast majority of Indian middle-class people are opposed to the privatization of nationalized industry.

So, I agree with Vir that there just isn't the kind of popular support for economic reform and growth that one would have liked. And I too think it is the result of our failure to communicate our successes.

Think about what India was like sixty years ago when we first became independent. There were strong doubts about the very survival of the country. Sixty years ago, 72% of the people were below the poverty line. Today the number is down to about 24% – a number that, although still too high, represents very real progress. And the country has moved forward dramatically in terms of education, health standards, and infrastructure. Now, if we want to continue our policy of higher government outlays on education and health care, we will need strong economic growth to provide the tax revenue needed to fund them. In the private sector, Arun has been able to invest heavily in growth because he's succeeded in providing high returns for his shareholders – and, as a result, they're confident and happy to let him invest their capital. By the same token, those Indian states like Kerala that have achieved higher levels of growth also have the highest levels of local government expenditures and the highest health and living standards.

So I think the message is a straightforward one: where you have economic growth, things like primary education and health care improve with them. My vision – and my goal – is to engage not just the Indian middle class but our other 800 million people in this process of brand-building. To the extent we succeed, our private sector will prosper – and its success will mean higher government spending and better lives for all.

Heyward: So you're saying that Indian politicians have been unable to persuade the people of the benefits of these economic reforms. What advice could we give the political party in India that wishes to win and stay in power?

Nilekani: Although we all talk about the benefits of economic growth and believe that only growth can alleviate poverty, it's important to keep in mind that elections in much of India are still decided on the basis of community and caste. There was a time in the 1970s when we had these great mandates that cut across caste and communal lines, when people voted not as Hindus or Muslims or Brahmans, but as Indians. But there are divisions in – in fact, I would say there has been a fragmentation of – our society that I think has been clearly reflected in our election outcomes.

As Amitabh said earlier, it's important to think of India as an aggregation of different states, each with its own people and interests.

You can talk about growth all the time in New York. But if a politician in Rajasthan really wants to build a shopping mall next to the Taj Mahal – as one nearly did – it's not easy to prevent it. Regional politicians are not responsible to anyone other than the regional electorates. And, unfortunately, electorates rarely vote politicians in or out on the basis of economic performance. They vote on the basis of caste. And unless we solve this conundrum, unless we find a way of making the electorate vote on the basis of growth or on economic issues, I think we have a problem.

Sorrell: This may not be the most politically correct way to make this point, but let me draw some parallels to France. When the French government decided to have a thirty-five-hour week, people who were working forty hours went to thirty-five. And in government establishments, they went from thirty-five hours to thirty hours a week. Friday has become a slack day and people have started to have three-day weekends.

Now, if you choose to do that, that's fine. But you have to make people understand the implications of that choice. Many people may, and probably will, be happier with the thirty-five-hour week. But companies are going to make less money, people are going to earn less money, and governments are going to have less to spend on the public services that we all claim to want.

My point is that if you pass these measures, you may please some people, but you have to live with the consequences. I think our challenge is to show people that, unless there's free trade and strong economic growth as a result, there will not be an increase in living standards. In 1991, communism disappeared as an alternative to capitalism; it's gone. But if the current democratic system is going to continue to prosper and deliver, you have to show people the consequences of electing politicians who pass measures that interfere with free markets and reduce economic growth.

I think that if India doesn't continue on the path it's established in the last few years, it will suffer as a result. And I think other countries will take up the slack. The world's economies are becoming more and more competitive. Look at the growth of Russia, China, Brazil. Look at Central and Eastern Europe as a whole, and the Middle East. Look at the growth of the Gulf States and of Africa. The world is becoming increasingly competitive. And I think you have to view it almost as a corporate race, if you like, to attract foreign interest and foreign investment. If you don't want to compete in this way, if you don't really want free markets, at least recognize the implications of your choices, the tradeoffs you're making.

Nilekani: On this question of getting popular or political buy-in, I agree with Vir and Amitabh that all the data indicate that people don't want privatization. Most people, especially those at the lower economic levels of society, want the state to be the guarantor of goods and services – which I think is a completely natural, and reasonable, response. So, where we have a big job ahead of us is in convincingly demonstrating the link between this economic growth and the resulting benefits for the masses of people, for the 800 million that Amitabh mentioned.

A big part of the problem here is that economic growth will definitely cause income inequalities to go up, at least initially. People who are educated and who have access to the global marketplace will do much better than those who don't – and that will accentuate income inequality. So, I think there's a big job ahead to show how this kind of reform process is actually good for everybody in the long run. It certainly needs to be done much better than it is now.

Sarin: Well, let me just point out that when we were making our own decision to invest in India, we were actually favorably impressed by the way the incremental GDP in India gets spread throughout the different economic strata. Our view at Vodafone is that a certain degree of wealth distribution within a country is necessary to support a deep market for mobile phones. And when making a major investment in any country, the extent to which wealth is distributed throughout the society is one of the key variables we look at. I will also tell you that we have looked at a number of countries where wealth is created, but remains highly concentrated in the upper classes. And we have been very reluctant to invest in countries where the wealth, because of political or social barriers, doesn't 'trickle down' readily. But, as I started by saying, India appears to us to have the kind of wealth distribution where, when the economy prospers, people in all levels of the economy seem to benefit.

Heyward: Arun, you spoke of the reverse synergies, or mutual learning, that has resulted from your $11-billion investment in India. At the same time, you own 3.5% of Mobile China. Do you believe that India's free-market democratic system allows for greater reverse synergies than China's state-controlled capitalism?

Sarin: Not necessarily. We are now the single largest foreign investor in Chinese mobile telecom. A few years ago, we invested $3 billion. As of yesterday, our investment there was worth $10 billion. And it has been very much a two-way, mutually beneficial relationship. We think we have brought a lot of valuable expertise and insight to our Chinese partner. At the same time, we have learned quite a bit from our partner and just from operating in the Chinese economy. I mentioned earlier that our company in China has 350 million customers. And we have learned a lot just from watching how mobile telecom has penetrated the Chinese rural networks. But we have also learned a lot from operating in other countries, countries such as South Africa and Egypt, and Romania and Turkey. We are continuously learning from our operations all over the world.

And having acquired all this learning and experience, we then try to apply it when we come to a new country like India. For example, there's a process called 'network sharing' that is allowing us to share the spectrum and the electronics in a way that is both cost-effective and energy-conserving, or what people now refer to as 'green'. Because only about 40% of India's population is covered by telecom networks, we are now building networks where there were none before. In the United States, by comparison, coverage is now at about 98% and in much of Europe, we are almost at 100%.

As a result, I would describe our operation in India today as a kind of pioneering venture. In a sense, we are leading the world in effective building. As we build out these networks over the next few years, we expect to learn more about how to make things even more green and conserve more energy. And when that happens, we will take those ideas out of India and bring them to the rest of the world.

Measuring Success

Heyward: Let me finish with one last question: how will you know that Brand India has been a success? And how will you measure the value of your brand once you've finished your campaign?

Sanghvi: There are two basic ways to measure how Brand India unfolds in the next five, ten, or twenty years. One is hard and the other is soft. The hard way would be to look at what happens in the country in both a macro and micro sense. Let's see if this nine or ten percent growth continues year after year. And let's attempt to measure whether the income increases are distributed, with all groups benefiting from economic reform. The soft measures would have to do with how people think about India today, as compared to how they thought about India ten years ago. And how will you think about India ten years from now? We need to track both types of measures for India to continue to make progress.

Kant: I agree that we need sustained levels of growth in the coming years. The period of remarkable Indian growth has been too short to have enough of an impact for people to really buy into it as a way of improving their lives. But it's also important, as Vir just suggested, that we function as an effective and fairly stable democratic system. Do we have elections at the right intervals – or do we have too many of them with too frequent changes of power?

I also think that, since Brand India is an aggregation of many local brands, effective and stable civic governance at the grassroots level is a key issue. And municipal elections are a good indicator of what's going on. My experience has been that wherever there has been good civic and municipal governance – where there is economic growth and investment in health and education – the local governments tend to remain in power.

Heyward: Vir, what are your thoughts on how a free media plays a role in the branding of a nation, a role that is different in India than in China?

Sanghvi: I think it's very important in any kind of branding for there to be free media. And, as you suggest, that's a major difference between India and China. India not only has a free media, but a vibrant media, and a vibrant popular culture. Bollywood is now bigger than Hollywood. Indian television channels are on par with the best in the world, and Indian newspapers are winning awards. And all this suggests to the world that India is a democratic state committed to human rights.

Heyward: Martin, any last words on the value of soft brands and how to value them?

Sorrell: I thought you would never ask, Andrew. At the risk of sounding commercial, let me just mention that there are at least two reasonable methods for quantifying the value of brands that I'm aware of. One, which is called Optimor, has been developed by Millward Brown. The other, which was developed by Young & Rubicam in work with the New York consulting firm Stern Stewart, is called Brand Asset Valuator. These methods can be used not just to value brands, but to identify various sources of brand value and ways of increasing it.

And as both of these valuation methods would tell you, the soft side is a major contributor to the value of Brand India. Much of this has to do with Vir's comment about the importance of India's commitment to democratic values. And I also agree strongly with Vir's point that Bollywood and the Indian media play a pivotal role in building Brand India, in influencing what people perceive India to stand for, and what it could stand for even more in the future.

Finally, I believe that India's media successes are providing us with just a glimpse of the creative capabilities of the 1.1 billion people in India. What we're seeing in India today is just the beginning, and the continued development of these capabilities will end up permeating everything. It will affect not just our creative services industry, but lead to innovations in marketing and design – and to improvements in business processes generally – in all kinds of organizations, public as well as private.

In terms of public organizations, we're seeing a big emphasis on country branding, and on regional and city branding as well. We're seeing presidents, prime ministers, governors, and mayors all focused on marketing their jurisdictions in a world that, over the past twenty years, has grown primarily through free trade. So, if you ask me, 'What has been the biggest driver of WPP's growth?', I will tell you that it's been the growth of free trade and the absence of protectionism. And I fully expect this to continue.

Heyward: Well, let's end on that note. I want to thank all the panelists for an entertaining and instructive discussion. And, again, my congratulations to you all on India's sixty years of independence. It will be exciting to see how things develop from here.

(The panel discussion Brand India – Where Next? *originally appeared in the* Journal of Applied Corporate Finance, *Volume 20, Number 1, Winter 2008, a Morgan Stanley Publication.)*

References

Crisis as catalyst : the making of a brand called 'Incredible India'

1 Clay Chandler, 'India's Global Reach', Fortune magazine, (Asia Edition, 29 October 2007).

2 D.A. Aaker, *Managing Brand Equity* (New York: The Free Press, 1991).

3 D.A. Aaker, *Building Strong Brands* (New York: The Free Press, 1996).

4 D.A. Aaker and E. Joechimschaler, *Brand Leadership* (New York: The Free Press, 2000).

5 T. Duncan and A. Moriarty, *Driving Brand Value Using Integrated Marketing to Manage Profitable Stakeholder Relationships* (New York: McGraw Hill, 1997).

6 B.B. Gardner and S.J. Levy, 'The Product and the Brand', *Harvard Business Review* (Harvard, March/April 1955).

7 K. L. Keller, *Strategic Brand Management* (Upper Saddle River, New Jersey: Prentice-Hall Inc, 1998).

8 P. Kotler, *Marketing Management* (Upper Saddle River, New Jersey: Prentice-Hall Inc, 1997).

9 T. Levitt, 'Marketing Success through Differentiation-of Anything', *Harvard Business Review* (Harvard, January/February, 1980).

10 J.R. Brent Ritchie and J.B. Robin Ritchie, 'The Branding of Tourism Destinations: Past Achievements and Future Challenges', paper read at Morocco (Morocco: AIEST 48th Congress, 1998).

11 National Tourism Policy, 2002, Ministry of Tourism and Culture, Government of India.

12 Travel and Tourism in 2020: The Key Drivers, prepared by the Future Foundation for Cendant.

13 Creenagh Lodge, 'Branding Countries: A New Field for Branding or an Ancient Truth?', in Research Report on 'Branding' published by Chartered Institute of Marketing, UK (London, February 2002).

'God's Own Country' shows the way: Kerala, where it all began

1 Amartya Sen, in *Development as a Freedom* (Oxford: Oxford University Press, 2001).

2 For further details on Kerala Travel Mart log on to www.keralatravelmart.org.

3 M.F. Husain and Shashi Tharoor, *Kerala: God's Own Country* (India: Books Today, 2002).

4 'Impact of Tourism in Kerala', a study by Tata Consultancy Services (2001).

5 'Tourism Satellite Accounts on Kerala', an analysis by World Travel and Tourism Council / Oxford Economic Forecasting (2002).

6 'Kerala's Approach to Tourism Development: A Case Study', a study by the Credit Rating information Services of India Limited for the Ministry of Tourism, Government of India (2004).

7 Conservation & Preservation Act, Kerala (2005). For details and full version log onto www.keralatourism.org.

8 Tourism Vision, 2025, Kerala. For details www.keralatourism.org

Infrastructure: propping up the fundamentals

1 'Evaluation Study in Selected Overseas Markets', Gallup Poll Organization for the Ministry of Tourism (2006).

2 'Advertising Effectiveness', survey conducted by Synovate on behalf of CNN (December 2006).

3 'Furthering the Process of Economic Development', Travel and Tourism Competitiveness Report, (Geneva: World Economic Forum, 2007).

4 'A Study to Prepare a Road Map for Tourism Infrastructure Development in India', report by Asian Development Bank (2007).

5 'Market Pulse Study on Manpower Requirement on Tourism Sector', study conducted for Ministry of Tourism, for details log on to 'Surveys & Studies' – www.tourism.gov.in

Air transport – piloting the growth of tourism

1 'The Impact of Civil Aviation Policy on Tourism in India', CRISIL, Mahajan and Aibara. See 'Surveys & Studies' – www.tourism.gov.in

2 'A Short History of Indian Aviation: Preface to a Long and Fruitful Future', Centre for Asia Pacific Aviation (2007).

3 'Total Tourism India', an analysis of one of the world's fastest growing markets, Pacific Asia Travel Association (PATA) (February 2007).

4 Quoted in *Business Today* (9 September 2007).

5 'Total Tourism India', PATA (February 2007).

6 'Financing Plan for Airports', a study by the Secretariat for the Committee for Infrastructure-Planning Commission.

7 'Indian Aviation: Market Overview and Outlook', a report by Centre for Asia Pacific Aviation (June 2007).

Hotels: creating room for growth

1 'Manpower Requirements; for Travel & Tourism Industry', a study by Market Pulse for Ministry of Tourism (2004).

2 'Total Tourism Study', PATA.

3 'Study to Prepare a Road Map', ADB.

4 Lodging Econometric International, quoted in *Mint* newspaper (22 November 2008).

5 Hugh & Colleen Gantzer, 'Highways are the New Frontiers', *Travel Biz Monitor* (21-27 January 2008).

6 For details on 'Incredible India Bed and Breakfast Scheme' go to www.incredibleindia.org.

E-business: making travel & tourism click

1 'The Emerging Online Travel Market Place in India', PhoCus Wright Inc. (2006).

2 Ibid.

3 'E Business for Tourism: Practical Guidelines for Destinations and Businesses', WTOBC (September 2001).

4 'Marketing Tourism Destinations Online: Strategies for the Information Age', WTOBC (1999).

5 Aaker and Joechimschaler, 'Building Brands: the Role of the Web', *Brand Leadership*.

6 David Kenny and John F. Marshall, 'Contextual Marketing: the Real Business of the Internet', *Havard Business Review* (Harvard, 2001).

7 Quoted in Aaker and Joechimschaler, 'Building Brands'.

Healthcare: holistic healing in India

1 Indian National Health Policy 2002, Ministry of Health and Family Welfare.

2 John Reed and Bernard Simon, 'GM workers call off strike after landmark healthcare agreement', *Financial Times* (27 September 2007).

3   Christopher Bow, 'US Hospitals' bad debt, add up to Healthcare woe', *Financial Times* (6 August 2007).

4. R. Martin et al, 'NHS Waiting Lists and Evidences of National or Local Failure: Analysis of Health Service Data', *British Medical Journal* Vol. 526, No.7382 (2003).

5   B. Jarman and S. Middleton, 'Hospital Waiting Lists and Pressures on the NHS', *British Medical Journal,* Vol. 330, No.1352 (2005).

6   Dr. Naresh Trehan, earlier with Escorts, quoted in 'Travel and Hospitality Industry Set to Tap into Asia's US$ 4 Billion Medical Tourism Market', *Travel Smart Asia.*

7   Report released by Deputy Chairman, Planning Commission of India on 2 April 2008.

8   Cover story on 'Medical Tourism' in US News & World Report 9 (12 May 2008).

9   Published in USA Today (15 April 2006).

10 Futurist Marvin Cetron. Quoted in 'Medical Tourism Growing Worldwide' (25 July 2005).

11 For details on Tom Keesling log on to www.indushealth.com.

12 I. Teh and C.Chu, 'Supplementing Growth with Medical Tourism', *Asia Pacific Bio Tech News* 9, No.1508 (2005).

13 Becca Hutchinson, 'Looking Ahead, Are There Any Medical Technologies or Procedures in which Particular Countries Excel?'

14 'Global Trends in Private Medical Insurance', a study by Swiss Re-insurance.

15 Jeffrey S. Schult, *Beauty from Afar* (New York: Harry N. Abrams, Inc, 2006)

16 Tilman Ehrveck, 'Medical Tourism can be a Marvel', *Business Standard* (14 June 2008).

Sustainability : the itinerary for the future

1   Robin Murray, *Zero Waste: Creating Wealth from Waste* (London: Demos, 1999).

2   *Indicators of Sustainable Development for Tourism Destinations,* a guidebook by the World Tourism Organisation (2004).

3   John Swarbrooke, *Development and Management of Visitor Attractions* (Oxford:

Butterworth-Heinemann, 2002).

4   For details log on to www.toinitiative.org.
5   S. Wearing and J. Neil, *Eco Tourism: Impacts, Potentials and Possibilities* (Oxford: Butterworth Heinemann, 2000).
6   H. Ceballos-Lascurain, 'Ecotourism as a Worldwide Phenomenon', in K. Lindberg, D. Hawkins and D. Western (eds), *Ecotourism: Guide for Planners and Managers* (North Bennington: Ecotourism Society, 1993).
7   M. Wood and S. Blangy, 'Developing and Implementing Ecotourism: Guidelines for Wild Lands and Neighbouring Communities' in Lindberg, Hawkins and Western (eds), *Eco Tourism.*
8   F. L. Fillion, J.P. Foley and A.J. Jacquemot, 'The Economics of Global Eco-tourism', paper presented at the Fourth World Congress on National Parks and Protected Areas, Caracas, Venezuala (1992).
9   Responsible Tourism Guidelines, South Africa Tourism (2002).
10 Report of the National Tiger Conservation Authority (February 2008).

Poverty alleviation: tourism as the key catalyst

1   'Tourism and Poverty Alleviation', a study by World Tourism Organization (2002).
2   Ibid.
3   'Poverty Alleviation through Sustainable Tourism Development', UNESCAP (New York, 2003).
4   'Tourism & Poverty Alleviation: Recommendations for Action', a study by Sustainable Tourism-Eliminating Poverty (2004).
5   Report of the Special Group constituted by India's Planning Commission to target ten million opportunities per year during the Tenth Plan period (2001).
6   'Socio-economic impact of tourism on folk artists and artisans of Kerala and Rajasthan', a study conducted by Ministry of Tourism (2003). For details, log on to www.tourism.gov.in
7   Evaluation of Rural Tourism Scheme for Ministry of Tourism by Matt McDonald Consultants (2006).
8   Lisa Singh, 'In Rural India, it (Finally) Took a Village', *Washington Post* (2 July 2006).

Through the looking glass: future of tourism

1   Travel and Tourism Economic Research, World Travel and Tourism Council (2007).
2   Total Tourism India, An analysis of one of the world's fastest growing markets, PATA (February 2007).
3   'Indian Tourists Outspend Americans in Britain', report in *Times* (London, 6 July 2008).
4   George P. Moschis, *The Maturing Marketplace* (Connecticut: Greenwood Publishing Group, 2000).
5   'Travel and Tourism in 2020'.
6   'India's New Opportunity: 2020', a report by the High Level Consulting Group – Boston Consulting Group for All India Management Association (2004).
7   'Indian Mobile Market World's Second Largest', *Hindustan Times*, (10 April 2008).
8   Rama Bijapurkar, *We Are Like That Only: Understanding the Logic of Consumer India* (India: Penguin, 2007).

9   Report of Intergovernmental Panel on Climatic Change: Summary for Policymakers (Cambridge: Cambridge University Press, 2007).
10 'Impact of Global Warming in India', *Hindustan Times* (17 April 2008). The article is based on a reply in Parliament by Minister of State for Environment.
11 'India to be 4° hotter in 40 years', *Times of India* (13 August 2008).
12 'Climate Change and Tourism', UNWTO.